# MENS CREATRIX

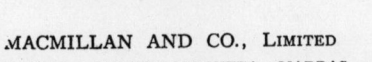

MACMILLAN AND CO., Limited
LONDON · BOMBAY · CALCUTTA · MADRAS
MELBOURNE

THE MACMILLAN COMPANY
NEW YORK · BOSTON · CHICAGO
DALLAS · SAN FRANCISCO

THE MACMILLAN CO. OF CANADA, Ltd.
TORONTO

# MENS CREATRIX

## AN ESSAY

BY

## WILLIAM TEMPLE

RECTOR OF ST. JAMES'S, PICCADILLY; HON. CHAPLAIN TO H.M. THE KING
CHAPLAIN TO THE ARCHBISHOP OF CANTERBURY
PRESIDENT OF THE WORKERS' EDUCATIONAL ASSOCIATION
FORMERLY HEADMASTER OF REPTON

MACMILLAN AND CO., LIMITED
ST. MARTIN'S STREET, LONDON
1923

*PATRI CARISSIMO*
*MORTUO PRAESENTI*

# PREFACE

This book was planned in the year 1908 when I was a junior don engaged in lecturing on Philosophy. At that time I had the presumption to believe that I was myself destined to be a philosopher. The course of events has led to my since being mainly occupied with what are foolishly distinguished as " practical affairs " (for what is so powerful in practice as a philosophy?), and the completion of this book has been the work of odd moments. It was partly written in Oxford ; partly at Repton, while I was Headmaster there ; but more than half of it has been dictated in spare half-hours since I came to London, indeed during the first six months of 1916. I have been eager to finish it, partly as a tribute to an old ambition, partly as a stimulus, if it may be so, to some real philosopher to do more adequately what I am only able to sketch out. We need very urgently some one who will do for our day the work that St. Thomas Aquinas did for his.

It would be impossible to give any adequate list of acknowledgments. It is said of Bishop Westcott that he held in especial veneration St. John, Origen, and Browning. I do not in any way claim comparison with that great scholar and seer if I say that the first name and the third, with Plato's in place of Origen's, would designate the master-influences upon my own thought. Among contemporaries I have derived especial advantage from close friendship with such thinkers as the authors of *Concerning Prayer* upon the one side and with so rigid an Augustinian as Father Kelly (of the Society of the Sacred Mission) upon the other, and with Bishop Gore as one who shares to some extent the view-point of both.

I have not hesitated to include practical matters. With Plato's example before one it is absurd to shrink from them.   Moreover, real political philosophy must deal with real politics.

My title is intended to indicate at once my debt to Bergson and my difference from him.

And so I offer to Christ and His Church what is likely to be my only extensive essay in the sphere which I once hoped would be mine.   May He pardon deficiencies due to negligence, counteract all tendencies to error, and allow to my work only such influence as may promote His glory.

W. TEMPLE.

St. James's Rectory,
Piccadilly, *October* 1916.

## PREFACE TO THE ISSUE OF 1923

This issue is not a new edition.   There is no part of the main argument that I wish to change.   Where topical allusions are become out of date I have added a footnote to point this out ; but no other alterations have been made.   I hope soon to complete a supplementary volume under the title *Christus Veritas* : that will be mainly theological, whereas this is mainly philosophical.

W. MANCHESTER.

Bishopscourt, Manchester,
*October* 1923.

# CONTENTS

ix

## CHAPTER XI

## CHAPTER XII

# PART III

## CONDUCT

### CHAPTER XIII

## CHAPTER XIV

## CHAPTER XV

## CHAPTER XVI

## CHAPTER XVII

## CHAPTER XVIII

# PART IV
## RELIGION

## CHAPTER XIX

## CHAPTER XX

# BOOK II
## GOD'S ACT

## CHAPTER XXI

## CHAPTER XXII

## CHAPTER XXIII

## CHAPTER XXIV

## CHAPTER XXV

## CHAPTER XXVI

# EPILOGUE

## CHAPTER XXVII

# PROLOGUE

*'Εν ἀρχῇ ἦν ὁ λόγος . . . καὶ ὁ λόγος σὰρξ ἐγένετο.—*St. John.

THE Argument of this book is as follows. It traces the outline of the Sciences of Knowledge, Art, Morality, and Religion, as the author understands these, not pausing to discuss what is disputable but merely affirming the position which is adopted. The four philosophical sciences are found to present four converging lines which do not in fact meet. Man's search for an all-inclusive system of Truth is thus encouraged and yet baffled.

Then the view-point changes. The Christian hypothesis is accepted and its central "fact"—the Incarnation—is found to supply just what was needed, the point in which these converging lines meet and find their unity.

Book I., entitled "Man's Search," is philosophical in method; Book II., entitled "God's Act," is theological. It will make my subsequent procedure more intelligible if I state what I conceive to be the difference between these two.

Philosophy is the attempt to reach an understanding of experience. It may be called the science of the sciences. It takes the results of all departmental studies and tries to exhibit them as forming one single system, just as these separate sciences themselves try to exhibit the facts which they study as united in coherent systems. Philosophy has no presuppositions or assumptions, except the validity of reason (or, to put it otherwise, the rationality of the universe). Philosophy assumes the competence of reason—not necessarily your reason or mine, but reason when free from all distraction of impulse—to grasp the world as a whole. It begins with experience, and may include within that all which we can mean by "religious experience"; it may even give to this the chief place among the various forms of experience; but it begins with human experience and tries to make sense of that. If it reaches a belief in God at all, its God is the conclusion of an inferential process; His Nature is conceived in whatever way the form of philosophy in question finds necessary in order to make Him the solution of its perplexities. He may be a Person, or an Impersonal Absolute, or Union of all Opposites— whichever will meet the facts from which the philosophy set out.

But religion is not a discovery of man at all. It is indeed an attitude of man's heart and mind and will; but it is an attitude towards a God, or something put in the place of a God, who (or which) is supposed to exist independently of our attitude. In particular, Christianity is either sheer illusion, or else it is the self-revelation of God. The religious man believes in God quite independently of philosophic reasons for doing so; he believes in God because he has a conviction that God has taken hold of him. Consequently, in theology, which is the science of religion, God is not the conclusion but the starting-point. Religion does not argue to a First Cause or a Master-Designer or any other such conclusion; it breaks in upon our habitual experience—"Thus saith the Lord." It does not say that as nature, in the form of human nature, possesses conscience, therefore the Infinite Ground of nature must be moral; it says that God has issued orders, and man's duty is therefore to obey. If the religion is one of fear, it may be something far inferior to naked ethics; but if it is of love, then it is far superior. Anyhow, it starts with God, whose Being and Nature are its primary certainties; it goes on to show, so far as it can, that God, as He has revealed Himself, is indeed the solution of our problems. In the language of the old-fashioned Euclid, philosophy attempts a problem—to construct a conception of God equal to the universe; theology attempts a theorem—to show that our God is equal to the universe.

Now, it is abundantly clear that a perfect theology and a perfect philosophy would coincide. There can only be one Truth. And it is one of the great glories of Christianity that it has fully recognised this. It insists that the Life of Christ is an act of God; Christ did not emerge out of the circumstances of His time; He is not just the supreme achievement of man in his search for God; He is God Himself, "who for us men and for our salvation came down from heaven." And yet He is also, in perfect manifestation, the Eternal Wisdom of God, which was in the beginning with God, and apart from which there hath never a thing happened. He is that which philosophers would have found if they could have collected the whole universe of facts and reasoned with perfect cogency concerning them.

But while theology and philosophy are ideally identical in result, though not in process, it is equally plain that they are not at all identical in their present stage of development. Philosophy working inwards from the circumference, and theology working outwards from the centre, have not yet met, at least in such a way as to present a single system whose combination of comprehensiveness and coherence would supply a guarantee of its truth. The Christian who is also in any degree a philosopher will not claim that by reason he can irrefragably establish his faith; indeed, it is possible that his search may lead him to nothing but perplexity, from which he saves himself only by falling back upon his unreasoned convictions, which come to him from the authority of the saints or from his own specifically religious experience. In the same way his theology may fail to give a satisfying account of empirical facts —of this war, for example, and all its horrors ; but he still believes that by loyalty to his central conviction he will find his way through the maze at last. We live by faith and not by sight. But the aim of this book is to indicate a real unity between faith and knowledge as something to which we can even now in part attain.

We shall watch the Creative Mind of Man as it builds its Palace of Knowledge, its Palace of Art, its Palace of Civilisation, its Palace of Spiritual Life. And we shall find that each edifice is incomplete in a manner that threatens its security. Then we shall see that the Creative Mind of God, in whose image Man was made, has offered the Revelation of Itself to be the foundation of all that the Human Mind can wish to build. Here is the security we seek ; here, and nowhere else. "Other foundation can no man lay than that which is laid, which is Jesus Christ."

Yet even at the last the security is of Faith and not of Knowledge ; it is not won by intellectual grasp but by personal loyalty ; and its test is not in logic only, but in life.

# BOOK I

## MAN'S SEARCH

### INTRODUCTION

# CHAPTER I

## INFINITE AND FINITE; THE METHOD OF PHILOSOPHICAL ENQUIRY

Ὁ γὰρ συνοπτικὸς διαλεκτικός, ὁ δὲ μὴ οὔ.—PLATO.

Ἐάν τέ τιν' ἄλλον ἡγήσωμαι δυνατὸν εἰς ἓν καὶ ἐπὶ πολλὰ πεφυκόθ' ὁρᾶν, τοῦτον διώκω κατόπισθε μετ' ἴχνιον ὥστε θεοῖο.—PLATO.

"There must be a systole and diastole in all enquiry; a man's mind must be continually expanding and shrinking between the whole human horizon and the horizon of an object glass."—GEORGE ELIOT.

PHILOSOPHY is, or should be, the most thorough-going effort that is prompted by the scientific impulse. It is not a visionary flight in realms of meaningless abstraction; it is a determined effort to think clearly and comprehensively about the problems of life and existence. No one is content with first impressions on all subjects; every one criticises, at least to some extent, the apparent deliverances of the senses; but for most of the purposes of life a small amount of such criticism is sufficient. I can confidently sit on a chair and eat my dinner off a table without knowing anything about the electrical theory of matter; it may be the case that the table and the chair and my body all consist of atoms, each of which is in itself something like a solar system of electrical forces; but whether it is true or not, the chair and table are solid enough for my purpose.

Yet thinking has had its effect on the most purely practical of our notions. Let us take an illustration

7

from contemporary life. When a sympathetic person meets a hungry man, the first impression is that it would be a good thing to feed him ; he does so, and is shortly afterwards severely reprimanded by the Charity Organisation Society for encouraging vagrancy, increasing pauperism, undermining the virility and independence of the entire population, and generally aggravating the evil he sought to cure. His hair naturally stands on end at the enormity of the crime he so innocently committed, and he now adopts as his guiding principle the maxim that nothing should ever be given to beggars. He fortifies himself in this position, if exposed to attack, by such portions of the 1834 Poor Law Report as have filtered into the minds of the young men who write leading articles for his newspaper. He now has, and acts upon, a theory. It is, as he thinks, self-evident that the chief aim of a patriotic rate-payer's existence should be to "reduce pauperism," and above all to take very good care that the state of the "pauper" is "less eligible" than that of the "independent labourer." He thinks he knows quite well what he means by the terms "pauper," "eligible," and "independent." *Hinc illae lacrimae* ; he has a theory, and condemns further theorising as "abstract" or even as just "theoretical." And yet all his three terms are ambiguous to a fatal degree. Technically a pauper is one who receives relief from the Poor Rate ; morally a pauper is one who is not self-supporting ; and it is by no means clear that the reduction of technical pauperism (by rigid application of another hopeless ambiguity called " The Workhouse Test ") tends to the reduction of moral pauperism ; for it is more demoralising to a man that he should live by sponging on his friends or exploiting his wife and children in "sweated" industries than that he should be "relieved" adequately and rapidly by the Society which his labour supports. So, too, "eligibility" of status depends on the moral and social standards of

the person who elects ; it is possible for a Workhouse
to appear "ineligible" to a self-respecting man and
"eligible" in the highest degree to a waster.   "Independence" may mean self-supporting, or it may mean
only "not supported by the Poor Rate"—which comes
near to being an "infinite" negation, for it does not
give us any answer to the question how the man actually
is supported.

   It is of course possible that what the Commissioners
of 1834 intended to say was quite right ; there is no
means of determining what they intended to say.   Their
value for our present purpose is this : that they have
provided the English people with a set of terms by
which to classify and understand the facts of Pauperism ;
and the most "practical" people are willing to accept
this intellectual apparatus without further criticism.
To that extent our practical people "think" about the
subject, and on the basis of their "thought" they
proceed to act, dismissing as academic hair-splitting the
complaint that all their leading terms are ambiguous.
But the truth is the exact converse of what they suppose.
It is not true that the "practical" person in touch with
affairs has the real perception of facts, while the academic
student follows the ramifications of some "abstract
intellectual plan of life quite irrespective of life's plainest
laws" ; rather it is the former who has put on the
blinkers of an unconscious dogmatism, so that he can
see only what his dogma tells him to look for, while
the philosopher is engaged in testing that very dogma,
not only by the intellectual criterion of self-consistency,
but also by the practical and empirical criterion of
applicability to the facts.

   Science and philosophy alike spring from the need
of man for fuller knowledge,—a need which may be
utilitarian, as when the knowledge is needed for the
guidance of conduct, but may also be quite ultimate, as
when the knowledge is needed for the mere good of
knowing.   Anyhow both science and philosophy are

rooted in the " Will to know "—a subject to which we must attend in detail later.   But that " Will to know " is itself the rejection of the claim advanced by other interests to interfere in the process which ends in knowledge.   Its satisfaction is found in apprehension of a reality which is presupposed to exist apart from its apprehension—and that, too, without any reference to the practical convenience of the judgment ultimately accepted as true.   It is a distinct and definite purpose, with a method of its own.   The formulation of that method is the task of Logic.

In an enquiry into the methods by which the intellect pursues its search for truth we must take account of the fact that the great bulk of our thinking is sub-conscious.   When some proposal is made which is entirely novel to us, we are inclined to say, " Let me stop and think about it."   The mind immediately goes blank and for a certain period remains so.   At the end of this period a man will look up and say how the proposal strikes him, or what there is about it which he disapproves of or does not understand ; he does not know, as a rule, what has gone on in the interval, neither does he know why the interval ends when it does.   In the subconscious regions of the mind some process has been at work resulting in a judgment or a question which appears within the field of consciousness.   All that logic, therefore, can do is to trace out these joints of thought which are all that is recoverable of the infinitely subtle process by which beliefs are formed.   This is true not only of theoretical opinions but of practical convictions.   We believe intensely many things for which we are unable to state the reason, though we also hold that our right to this belief depends on a reason being discoverable.   In regard to the great conventions of life there is nearly always a vast inductive process through which the human race has passed, and of which no individual has ever been at all fully conscious.   An infinite number of facts in the experience of men has led them to believe that certain courses of conduct are vital to the well-being of society. The conclusion is a truly scientific induction, yet no one ever consciously drew the inference, and the facts which form the data are so numerous and so subtly differentiated that their statement in words could never represent the full weight which they possess in experience.

Far from being less reasonable than consciously formed theories of life, these convictions have probably far more reason, a far greater empirical basis, and have been reached by a far more cogent inferential process. For when a man sets out an array of facts and then draws conclusions from them after the manner of a physicist or chemist, he is inevitably omitting a great number of the facts that are relevant. One may take as an extreme instance Mr. Bernard Shaw, who with perfect logic deduces conclusions from quite accurate observations ; but what he observes is a very small portion of all the facts of human nature, inasmuch as he seems to be entirely blind to the whole sphere of human sentiment and even passion ; consequently, however sincere and cogent his argument, we all know that his conclusions have no applicability, and this we know by what seems an instinct but is really the deposit in us of the whole process of human reasoning, some small part of which has been conscious in a few individuals, but the vastly greater proportion of which has never become conscious at all.

None the less it is only with consciousness that the philosopher can deal, and it is to this, therefore, that we must address ourselves, remembering throughout how small a part of human thought it is, and recalling this truth to mind at the points where to forget it is most likely to be a source of error.

Here I would venture, with much hesitation, to suggest that it is in Logic more than anywhere else that philosophers have given ground for the accusation that they leave facts behind them when they come to

make theories. No doubt this accusation is in part due
to the fact that many people expect Logic to do the
work of Psychology and tell them how they actually
pass from one unwarrantable conviction to another ; for
this is often the character of our "thinking." But Logic
is the *science of mental process, so far as this leads to
knowledge ;* it studies the method of the Will to Know,
not the fortuitous emergence of those opinions upon
which "practical" men are ready to take action of
momentous consequence. And finding two main
directions in which scientific thought may move, Logic
has, for purposes of investigation, separated these and
set them up as the Deductive and Inductive Methods.

Now, scarcely any one ever thinks deductively,
according to the patterns of deduction provided in the
text-books. The authority of the Syllogism has, it is
true, been broken for a quarter of a century at least,
but having held the throne for two thousand years, it
still exerts a subtle and malign influence. The chief
trouble about it is familiar enough ; it lies in the Major
Premise. In some manifestly valid arguments there
is no room for any Major Premise ;[1] and where such a
Premise is employed, it is very hard to justify. Even
in the case of our old friend—

> All men are mortal—*or* Man is mortal,
> Socrates is a man,
> Socrates is mortal—

the difficulty appears. If the major is enumerative we
have no right to make it until Socrates (and we ourselves) are dead ; and the charge of question-begging
is irrefutable. Or if it is a true generic judgment
representing our knowledge of the present physiological
conditions of human life and their inevitable result in
death, the proposition seems to become a definition, and
it is doubtful whether the minor can be referred to it ;

---

[1] As, *e.g.*, in Mr. Bradley's instance—A is 10 miles north of B ; B is 10 miles
west of C ; C is 10 miles south of D ; therefore A is 10 miles west of D.

for until Socrates has died, we cannot be sure that he comes under the definition ; it is always just possible that in him biological evolution has produced an organism which replaces its own decay, and is human in every respect except those which lead to mortality. In short, universal propositions are only possible as definitions,[1] and there are traces of Nominalism about our best-established generalisations. All we can be sure of is that if *a* is the cause of *b*, whenever *a* occurs *b* will follow ; for it is part of the being of *a* that it produces *b*. But we may come upon an object which resembles *a* in every observable respect, and look for the appearance of *b* ; if instead of *b*, β emerges, we shall have to say, " It was not *a* after all, but *a*." That is, we make production of *b* part of the meaning of our term *a* ; but then we can never tell whether or not any given object is *a* until *b* has followed. Only by making " productive of *b* " part of the meaning of the term *a* can we make the proposition " *a* produces *b* " strictly universal ; but this proposition is now so purely analytical as to be a tautology. Thus the only sense in which the Uniformity of Nature is certain is that which makes it a statement of the Law of Identity :—A is A.[2] It is in this sense that the Uniformity of Nature is a necessary postulate of thought.

It was possible for our forefathers to transfer the unconditional certainty of the Uniformity of Nature thus interpreted to specific " causal " relations because they believed in Real Kinds, each self-contained and essentially distinct from all others. Whatever was true of the Kind was therefore true of each instance ; and every phenomenon was an instance of a Kind or Genus. Biological evolution, with all the scientific development it has assisted, has destroyed the basis of that way of thinking ; we are no longer at liberty to believe in Real Kinds as thus existing distinctly and unalterably

---

[1] Cf. Poincaré, *Science and Hypothesis* (E.T.), pp. 48-50, 135-139 and *passim*.
[2] Cf. Joseph, *Introduction to Logic*, chap. xix. (specially pp. 376-390).

over against each other. It is very hard to say where
the line should be drawn between, for instance, the
animal and the vegetable. No doubt the elephant is an
animal and the cabbage is a vegetable, but what about
the Sun Dew or Venus' Fly Trap? Whether these are
vegetable or animal will depend on *our* definition. The
tiresome Nominalist element appears in all our attempts
to reach universal judgments. Absolute divisions of
kinds do not exist in nature any more than between the
periods of a human being's life. A boy of ten is a
boy; a man of fifty is a man. The law must fix a
definite point for the transition and selects the twenty-
first birthday; but no one supposes that Boyhood is
one fixed type and Manhood another, and that every
English male miraculously passes from one to the other on
becoming twenty-one years old. Syllogistic inferences
from Major Premises about Boyhood and Manhood are
likely to be most misleading.

The ancients at least avoided the blunder of supposing that exact knowledge of Real Kinds was in itself
exact knowledge of particular cases; in fact both Plato
and Aristotle regard particulars as not strictly knowable at all.[1] So far as Matter is indeterminate, as it
usually and perhaps always is to some extent, we are,
according to Aristotle, in a region of uncertainty, and
the educated man will not demand more exactitude in
the science than is permitted by the subject-matter of
enquiry.[2] Yet the method of science remains for him
the construction of Universals through the five-staged
process of $\alpha\check{\imath}\sigma\theta\eta\sigma\iota\varsigma$, $\mu\nu\acute{\eta}\mu\eta$, $\dot{\epsilon}\mu\pi\epsilon\iota\rho\acute{\iota}\alpha$, $\dot{\epsilon}\pi\alpha\gamma\omega\gamma\acute{\eta}$, $\nu o\hat{\upsilon}\varsigma$
(where the last universalises, on its own authority,
the product so far reached and makes of it a definition,
$\dot{o}\rho\iota\sigma\mu\acute{o}\varsigma$),[3] followed by deduction of properties from the
definition of essence thus formed. Science for him
rests on the assumption of Real Kinds.

[1] Cf., *e.g.*, Plato, *Republic*, 476 A-480 A.
[2] Cf., *e.g.*, *Met.* 1027 a 13-17 ; *Eth. Nic.* 1094 b 11-28.
[3] Sensation, Memory, Competence due to experience, Adduction of instances,
Reason. Cf. *Anal. Post.* 99 b 15-100 b 17.

The difficulty about Deduction is that we have no certain right to our starting-point. The difficulty about Induction is that we have no certain right to any conclusion. The only way to prove a conclusion inductively would be to form a complete list of all possibilities and disprove all but one ; but the formation of such a list is impossible, except in mathematics. In mathematics it is possible, because there terms mean exactly what we define them to mean and have no tiresome fringes where one is doubtful whether the name can be applied or not ; but this advantage tends to disappear the moment we try to apply the results. A triangle is what the geometrician defines it to be ; whether any apparently triangular piece of wood is really a triangle is another, and perhaps an unanswerable question ; presumably there is no rectilinear figure in matter.

These considerations are less disastrous than might be supposed, because no living thought is either Deductive or Inductive : it is always both at once. The student or investigator does not approach his subject with a perfectly blank mind ; he assumes at least that the group of facts before him forms some kind of system, and generally he has some conception, however vague, of this system's nature. His study of the individual facts modifies the system in which he holds them together ; the modified system suggests new points to be examined in the facts. In the former phase his procedure is predominantly inductive, in the latter predominantly deductive. But his method is a see-saw between the system as a whole and its constituent parts ; his knowledge of both grows together. We may imagine a Royal Commission setting out to investigate Unemployment. Their aim is to relate all the facts to one another within a system of thought. They will not try to establish universal laws and argue from them ; nor will they try to arrive at some universal formula by induction ; but they will try to find the ground of the various types of unemployment in the whole tissue of the social and economic conditions of the world, and to gain such an apprehension of those conditions as will reveal the ground of all types of unemployment.

Plato presented the ideal method (at one period) [1] as a single ascent to the supreme principle and a single descent from it to the particular manifestations of it— the latter being required for practical, not theoretical, reasons. But indeed it is necessary to turn from generalisations to particulars and back again as often as possible. We cannot begin with generalisation ; but neither can we begin with "facts," as Induction requires ; we cannot "build upon the facts" because, until our structure is complete, we do not know what they are ; the aim of our whole enquiry is to find them. Facts are not always the original data, nor are these always facts. The truth about the Earth and the Sun is not what the senses suggest (that the sun goes round the earth), but what science establishes (that the earth goes round the sun). It is at the end, not at the beginning, of our intellectual process that we are in possession of the "facts." Hence our "conclusion" should always modify its own premises ; for our goal is not the forma- tion of one judgment whose truth is guaranteed by others, but a whole system whose parts support each other and in which all the "facts" are found.

Deductive or Inductive Logic arranges its terms in triangles ; at the apex is the Genus, below it stand the Species, below each of these the sub-species, and below these again the individuals. Whatever was true of any term in this pyramid of classification was therefore true of every term falling under it. This is an excellent method of argument ; if one's opponent will admit a proposition he can be forced to admit its consequences. But it is a device rather of Rhetoric than of Logic, except in so far as a man may argue with himself in

[1] *Rep.* vi. and vii.

the search for truth. Even the Syllogism has great rhetorical value.

But living thought is circular ; it moves round and round a system of facts, improving its understanding of the system and its constituent parts at every stage. The Middle Term in such inference is clearly the system itself as a whole—not any abstract quality nor any fixed genus ; the better understanding of this " concrete universal " and the better apprehension of its particular " differences " are one and the same thing. Thus tridimensional rectilinear space is the system articulated in Euclidean geometry ; and the process results in a fuller knowledge of the system than was possessed at the outset. Thus the Poor Law Report of 1909 investigates the fact of Unemployment ; but Unemployment is not a mere being-out-of-work, but is a whole system of fact, set out in detail in the evidence and grasped as a unity in the Report.[1]

How effective in practical life a purely logical doctrine may become is made clear by the feudal system, which is simply Deductive Logic in practice. The satisfaction of that logic was reached when terms were arranged in pyramids, with the *summum genus* at the top, the various *genera* below, the *species* arranged each below its own *genus*, and the individuals again below these. So in Feudalism the King stood at the top ; below him were his vassals ; below them again the sub-vassals. It is interesting and typical that France alone adopted Feudalism in its most " logical " shape. Further, all Europe constituted a still further and inclusive pyramid, for all kings were (in theory) vassals of the Emperor ; similarly the Pope stood at the head of the ecclesiastical system, and the pyramid was finally completed, according to the Imperial Theory, by the fact that both Pope and Emperor derived their right from God, or, accord-

---

[1] For this reason the exposition of a body of truth is bound to contain many repetitions. The old deductive method avoided this. The exposition moved steadily down the chain of argument. But if the system consists of interlocking parts, not of one straight chain, repetition is unavoidable.

C

ing to the Papal Theory, by the fact that the Emperor
was a vassal of the Pope—God's earthly representative
(for had not the Pope bestowed the imperial crown on
Charlemagne on his own initiative in St. Peter's Basilica
on Christmas Day, 800 ?).

It is interesting also to notice what happened to
so vigorous an intellect as that of Hobbes when the
Reformation had knocked off the apex of the pyramid.
He has to make the citizens (*infimae species*) produce
their own *summum genus* by contracting away their rights
to an absolute monarch. And the frontispiece of the
*Leviathan* represents the monarch (whether Cromwell
or Stuart) as such an apex, the source of civil authority
represented by the sword in the right hand and the
symbols below it, and also of ecclesiastical authority
represented by the pastoral staff in the left hand and
the corresponding symbols below it. The Royalist
theory that the King had Divine Right (*i.e.* "held of"
God without intermediary) is a precisely similar attempt
to retain the mediæval form of political thought after
the life was out of it.

Democracy, on the other hand, consorts well with
the modern method in logic. Here there is no source
of authority over against the individuals, but the individuals constitute the system which they obey and obey
the system which they constitute. And it may be
noticed that whereas the old form of Government was
rigid in principle whatever development it may have
permitted in detail—so that progress was only possible
through compromising the fundamental article as was
done by Locke—the modern form becomes perfectly
plastic so that every particle of the machine of
Government may be changed at the will of the
sovereign people without any derogation of its
sovereignty. Just so in science, the old method depended on the rigidity and permanence of its *Genera*
or Kinds, while the modern enquirer allows new facts
to modify his system, and his system to throw new

light on the facts, to any degree, without check or hindrance.

The enquirer then must perpetually allow his generalisation to help him in the apprehension of particulars, and the further apprehension of particulars to react on his generalisation. Only so can he do full justice both to the particular and to the universal function, which coexist in every individual fact.[1] But in no sphere is this more important than in philosophy. Perpetually generalisations are reached and accepted as final, or definitions are received as fixed, while modification is still called for. We need to come back to the world with our generalisation in our mind, and see the world again in the light of it ; and then to return to the generalisation with the new material obtained by our last vision of the world. " A man's mind must be continually expanding and shrinking between the whole human horizon and the horizon of an object glass." Thus we may consider what things are good and so reach a general conception of Good, perhaps as that in which the soul finds perfect satisfaction ; but then we must see what are the things in which the soul finds satisfaction, a process which may leave the formula untouched but will almost certainly modify its content. We may have interpreted the formula in a hedonistic way ; we generally do at first ; and then we may have found that a great act of self-sacrifice may be peculiarly satisfying to the soul ; this would kill our hedonism forthwith, and therefore alter our general conception of Good. The same process needs very vitally to be applied to such terms as Liberty, Justice, Right, Responsibility, Empire. In the case of the term Socialism it is going on before our eyes. With thought-systems so complex as those denoted by these names, many a swing backwards and forwards, from the One to the

---

[1] Nothing is merely "This" ; to be at all, it must have some character—be of some sort ; every existent is τόδε τοιόνδε—This-and-nothing-else and this-sort-of-thing.

Many and from the Many again to the One, will be needed before anything like truth is found. One chief duty of the philosopher is to keep each Universal plastic, until he is certain that all the relevant facts are coherently united under it.

This means, no doubt, that absolute and final certainty is not attainable outside the sphere of mathematics. But it does not mean that advance in knowledge is impossible. Modern science is far nearer the truth than the fantasy of a medicine-man ; it holds in a comprehensive grasp far more of the relevant facts ; its generalisations are far less arbitrary, its universals more concrete ; the Nominalist element in its definitions is being perpetually reduced.

Nowhere is the danger of resting in abstract universals more serious than in Theology.[1] We are liable to argue in support of the Being of God, without troubling ourselves as to what sort of God we are establishing. He emerges in the argument perhaps as the Ground of existence. But it is not thereby clear that He deserves our respect, to say nothing of worship ; this will depend on our view of the existence He has produced and His own attitude towards it. There is a tale of a member of Parliament who was prepared to tolerate diversity of opinion in non-essentials ; but Charles Bradlaugh, positively an Atheist, he could not allow to take his seat unhindered. " Mr. Speaker," he said, " we all believe in a sort of a something." The religious value of such belief is perhaps open to question.

Our method, then, must be simply the progressive systematisation of our experience as we apprehend it ; we shall not argue from Universals to Particulars or from Particulars to Universals or from Particulars to

---

[1] An "abstract universal" is a principle of unity imperfectly apprehended, so that only some of its real content is before the mind, e.g. "Dog," conceived, not as a Notion requiring all the kinds of Dog for its full manifestation, but as the mere quality of "Dogness" which is identically the same in all Dogs. It is not clear that there is any such quality.

Particulars. All these phrases describe passing moments in the activity of thought, which never exist in isolation. And when we are told that the French are a logical nation, because having adopted a principle they " see it through," we shall say, " That may prove that they are a very deductive nation, but not that they are peculiarly logical." [1] Or if we are led to say that we believe in equality of Opportunity and some friend urges, " Then do at least be logical and abolish the family," we may find ourselves answering, " That would indeed facilitate the equalising of opportunity, but it would not be at all logical, because it would do more to frustrate than to further that improvement of life for the sake of which equality of opportunity is desired." There is nothing logical in forcing a principle upon circumstances to which it is inapplicable ; the logical course is rather to find out precisely the sphere of its applicability. Compromise is inherently just as logical as fanaticism, and in most circumstances is a great deal more rational.

So when we come to consider Reality as a whole, we shall not be agitated by meaningless dilemmas as to whether it is One or Many, and whether we ourselves are Monists or Pluralists. We shall say that no doubt it is both One and Many, and shall set about seeing in what senses it is either ; we shall not expect to see the unity swallow the plurality nor the plurality break up the unity. Lastly, we shall not set Infinite and Finite over against one another as if one must oust the other ; but we shall say that the Finite is that whose explanation is in something other than itself, and the Infinite is just the whole whose explanation must be within itself : if this involves endless extent in Space and Time, we shall accept that implication. But just as for us a universal is not something diverse from a particular, but is just

---

[1] This deductive quality of the French mind is rooted in a noble passion for intellectual integrity. As Mr. Clutton-Brock wrote in *The Challenge* (May 31, 1916): " There is a peculiar beauty in the French logic : it is thought become passionate but not bewildered with passion, the idea pushed as far as it can be pushed, for the love of it, as the Gothic idea was carried as far as it could be carried at Amiens or Rheims."

the system of particulars, so the Infinite will not be something diverse from the Finite, but just the system of the finites.

Every special science deals with some group of facts provisionally assumed to constitute an independent system. Philosophy attempts to deal with all facts as related in the one system of the Universe, and with that one system as uniting them. And its method is neither Inductive nor Deductive. It aims at a comprehension covering the multitude of particular facts and penetrating to the principle of unity which holds them together ;[1] it does not proceed from first principles or to them,[2] but it allows particulars and universals, differences and unity, parts and whole, to influence one another in the intellectual construction which it forms, until all facts are seen knit together in one system whose principle is the explanation of the world.

This is the work of thought, and must follow the laws of thought. The intellect's demand for coherence must therefore govern it. But coherence alone will be found inadequate as the all-explaining principle, for the simple reason that coherence must always be coherence of something. When we come back from this demand for coherence, which is the universal principle first given, to study the facts which are to be exhibited as cohering, we shall find that the principle of their unity must be more than intellectual or intelligible. The particulars of experience are given on one side, the intellect's demand for coherence on the other. As these two data influence each other, both are affected. We begin to "understand" the particulars ; that is, we begin to experience them more completely as related parts of a system and not only as isolated entities. And we begin to give content to our principle of coherence ; it passes from the mere absence of contradiction into the concrete harmony of different elements.

---

[1] Εἰς ἓν καὶ ἐπὶ πολλὰ ὁρᾶν (Plato, *Phaedrus*, 266 B).
[2] Ἀπὸ τῶν ἀρχῶν ἢ ἐπὶ τὰς ἀρχάς (Aristotle, *Eth. Nic.* 1094 a 31).

But so we pass beyond Intellect, as the word is commonly used, to Imagination and to Conscience. But all of these are functions of one Mind or Reason, and the later or higher functions are already implicit in the scientific intellect. Art and Science are in principle utterly distinct; but they are complementary to each other, as will be more fully seen later on. And Philosophy—the attempt to grasp the whole as a whole—requires Imagination as well as Intellect, the artistic as well as the scientific capacity. Plato's supremacy among philosophers is due to just this combination.

In the discussions which follow we shall try to adopt the method we have outlined in dealing with some of the problems confronting those who try to think about the four main departments of Mind's activity—Knowledge, Art, Conduct, and Religion. We shall try to find a principle capable in its own nature of uniting and so explaining the facts thus brought before us; and we shall consider whether the facts themselves give any ground for accepting this principle as their explanation. The enquiry is tentative; but for the sake of clearness and brevity the exposition will be confident. Views not accepted will only be mentioned when the ground for their rejection seems to be also ground for the acceptance of others. At the end we shall be near the vision of the " Idea of Good "; but we shall still have to rest content with the confession, with which for that reason we commence : δοκεῖ σοι δίκαιον εἶναι περὶ ὧν τις μὴ οἶδεν λέγειν ὡς εἰδότα; . . . ἀλλ', ὦ μακάριοι, αὐτὸ μὲν τί ποτ' ἐστὶ τἀγαθὸν ἐάσωμεν τὸ νῦν εἶναι· πλέον γάρ μοι φαίνεται ἢ κατὰ τὴν παροῦσαν ὁρμὴν ἐφικέσθαι τοῦ γε δοκοῦντος ἐμοὶ τὰ νῦν· ὃς δὲ ἔκγονός τε τοῦ ἀγαθοῦ φαίνεται καὶ ὁμοιότατος ἐκείνῳ, λέγειν ἐθέλω, εἰ καὶ ὑμῖν φίλον, εἰ δὲ μή, ἐᾶν.[1]

We count not ourselves to have apprehended.

---

[1] Plato, *Republic*, 506 c-e.

# BOOK I—*continued*

## PART I
### KNOWLEDGE

# CHAPTER II

## THE WILL TO KNOW

Πάντες ἄνθρωποι τοῦ εἰδέναι ὀρέγονται φύσει.—ARISTOTLE.

"The region of intelligible necessity, which ought only to be vitalised by a general *will to know*."—BOSANQUET.

IT is perfectly clear that knowledge is very seldom attained without serious effort ; and men do not embark on serious effort unless they think there is something to be gained by it.   With what object, then, do men undertake the effort whose result is the attainment of knowledge ?

Often, no doubt, the object is of the kind distinguished as practical ; that is to say, the knowledge, when reached, is to be not only possessed or enjoyed, but utilised. But there is also a definite and distinct love of knowledge for its own sake, an intellectual interest whose satisfaction may lead to no results beyond itself.   And it is sometimes suggested that one or other of these impulses to learn has a priority over the other.   This suggestion seems to be groundless.   For the method of enquiry and the result reached are identical, whichever form of the impulse may have led to the commencement of the effort.   The only distinction which can be drawn between them is this : the "practical" interest may be satisfied with a provisional answer ; we may know enough about a subject "for practical purposes," and therefore close our enquiry ; whereas the "speculative" interest can only be finally satisfied when the subject of

27

enquiry has been grasped in all its relations, or, in other
words, when a complete theory of the Universe has
been formed.

This distinction may be important. It is possible,
for instance, that a student of Logic may be perplexed
when told that, if once the mind has made a judgment,
it cannot rest short of omniscience. When we are told
that Reality is the subject of all judgments, or that
from categorical judgments we are necessarily driven
to hypothetical, and from hypothetical again to disjunctive, we are disposed to protest. When I say,
" Charles I. was executed," I am not thinking about
Reality as a whole at all; when I say, " Tragedy is a
species of drama," I am not even leading up to a
complete disjunctive judgment about the drama. And
all this is true, because most of our judgments are
framed under the influence of " practical " interests ;
and when we know "enough for practical purposes,"
we are content. But if our interest were speculative,
and we were determined not to rest until we understood
fully every term employed, then we should find these
doctrines of the Logicians verified ; for when our
procedure is " vitalised by a general will to know,"
we go on asking " why ? " of every statement made,
until the circle is complete and all our statements
support one another in a system known to include all
the facts ; but unless the Universe consists of several
unrelated parts, this system is itself quite plainly a
disjunctive judgment with Reality for subject. For as
long as any of the relations of any of the terms
employed are still unknown, the speculative intellect
will pursue its enquiry ; and short of universal truth
there is no stopping place. For even if (as is almost
incredible) the universe consists of parts coexistent and
otherwise unrelated, coexistence itself is a relation.
And so, as we proceed under the influence of the
speculative impulse, we find that nothing less than
Reality is the ultimate subject of our thought, and

nowhere short of omniscience can we rest content.
In this point the will to know is typical of that effort
for self-transcendence of which it is a case.    It is this
effort to escape from one's own particularity and realise
one's membership in a whole which prompts alike the
search for knowledge, the creation of beauty, devotion
to duty, and worship of God.    Man is a finite mind ;
but because he is Mind he cannot be content with his
finitude.    And one of the ways in which he tries to
rise above it is in the pursuit of knowledge for its own
sake—a pursuit which, once started, never stops until
the whole Universe is focussed in his intelligence.

But while it is true that the practical and speculative
interests differ very much in the thoroughness of the
enquiry to which they prompt, it is equally true, and
for our purpose more important, that the method of
the enquiry is the same in both cases.    The speculative
enquirer may use experiment to verify his hypothesis,
and the practical enquirer never dreams of dispensing
with the demand for self-consistency.    Once the
enquiry is started, our purposes and choices have no
more control over its result.    If Pragmatism thinks
otherwise, it is simply and plainly wrong.[1]    We test
many of our ideas by finding out whether they
" work " ; but whether they " work " or not depends
on whether they are true.    And in our intellectual
experiments we are, as William James and other
Pragmatists have admirably insisted, perpetually checked
and guided by the resistance of the object-world.
Indeed, the true Pragmatism and the facts of experience
seem to be at one in teaching that our personal preference only operates in selecting among various alternative
hypotheses ; the hypothesis selected must then submit
to tests which are wholly independent of our preference.

---

[1] I should not dream of accusing Pragmatism of this, were it not for one or two
casual sentences in other writers, and this sort of absurdity in Mr. Sturt : " Our
belief that the human consciousness survives bodily death is to be established, like
other dogmas, by the consideration that it lends interest, dignity and comfort to our
present life " (*The Idea of a Free Church*, p. 137).

The reason why different people are able to rest satisfied with different convictions about the same subject is often that they have asked different questions, to which different answers are needed. It can hardly be too often insisted that while all our knowledge is, in the end, rooted in some interest, that interest only dictates our question and not our answer to that question. I may treat a human being as so much physical mass, and weigh him ; I may consider him æsthetically, and estimate his beauty or ugliness ; I may consider him ethically, and pronounce him good or bad. I thus get different answers to different questions about one subject. They are in no way contradictory or incompatible, though the æsthetic and ethical judgments might be so worded as to be contradictory in appearance ; my interest determines which question I am to ask, but in no way affects the answer I ought then to find.

According to the ordinary use of language, the word "logical" seems to be used only of the process by which we find an answer to our question, while the larger word "rational" is used alike of the question and of the method adopted to find the answer. Logic is therefore the science of intellectual process so far as this leads to knowledge ; choice and preference have nothing whatever to do with it. But it needs some non-logical impulse to set this intellectual process in motion. Thus a man may want to know how many shillings must be piled one on the top of another to make a column that would touch the moon ; in fact, one gathers from some journals that there is a whole public possessed of an appetite for such knowledge. The desire to know this is neither logical nor illogical ; but there are logical and illogical, that is correct and incorrect, methods of satisfying it. The question, however, whether the desire to be satisfied is rational or irrational is quite legitimate.

Scientific procedure "ought only to be vitalised by a general will to know." Certainly ; but to know what ?  To know the answer to some question set by a practical aim or a speculative impulse.  And whether or not we regard the whole enquiry as " rational " depends partly on the logical value of its method, partly on our sympathy with its aim.

> One friend of mine wears out his eyes,
> Slighting the stupid joys of sense,
> In patient hope that, ten years hence,
> " Somewhat completer " he may say
> " My list of *coleoptera* ! " [1]

And some at least will say that however logical, and even intellectual, his procedure may be, it is not rational.

We come here to ultimate value-judgments.  So far as we want knowledge to guide us in conduct, we know where we are.  The value of the knowledge is determined by the value of the end it will help us to reach.  But when we are following the speculative impulse, which any one who pleases may dismiss as " mere curiosity," the matter is more complicated.  We may defend this impulse in general terms on the ground that very nearly all knowledge turns out to be of some use, and it is unwise to check enquiry because we do not at the moment see in what way it can be useful.  But this is to defend the " speculative impulse " on " practical grounds," which the owner of the impulse invariably dislikes.  And the answers to some questions are certainly useless ; if we know how many shillings would reach from here to the moon, we can do nothing with the knowledge.  Is the enquiry in such cases rational ?

The answer seems to depend on the amount of effort required in any given case, and the amount of other valuable activity displaced.  To satisfy any desire is good ; whether it is to be done depends on the amount of other good so prevented from being realised or the amount of harm incidentally involved.  The

---

[1] Browning, *Easter Day*.

impulse of curiosity, like any other impulse, may in particular circumstances be a temptation.

But it is to be noticed that the great problems of philosophy are not of this kind. Questions concerning the Being of God, the Doctrine of Immortality, and the Freedom of the Will are not unimportant to any man. Our answer to them may not alter our conception of what we ought to do, nor increase our knowledge of how to do it; but it may very vitally affect our resolution to do what we know how to do and believe we ought to do. We may not be able to use for our ends any faith we reach with regard to these matters; but it may use us; and it may even be true that in letting it use us we find the fulfilment of our own destiny. Anyhow, these questions are important. Let us just consider how three non-practical sciences have affected some men's view of life.

Our forefathers believed that the world was made in a week, precisely in order that men may dwell upon it; the heavens were spread as a canopy over men's heads, and the sun and moon were designed to give light upon the earth. But astronomy came and showed us that this earth of ours, the scene of all our endeavours, is a twirling speck, revolving with quite startling futility about one of the minor stars, always coming back to the same place and always setting out on the ridiculous round again; and it is growing cold, and where, then, will be our aspirations and struggles and the cities we have built? Surely every one who has looked at the sky on a starry night must have wondered if he is not the merest accident. The feeling is old enough, but astronomy has intensified it: "I will consider Thy heavens, even the works of Thy fingers, the moon and the stars which Thou hast ordained; what is man that Thou art mindful of him, or the son of man that Thou visitest him?"

And, as if this were not enough, Geology followed and revealed incredible vistas in the past history of the

earth ; and Biology reduced humanity to a single phase
in an endlessly changing life - process.   Astronomy
made our world a tiny atom in infinite space ; Geology
made our whole history a moment in infinite time ;
Biology made our boasted faculties an incident in a
process whose beginning and end are alike unknown.
And so we are left, helpless in a vast machine-like
universe, whose indifference to us can only be symbolised
by—

> The august, inhospitable, inhuman night
> Glittering magnificently unperturbed.

We find ourselves in a world over whose destiny, in
the main, we have no control whatever.   It is an ordered
world ; and the most important question we can ask is
the question—What is the nature and character of the
Power or Force that orders it?   This governing
principle is not anything that we can do or possess :
knowledge of it will not add to our skill in weaving or
in carpentering, in medicine or in generalship.[1]   But
without it everything is uncertain, and all resolution
becomes infected with ultimate doubt.   This knowledge
will perhaps not help us to do what we want to do, but
it may help us to want to do the right thing.

In fact, the truth seems to be this.   So far as the
possession of knowledge is the exercise of a natural
function and the satisfaction of a real impulse, it is a
good thing ;  the knowledge of great subjects, the
science which is itself on the borderland of art, is one
of the best things in life.   So at least most of us
deliberately judge.   But there is a petty kind of
knowledge, the pursuit of which is pedantic and
contemptible.   Even in the sphere of the great sciences
and of philosophy itself, we very rarely, and perhaps
never, find a pursuit of knowledge for its own sake
alone.   Like justice in Glauco's classification, knowledge

---

[1] Ἄπορον δὲ καὶ τί ὠφεληθήσεται ὑφάντης ἢ τέκτων πρὸς τὴν αὑτοῦ τέχνην
εἰδὼς τὸ αὐτὸ τοῦτο ἀγαθόν, ἢ πῶς ἰατρικώτερος ἢ στρατηγικώτερος ἔσται ὁ τὴν
ἰδέαν αὐτὴν τεθεαμένος (Aristotle, Eth. Nic. 1097 a 8-13).

is valued both for its own sake and for its results.[1]  It is one of the good things in life, and is also the means of attaining others.  And its own inherent value is increased by its living relation to all our other interests and pursuits.  As Tennyson shrewdly observed—

> Beauty, Good, and Knowledge are three sisters,
> And never can be sundered without tears.[2]

Knowledge divorced from other goods becomes pedantry and dry-as-dust.  Its value is then slight.  But the exact knowledge of the man of wide culture and sympathy is undoubtedly one of the best things in the world.  Knowledge is therefore to be pursued for its own sake, but not for its own sake alone, nor in isolation from all other interests.

This is what we should expect.  For the procedure which leads to knowledge must be vitalised by a will to know.  But no one has or can have this in a perfectly general form.  If the necessary effort is ever to be started, the will to know must take a particular form: it must begin somewhere ; it must become an effort to know this or that.  And its field of investigation is bound to be determined by interest of some kind.  The determining interest must result from general psychological conditions ; it cannot live in the soul entirely apart from all other psychic activities.

For it only exists, so far as we know, in actual persons ; so far as *my* knowledge is concerned, it is rooted in *my* will to know ; and this is not only my will that there shall *be* knowledge, but also my will that *I* may have that knowledge.  Knowledge is desired as good, and as good for me.  But while all knowledge may be good for me in some degree, unquestionably knowledge of some things is better for me—both in itself and in its consequences—than knowledge of some other things.  Which departments of knowledge have

---

[1] Plato, *Republic*, 358 A.
[2] *The Palace of Art : Dedication.*

this superior value for me is determined by my whole character and circumstances. The starting-point of my search, the questions I ask, are given me by my individual personality.

Knowledge, in short, is one of the good things of the world ; and, as we shall find to be the case with all good things, its value lies in its relation to some individual personality. It may be as good—for some people—as anything else whatever ; it is not for anybody the highest good, for the highest good is a condition of the whole soul in which knowledge takes its place with other good things. It is one of the proper treasures of a complete personality, the first and simplest deliberate work of the creative mind.

# CHAPTER III

## INTELLECT AND IMAGINATION

Οὐδέπ ͦ τε νοεῖ ἀνεῦ φαντάσματος ἡ ψυχή.—ARISTOTLE.

"Aliquis forte putabit quod fictio fictionem terminat, sed non intellectio . . .
"Cum non distinguimus inter imaginationem et intellectionem putamus ea, quae facilius imaginamur, nobis esse clariora et id quod imaginamur, putamus intelligere."—SPINOZA.

BEFORE the mind ever starts upon any deliberate and self-conscious activity, it has before it a vast amount of material. This is not altogether raw material, for, as we all agree, it is impossible for a rational being to apprehend anything at all without rationalising it in the process. •We start of necessity from our sensations. But we never have a mere sensation, which is a sensation and nothing more ; or, if we have it, we are unaware of it. We may say, if we like, that every stimulation of the nervous system which has any effect on the outermost fringe of consciousness, though it never itself comes into the field of consciousness at all, is really a sensation. In that case I have a sensation of those innumerable sounds which fill the air in most parts of a country like our own, but of which I am totally unaware until I notice their absence in the silence of some remote valley among the hills. Such "sensations" may give a colour and tone to the operations of the mind, but are not themselves material for it. We do not find that material until we reach those definite and individualised sensations to which we give names. But these names are of necessity Universals.

36

As soon as an element in experience is so fully realised
that it can be made material for thought, it is more
than a mere " this." It is already " this instance of
such and such a thing "—it is τόδε τοιόνδε. This
complex character it never loses, and the elaboration
and articulation of this complexity is the whole task of
science.

But the whole emphasis of science is on one of the
two elements in the complex fact. It is bound to
ignore as far as possible the " this " in its effort more
perfectly to understand the " such." It passes from
perception to conception ; but it never leaves perception
altogether. Euclid is concerned with the isosceles
triangle as such ; but he cannot move a step without
the particular triangle A B C. Plato indeed regarded
the need of the figure as a weakness, and desiderated
an activity of pure thought. But this weakness, if
such it be, is inherent in all thought. Just as a mere
particular can never be an object of experience, so a
mere universal can never be entertained in thought.

What then becomes of all our universals ? When I
say, " This rose is red," I am no doubt analysing a
particular red rose. But the Predicate contains a wider
meaning than the redness of the rose before me ; it
refers the Subject to the whole class of red objects, and
thus to a place in the intellectual construction which we
call the science of Optics. Moreover, a judgment of
this type may be almost entirely synthetic. I may ask
somebody to find a book for me ; he asks what it looks
like, and I answer, " The book is red." For me the
judgment is mainly (though not entirely) analytic ; for
him it is entirely synthetic. A new content—redness
—is added to his idea of the book ; what is so added
is a quality, a universal. Without a particular instance
of this universal before him, he yet holds it in his mind,
so that he knows what is meant when its name is spoken.
Is he not then holding in his mind the universal bare
and unalloyed ?

If we examine the action of our own minds, I think we shall find that this is not so. Certainly I myself am quite incapable of holding a general idea in my mind without the help of its name or some other symbol. If I want to think of "ten," I have to imagine either the sound or the appearance of "ten" or "10." If I want to think of "red," I need the word "red" or some imagined spot of red colour to help me. Without some percept or image I cannot hold a concept in my thought.

Meaning cannot exist without expression, nor logical content without mental image or symbol. If I tell a man who never saw snow that snow is white, and he understands, it must be because he knows the meaning of the term white ; and that meaning cannot exist in his mind without some image any more than it can exist all alone in nature. In this case the image is almost certainly a white-coloured area ; but it might be only the name "white," whose scientific definition or whose emotional associations are remembered ; if what is understood is really what snow looks like, then no doubt the image must be a white surface, for colour as a form of experience is not expressible in any other terms than its own. But image of some sort there must be, to make understanding possible at all. All thought must be about something, which it takes as, for the time at least, extant ; if thought is its own object, it must be either treated as an objective process, or analysed into thoughts which are endowed with a quasi-independence for the occasion. When Shelley says of Prometheus—

> He gave Man speech and speech created Thought
> Which is the measure of the Universe,

he insists on a very profound truth, if by speech we mean symbolism of whatever kind. Our thought must have some real object, or equivalent of a real object. If it cannot find in the world of perception a suitable embodiment of its meaning, it constructs one in the world of imagination. The Idea as " meaning " can only exist in and by means of the Idea as " mental image," whether this image originates in perception or imagination. For we know that an abstract or isolated universal is nothing at all. Many things are yellow ; but yellow itself is nothing. We cannot think for a moment without imagery or symbolism of some kind ; and we shall find that one main function of Art is to supply adequate, or at least comparatively adequate, imagery for our concepts.

Logic is bound to deal with the correlation of ideas, that is, of our apprehensions of facts, and not with the facts " in themselves." We therefore speak of the two elements—image and meaning—in the idea rather than of the particular and universal in the thing. But it is to be noticed that it is no mere mental creation which is at once particular and universal in the way described. It is the object itself as given in the most elementary apprehension of it. Consequently the intellect in attending only, or mainly, to the universal aspect or function is ignoring some element of the reality itself ; and when Art inverts the scientific process by attempting to understand the object from within instead of through its external relations, it is supplementing our full understanding of the reality. It is not a mere play of the mind working independently of fact, but it is a complementary activity equally necessary to the full understanding of the real world. It is only by the union of Science and Art that genuine knowledge can be reached, and just because the artistic process is complementary to the scientific its inherent principle is the same though it applies that principle differently. A great work of art is not only as logical in structure as a geometrical proposition, but its logic is far more subtle and minute. The intellect as distinct from imagination can only deal, as we have said before, with the outstanding features or joints of the logical process. The infinite delicacy of the logical structure in the real world is only grasped by imagination when it apprehends the real in its concreteness with all that minute articulation which can never be artificially constructed by the intellect.[1]

Words, whether visible or audible or both, are the commonest form of imagery. Thus Justice is a word which is no doubt to many people the only symbol they have of a most important abstract Universal. Words are in one way peculiarly well fitted for this use, for their connexion with their meaning is, from our present point of view, arbitrary; the connexion between "Justice" and its meaning is indirect and historical, and so, for any one but a philologist, accidental and arbitrary; and this makes thinking about it more free than it would be if the word at once suggested some easily visualised object, as "Equity" suggests two or more equal quantities; and in this sense modern terminology is a great advance upon hieroglyphics, quite apart from its greater convenience. But there is on the other side the danger of verbalism. Some words have so little essential connexion with their meanings that if we are not careful we may attach great emotional value to them without at the same time meaning anything by them at all. Hence shibboleths, party-cries, and catchwords.[2] But in spite of the danger of verbalism, words are the best type of image or symbol for purposes of pure logic, because in logic we are concerned with an idea (or fact) *qua* "meaning," and not *qua* "mental image" or "occurrence," though the latter element can never be eliminated. And words are the best symbols for logic, because they do not attempt to embody the meaning concretely; they only stand for it, and the understanding is thus free to define as it will, unfettered

---

[1] Cf. pp. 153-155.

[2] Cf. the political debates about Chinese Labour in South Africa. Very few politicians discussed the question whether the system was good or bad; they only discussed the appropriateness of making the noise "slavery"; because if that noise is made, much English blood will boil, while if it is not made, the worst of systems may be endured or even approved.

by the suggestions of the image. But it is a mistake to suppose that words are not images or symbols ; they are symbols, in which the representative element is at a minimum; they are formal symbols, and are on that account the best symbols for logic or for pure thinking. While we are thinking, our emotions should be, so far as possible, at rest ; and it is the image-element in our ideas which most easily arouses the emotions. Moreover, the more fully developed this image becomes, the more completely does it limit the content with which it is connected. The meaning of a word may be modified indefinitely ; but the meaning of a picture or a poem or a moral act (all of them symbols or embodiments of " meaning ") is fixed.[1]

The unconscious confusion of image and meaning is the cause of most error. Without an image we cannot think at all ; and we are liable to treat the image as exhausting and limiting the meaning for which it stands. There are many people for whom names are a substitute for thinking. They attribute heat to a substance called caloric, whose property is to give heat to bodies in which it is present ; they attribute moral judgments to a faculty called conscience, whose property it is to pronounce moral judgments ; they attribute the motion of bodies to a force called gravitation, whose property it is to make bodies move as they do. And this mere naming of facts they dignify with the title of explanation. This leads to endless confusion. And Science is at first precisely the liberation of thought from the control of the imagery which yet remains an indispensable part of its machinery. For Science the image is necessary but irrelevant ; and it should therefore be one which expresses the meaning by convention and not by

---

[1] We can still say the Nicene Creed, though our thought is not that of the Nicene or Constantinopolitan Fathers, because we have by imperceptible stages modified the meaning of many of their terms to suit our own habits of thought ; but few of us can read *Paradise Lost* without raging inwardly, because the words of the poet are combined into an artistic whole whose meaning is not plastic and is not ours.

direct suggestion or reproduction ; thought is thus left free to articulate and correlate its meanings according to its own principles.

But also thought is thus left finally and irrevocably abstract. It abstracts from the whole setting of imagery or perception and attends only to the "such" while ignoring the "this." It is right to take this course, but its work is provisional. At the end it must relate its abstract "truth" to the real world ; and if there is in the world of perception no object which embodies the "truth" in which Science culminates, it must call in the imagination, not as servant but as colleague or even as master, to create through Art what is not found in normal experience. The true beauty is something greater than what most men see in mountain or sky ; we do not see it till the artist has thrown upon "the earth and every common sight,"

> The light that never was, on sea or land,
> The consecration, and the poet's dream.

But that light transfigures and transforms what it illuminates. It adds new values of its own.

Because the intellect alone can never fully grasp its own subject-matter, owing to its initial act of abstraction, it is condemned never to escape from its own restlessness so long as it remains itself. Restlessness is the essence of Science ; it asks why ? for evermore, and of every answer it asks why ? again. But Art is essentially at rest, because the imagination rounds off the experience it handles into a (relatively) complete whole. No doubt the intellect may take hold of the artistic product and handle it scientifically ; this is criticism. But none the less, Art remains the natural culmination of Science, as Plato saw when he closed the argument with the myth.

Art is the climax of the speculative or contemplative activity of mind ; its *product* is generically superior to

that of Science, for it is capable of including this with
other aspects of reality in addition.   But the *method* of
Art is neither superior nor inferior to that of Science, it
is simply different ; and we must investigate them
separately.

# CHAPTER IV

## KNOWLEDGE, TRUTH, AND REALITY

Τὸ παντελῶς γνωστὸν παντελῶς ὄν.—PLATO.

" Summus Mentis conatus summaque virtus est res intelligere tertio cognitionis genere."—SPINOZA.

FROM Plato onwards Mathematics has appeared to claim the place of the typical science. And we can easily understand how this occurred, and also how it came about that for Plato Geometry was the dominant branch of Mathematics. It is natural that Mathematics should be the first science to develop, because it is necessary to all other sciences, and also because its subject is the most abstract and simple. It is the science of the category of quantity—the most abstract of all categories. But in Greece one branch of the science, and that the most elementary, was hampered by its symbolism ; to solve complicated arithmetical problems in Greek notation may well be conceived as constituting the main occupation of Ardiaeus the Great in the underworld. Whether for this reason or for some other, Geometry was the branch of Mathematics that most affected Plato. But it differs from other departments of knowledge in two very vital respects : its subject-matter is not reality as given in sensation, but certain terms defined quite precisely at the outset ; and it stands in no relation whatever to Time or Change. Ground and consequent are here simultaneous ; the equality of the angles at the base of the isosceles triangle follows in none but the logical sense from the equality of the sides ; it follows from it, but does not arise after it. Now this marks a great difference between Mathematics and most if not all other branches of Science. In physics and chemistry cause precedes effect temporally ; in biology and human history the material itself changes, new types are evolved, and different emotions or aspirations become prominent ; in fact, the less abstract the subject-matter, the more important is the part played by Time. This distinction is fundamental ; for by no means can the successive be so interpreted that its successiveness disappears without fatal distortion of the facts. Thus, for instance, when logicians reduce Cause to Totality of Conditions, and then tell us that as soon as the Cause is complete the Effect is there, so that the succession seems to disappear, we can only reply by asking—" But why does the incomplete cause become complete ? You have indeed proved the continuity of cause and effect, but you have not explained away the successiveness of the phenomena ; you have only put it all inside one of the two terms—namely, Cause. Our problem now is, How does the cause come by its completion ? And if all causal sequences are really relations of ground and consequent after the manner of geometrical relations of ground and consequent, why is there any process in the world at all, or why do we think there is ? " We will suppose that our logician leaves the latter question alone, and urges that succession is only Appearance, on the ground that the advance of knowledge sets us more and more free from the time-process and converts our knowledge more and more into apprehension of necessary connexions of content ; let us see how far this carries us.

Now it seems to be true beyond all possibility of dispute that the advance of science leads to judgments more and more independent of Time. There is nothing mystical about this timelessness ; it only means that there is a class of judgment to which Time is wholly and entirely irrelevant, such as $2 + 2 = 4$, or any other mathematical judgment. It seems indisputable that science leads more and more to such judgments; the law of Gravitation is a judgment of this nature, and so is any conceivable formulation of the principle of Evolution. Scientific truth seems to be Timeless, and we may admit that once true is always true; but when Mr. Bosanquet speaks of "the nature which reality has for us as a construction which more and more emancipates us from space and time" we say that we believe scientific truth to be such a construction, but whether or in what sense Reality is so is a question calling for further enquiry. In the case of Geometry or Mathematics generally we may admit that the Truth reached fully represents the matter of study; but how far is that matter of study real? What kind of Being do we attribute to $2 + 2 = 4$? Outside the sphere of Mathematics, at any rate, it is impossible to admit that the scientific truth fully represents the matter of study. The formula of the principle of evolution may be timeless; but the evolving species and individuals are not. A law of causation may be a timeless judgment in hypothetical form, but the sequence of cause and effect is not timeless at all; not only is temporal sequence essential, but the order of events has to be maintained; to invert the order is to contradict the facts, and to juggle with the order is to alter the facts. With the single exception of Mathematics, all Science seems to aim at the discovery of timeless judgments formulating the unchanging principles which govern the world's course of change. If we take Mathematics as our typical science we may forget this, and be led to the belief that because the principles to which we are led by Science stand unaffected by time and change, the reality whose principles they are is similarly unaffected; but Mathematics is peculiar in this respect. In all other departments Truth of the kind established by

Science may be timeless, but the object, concerning which it is true, is successive.[1]

This peculiarity of Mathematics is rooted in the other which has already been mentioned. In Mathematics our subject-matter is given in certain terms which mean precisely what they are defined to mean ; a triangle is a plain figure bounded by three straight lines, and in that definition its whole essence is given. There is no danger of our purely mathematical reasoning becoming disturbed by a triangle whose sides are just a trifle crooked ; a figure with such sides is simply not a triangle. Consequently it is possible in Mathematics to reach really necessary connexions of content and quite absolute demonstration within the limits of the initial definitions. But the moment we apply our Mathematics to the physical world, this certainty vanishes, and we have to say, " If this is a triangle, its internal angles are equal to two right angles," or, " The sum of the internal angles of this figure approximate to 180° in whatever degree the figure itself approximates to triangularity." We may conceive space in a variety of ways ; the simplest and, as far as Mathematics has yet gone, the most scientifically useful is the familiar tri-dimensional conception according to which the twelfth axiom of Euclid is valid ; the articulation of this conception is given in Euclidean geometry, which is a statement of fact in the terms of that initial conception, and is correct so far as that initial conception is correct. But it is not the only possible geometry, as Riemann and Lobatchevski have shown.

Concentration on Mathematics as the typical science tends to conceal the fact that certainty is only

---

[1] There is, of course, a great deal more to be said about this. At present we may remark that the Truth or Formula may be a mere Abstract Universal : e.g. the formula of gravitation in the mind of one who knows no physics. But it may also be the summary of a knowledge which grasps the whole successive process in a single experience, which in itself transcends succession—a concrete universal which is itself timeless, but whose constituent elements are successive. But here the artistic function of mind is added to the scientific.

obtainable by means of abstraction, which always may involve falsification. But as we pass to more concrete sciences this becomes manifest. Physics is highly mathematical, and the enticement of a complete certainty draws it perpetually closer to Mathematics. It is to be noticed that Materialism, as a popular philosophy, always seeks a physical and mechanical mode of statement, rather than a chemical, presumably because in chemistry we have already left behind the region of thought where the consequent can be precisely calculated from the antecedent ; this is no doubt due, as Materialism itself is due, to a desire for absolute exactness and cogency of reasoning. But this exactness is not compatible with complete truth. The intellect alone cannot deal with the whole world of fact ; and if we are determined to follow intellectual methods only, we shall end with a Scientific Truth which states so much of the real world as its methods can reach—a dissected corpse.

The intellect must be allowed the use of universal propositions; but it never has the right to make one except as a definition, and these definitions can never be freed from some degree of arbitrariness. We experiment with one after another, and are bound to use, alike in science and in practice, the one that fits most of the facts which appear to be intimately related to each other. Every scientific universal is a system of fact grasped as a unity ; but the outline of that system is seldom clearly defined until we define it. Some points are better than others for drawing the line, but there is no one point where it must be drawn.

Only by the assumption that our definitions are final can perfect intellectual satisfaction be attained. And if we make this satisfaction our criterion, we shall find ourselves at one with Plato and Aristotle in placing the subject-matter of knowledge outside what we usually regard as the real world, that is to say, the world of sensation. It is worth while to remember where this leads us ; Aristotle's God, just because He is omniscient, knows nothing about this world of ours ; for His intellectual life is to be perfect, and the object of His thought is therefore to be found only in the eternal Forms, and not by any means in the material world, which is only in part determined by them.   Now it must be true, if thought is valid at all, that the world of our experience is governed by some one principle accessible to thought ; and from knowledge of it, all events and phenomena would be deducible; but we shall find reason for believing that this one principle can only be discovered in the moment when all events and phenomena are already known.   Knowledge of the one principle of the universe and knowledge of all its parts are one and the same ; and therefore to us the one principle is never fully knowable.   No other principle or definition has final certainty ; and our whole intellectual life is therefore, in greater or less degree, experimental.  We reach a provisional certainty by turning a general statement into a definition, and deducing the properties involved in the essence so defined.   But we are never quite sure that our result is true of any given fact before us, because it is always possible that it contains elements which at once modify the properties and exclude the fact from the definition.   We can only reach absolute cogency of reasoning at the cost of surrendering applicability to fact.

Yet the whole process of science insists that this method is valid, even though its validity can only be fully established when Omniscience is reached.   The abstractions of science do help us both to understand and to control the real world ; those which help us most in this theoretical and practical aim are the best established ; and the difficulties in them which remain are often to be solved by a return to particulars, whether of sense or of imagination.   Spinoza's *scientia intuitiva* is not only the proper climax of the generalised *scientia secundi generis*, but contains the solutions of its

E

problems. Even Aristotle, despite his insistence on the universal as the sole object of knowledge, is ready to regard ἐπιστήμη as a δύναμις whose ἐνέργεια is θεωρία.[1]

Scientific Truth, then, is that ideal intellectual construction which would reveal the principles governing the real world in their complete nexus. Some parts of this construction we seem already to possess, e.g. 2 + 2 = 4. That is not a fact ; it is a truth. And whenever we have perfect intellectual satisfaction, we have Truth : τὸ παντελῶς γνωστὸν παντελῶς ὄν. This Truth may be a statement never precisely verified in experience ; no geometrical truth has a perfect material counterpart. Straight lines do not exist (in all probability), except as the product of an analytic mind ; there is a shortest distance between two points, but there is no straight edge. Truth is the ideal intellectual construction by means of which all experience would be correlated ; it is not a variable ; to say it was once true that the sun went round the earth, because that idea " worked " pretty well for the folk who used it, is an abuse of language. Truth is that system of notions which would give perfect intellectual satisfaction ; if no one at all possesses it, that does not affect its nature or the meaning of the term. And particular statements are true if they can make good their claim to be elements in this whole system.

But Truth is not Reality, not because it consists of a different kind of entity called Ideas, beyond which Reality lies, but because it is only one element in Reality which is compact of it and many others besides. It is easy to say that we can only know what falls within our own experience, and of course this is so ; but when it is argued from this that the mind knows primarily its own ideas and from them infers a world outside, a grievous fallacy is introduced. An idea is not an object of the mind standing somewhere between the mind itself and the reality which it would know ;

---

[1] *Met.* M 1087 a 10-25. Cf. *De Anima*, ii. 417 a 21-29.

an idea is a mental apprehension of reality ; it may be adequate or inadequate, just as the image on the retina of the eye may be correct or incorrect according to the health of the whole eye ; if it is incorrect we see the object amiss, but it is perfect nonsense to say that what we see is the image on the retina ; this is the one thing which we can never see at all, for it is that by means of which we see anything.

Similarly, if our mental grasp is either distorted or inadequate we may express this by saying that we have a wrong idea, but it is only for subsequent reflection that this idea becomes itself the object of thought ; it is essentially the thinking mind, but because the mind is self-conscious it can think about itself *qua* thinking, and therein make its own ideas into its objects. Psychologists and logicians are always doing so, but they must not allow the process which constitutes their science to lead them to believe that the thinking which they study follows the same process. Thought itself is primarily concerned with the world ; but this thought is itself part of the world, and there is therefore a special science of thought just as there is a special science of chemistry. If we begin with the notion that the mind never has any objects except its own ideas, we can never argue to a world beyond at all. Reality is the presupposition of all thinking ; in actual fact the distinction between mind and its objects is drawn within the given *totum* of experience, and we have knowledge of the object or not-self before we have any knowledge of the subject or self. Self-knowledge, even knowledge of our own existence, is more inferential than knowledge of the world about us, just as, in its content, it is, as a rule, far more rudimentary.

Now we have seen that Truth is not the whole of Reality, and the knowledge which grasps Reality must therefore be something more than that scientific knowledge which grasps Truth, and whose perfect type is Mathematics. Let us, however, attend first to the method of scientific knowledge and some of its peculiarities.

# CHAPTER V

## THE JUDGMENT

"In abstract terms a Judgment is expressible in the proposition : The individual is the universal."—HEGEL.

THE unit of thought is the Judgment. This has been obscured to some extent by the fact that the verbal expression of any judgment requires at least two words, and, in English, three. From this fact has arisen the suggestion that the judgment is a union of two ideas, and other similar doctrines. But we find that the two terms of the judgment—the Subject and Predicate—can only exist as terms of a judgment. The mere act of naming a thing or a thought is an implicit, and usually even an explicit, judgment. Our consciousness registers something simpler than a judgment only, if at all, in an apprehension whose only expression is an ejaculation ; and even this becomes a judgment as soon as it is made in the very least degree an object of reflection.

The essence of the Judgment quite plainly lies in the assertion that the Subject is the Predicate. "S is P" is its rudimentary form. And plainly the value of this statement depends on there being a real difference between S and P. The Judgment, then, is the conscious apprehension of a complex unity—or, in other words, of a system. The development of the Judgment from its simplest to its most fully elaborated form is simply the growth of articulation in the expression of this fact.

52

The system apprehended is, of course, real. There can be no occasion to discuss whether the "copula" (the word "is") has any existential value when used in a predicative sense. It is enough to remind ourselves that we do not as a matter of fact exercise our minds upon nothing. The Judgment is assuredly an apprehension of reality, though, of course, reality is not to be limited to the world of our sense-experience. Alice when "through the looking-glass" is quite real, and so are the Red Queen, and Humpty Dumpty, and the White Knight (bless him!), for they are all characters in real fiction. All judgments, then, are in their various ways apprehensions of—statements about—reality.

The direct Judgment pure and simple is the Categorical. Its form is the normal form of Judgment; and while, in the effort to understand it, we shall find ourselves driven to change that form, yet at the end of the enquiry, when we have reached the most complete and perfect form—the Disjunctive—we shall find that it is again Categorical. Let us, however, begin at the beginning with a simple judgment of perception—e.g. This is red. Clearly the object before me is "this red (flower or other object)." The judgment, therefore, has analysed "This red" into the fact that it is the object occupying attention—"This,"—and the further fact that its colour is red. The judgment, in fact, is analytic of the experience. But it is also synthetic, for it adds to the content of the experience by naming the object red, and so relating it to all other red things and to a place in the scheme of colour. In this sense of the words every judgment is both analytic and synthetic; and it may be well to remark that it is in this sense that I use the words unless the contrary is specially stated.

For there is another sense in which these words are used of judgments—the sense in which they were used by Kant. According to this use of terms a judgment is analytic when the Predicate adds nothing to the meaning of the Subject but only states explicitly part of that meaning ; whereas a judgment is synthetic when the Predicate increases our knowledge of the Subject. Thus Kant gives as an instance of the analytic judgment, " Matter is extended in space," on the ground that extension is part of what is meant by Matter ; while, as an instance of the synthetic judgment, he gives, " Matter is ponderable," on the ground that weight is not part of what is meant by matter.

The two uses of the terms do not lie very far apart, for it is clear that, in our former instance, it is the Redness of This which enables us to say, " This is red," so that our statement might be put, " This red thing is red." Kant's use of the terms is the less valuable of the two, because it really depends not on anything essential to the judgment but on its verbal expression in the Proposition, and, further, it gives no expression to the synthetic element in judgments which are, in Kant's sense of the term, analytic. For if I say, " This red thing is red," I am insisting precisely on the redness of the red thing, that is, on its relation to other red things and its place in the scheme of colour, in opposition (perhaps) to some one who thought it would look particularly well if placed next to a bright magenta-coloured object. *And it is only for the sake of this synthetic element that the mind proceeds from perception to explicit judgment at all.*

In every perception we apprehend a complex unit, for the object perceived is at least " This instance of a Kind "—τόδε τοιόνδε, *e.g.* This red thing. But I only convert this perception or implicit judgment into an explicit judgment for the sake of some increase of knowledge which this brings. This knowledge may be my own or some one else's. To take our former illustration : [1] I may ask a friend to fetch a book

[1] Chap. III. p. 37.

for me from another room ; he asks what it looks like, and I reply, " It is a red book," or, " The book is red." Here I have before my mind the red book ; part of that complex unit my friend too has before his mind, for he knows that the object in question is a book. I analyse the real object grasped by my mind in order that I may add the element Red to the element Book already grasped by his. And we find that here, as in all other cases, *the analytic element is what makes the judgment possible and conditions its truth, while the synthetic element is what makes it interesting and conditions its occurrence ; for I shall not make it unless I have some interest in making it.*

But as we attend to our Judgment —" This is red " —with a view to understanding fully what we mean by it and what grounds we have for making it, we become aware that we have to think about a great many things besides the immediate object of our interest. Science with its perpetually reiterated question " Why ? " endeavours to see the original subject of enquiry in an ever-widening context of relations. If our aim in making the Judgment is purely practical, we may feel at any moment that we have enough knowledge to guide our action, or that we are now bound to act on such knowledge as we have, however defective it may be. But the Will to Know is not thus satisfied ; nor will it be satisfied until it is impossible to ask " Why ? " once more with any intelligible meaning. But if the universe is a single system, as philosophy presupposes and experience increasingly testifies, no one part of it can be wholly unconnected with any other part. And thus our enquirer, who is impelled by the Will to Know, finds that wherever he starts, he is bound to make the entire universe the object of his thought. This is what logicians mean when they tell us that the logical subject of every judgment is Reality as a whole ; for if all the implications of any judgment are fully thought out, the judgment itself becomes something requiring for its expression a phrase like " Reality is such that, etc."

Perhaps this is clearer in less elaborately simple instances. Suppose that a man inspired or afflicted with the Will to Know is confronted by the statement that " John Brown's character was profoundly modified by the peculiar tone of his Public School." At once he will want to know what this " tone " was, wherein it was " peculiar," and therefore what is the general and characteristic tone of a " Public School," why Public Schools have such general characteristics, and so forth. Plainly he is launched upon an enquiry into English History. He will also enquire what John Brown's character is now, what it was before he went to school, what other influences besides those of school have affected him, what his home was like, why his home was of such a sort, how far the Industrial Revolution had affected the economic position of his family, why the Industrial Revolution took the course it did, and so forth. This line of enquiry also has led to English —indeed to European History. But the full understanding of this depends on some knowledge of the geographical and climatic conditions of this and other countries, which leads in due course to the nebula theory of the formation of the Solar System. Now if the interest prompting the original judgment is the doubt whether or not John Brown should be appointed to some post requiring special aptitudes, part of this prolonged investigation may be omitted ; but if the interest is precisely a desire to understand how John Brown came to be what he is, as much of it as there is time for must be undertaken, and the Will to Know is unsatisfied until it has been carried through. Consequently there must be in all scientific thought an explicit or implicit reference to the system of reality as a whole.

In the elementary Judgment from which we set out there is one term which especially challenges further consideration. If I am to say with full right, "This is red," I must know what is meant by the term Red, and I must know (which is part of the same thing) to what objects it is applicable.

But the knowledge here desiderated is a knowledge of Universals ; and when we examine the Judgments which constitute this knowledge we find that they take two forms—Enumerative and Generic ; *e.g.* "All men are mortal," and "Man is mortal."[1] Of these the former clearly depends upon the latter ; for, strictly speaking, we can have no right as a mere result of enumeration to say that all men are mortal until all men, including ourselves, are dead. Our right to make any such judgment must be derived from the judgment "Man (as such) is mortal" ; and if that can be shown to be true, then of course all (individual) men must be mortal. The stock instance of a purely enumerative universal is, "All swans are white," which almost any one would have assented to before the discovery of black swans ; but the only justifiable judgment would have been, "All swans hitherto observed are white."

The generic form of the Universal proposition is no doubt formally valid, whereas the enumerative form is not formally valid inasmuch as the enumerative universal derives its validity from the generic for which it has been substituted. But, as we have already seen,[2] this generic knowledge—Spinoza's *cognitio secundi generis*— of which mathematics is the chief and perhaps the only perfect instance—is not directly applicable to the physical world. We cannot argue from the definition of Man as mortal to the mortality of any particular biped hitherto regarded as human, because there always may be some peculiarity about him which exempts him from the law of the class to which in most respects he belongs. So that in the syllogism proving the mortality of Socrates, if the Major is stated enumeratively it is

---

[1] Cf. Chap. I. p. 12.
[2] Cf. Chap. I. p. 13, and IV. p. 49.

itself unwarranted, and if the Major is stated generically
the Minor is unwarranted : either " All men are mortal "
or " Socrates is a man " carries us further than we have
a right to go.

Consequently the Will to Know throws its proposition into hypothetical form—" If man, then mortal."
To this as it stands no exception can be taken, but the
" reference to reality " is now very thin ; and the
question how we can find warrant for the inference is
very pressing. It is not the case that the Hypothetical
Judgment affirms nothing ; quite clearly it affirms a
connexion of content. But its warrant for this must
come from a perception that the two " contents " are
mutually implicated in a system which contains them
both ; and the full understanding of it will require the
articulation of this system. And so the Will to Know
presses on from the Hypothetical judgment (if A then
B) to the Disjunctive, which is the form adapted to the
articulation of a system. This is not the kind of
Disjunction where the subject is an individual particular,
and the Predicate gives a list of alternative determinations—*e.g.* This wooden triangle is *either* equilateral
*or* isosceles *or* scalene ; for our right to make this
Judgment depends on previous knowledge of the
possible modes of triangularity. The Disjunction we
require is precisely that which states this previous
knowledge—where a system is stated in its unity by the
Subject and in its differences by the Predicate ; *e.g.*
Triangle (*or* triangularity) is equilateral, isosceles,
scalene : the three alternative predicates exclude one
another, but the subject includes them all and only
through all of them finds its full expression.

In this way the Disjunction, as the form of the
articulation of system, is the proper form of knowledge ;
it is the form of Omniscience, which may be represented
as a Disjunctive Judgment in which the Universe is
the subject and its whole wealth of variety the predicate.
But this predicate does not give a mere list of observed

determinations of the subject ; the alternatives must be
at once mutually exclusive and exhaustive, as in our
geometrical example every triangle must be either
equilateral or isosceles or scalene, but cannot be more
than one of these.    This so far realises the ideal of
knowledge, which is, as Plato says, not only to group
the Many under the One but also to insert How many
(ὁπόσα)—after which the Many may be allowed to go
to infinity.[1]    It does not matter for geometrical
purposes how many triangles there are ; what matters
is how many modes of triangularity there are.

We find, then, that the effort to understand fully
what is contained in the simplest act of thought will
carry us from the initial categorical judgment of perception to the disjunctive, in which we return to the
categorical form (S is P) after passing through the
hypothetical (If S, then P).    And the reason why we
are thus carried forward is that from the very first we
are engaged with a system—a unity of differences—and
only the Disjunctive Judgment gives adequate expression
to this systematic character of our experience.    In other
words, our process is the gradual elucidation of the fact
that "the individual is the universal."    At first we see
the subject merely as an individual marked by certain
features ; but the effort to understand this reveals the
individual as the concrete universal of its own com-
ponent elements or modes of actuality.    So Triangle
is the concrete unity of Equilateral, Isosceles, and
Scalene ; so Athens is the concrete unity of Pericles,
Phidias, Aeschylus, and Plato, and all its host of citizens ;
so a man's Self is the concrete unity or universal of his
actions and his varying forms of property, which are
united in a system by their relations to him.

The development of the Forms of Judgment which
we have traced is not a mere accident.    It results from
the nature of experience itself.    It represents the increasingly adequate expression of the systematic nature

[1] *Philebus,* 16 D, E.

of the world which all science and philosophy presuppose, and experience perpetually reaffirms. The simplest and most elementary judgment is an apprehension of unity in difference ; the fullest and most elaborate is at once the apprehension of differences held together in the unity of a universal, and the articulation of a universal into its differences.

We saw, however, that any given Judgment is formed as a separate affirmation only for the sake of an addition to knowledge—our own or some one else's. In the direct grasp of any object or system of truth judgments are implicit but not explicit ; a man absorbed in contemplation of a picture is not actually forming judgments ; but his experience contains the material for very many judgments, which are really *in* the picture (or his experience of it) and are not only made *about* it, but which none the less remain latent and implicit.

It is especially important to remember this in relation to the *Negative Judgment*. Negation, as the mere form of difference or distinction, is as all-pervasive as affirmation, the form of identity.[1] But a man does not make a specific and explicit negative judgment except to correct some actual or possible error of his own (*i.e.* to add to his own knowledge), or else to correct some actual or possible error of another man (*i.e.* to add to that other's knowledge). We may illustrate the positive value of the Negative Judgment by the part it plays in the game of Twenty Questions, where some one member of the party has to discover an object agreed upon by the rest in the course of twenty questions to which the answer must be either Yes or No.[2] The only skill in asking the questions is to choose questions to which the Negative answer is as instructive as the Affirmative. Thus, for purposes of

---

[1] Cf. Plato, *Sophist*, 255-258.

[2] The first question is always, "Is it animal, vegetable, or mineral?" and here one of the three may be named in the answer : this exception to the rule implies that the question is understood to be a complete disjunction of the universe. I may add that in my experience the questions only serve to narrow the field of attention ; when that is done, the precise object is reached (if at all) by telepathy.

this game, Europe and non-Europe are almost equally large, owing to the players being far more fully acquainted with Europe. So the question, " Is it in Europe?" just about halves the field of enquiry, and the answer "No" is just about as useful as the answer "Yes." And in either case, the judgment is analytic to the person giving the answer, and synthetic to the questioner, for whose sake it is made ; the analytic element is what makes the judgment possible and conditions its truth ; the synthetic element is what makes it interesting and conditions its occurrence.

The amount of positive knowledge gained by a negative judgment depends upon the number of terms in the Predicate of the Disjunction within which the negation is made. Let us suppose (*per impossibile*) that a man has a desire to go to Bletchley. He may be resident in Oxford, and know that there are two and only two railway stations in that " Academical Retreat," one of which is " right for " Bletchley. He goes to the Great Western Station, and is told, " This is not the station for Bletchley." This negative is precisely equivalent to the positive judgment, " The North-Western is the station for Bletchley." But if he were resident in London and began with Charing Cross, the discovery of his error would hardly help him at all. The number of railway stations in London is presumably finite, and he would therefore inevitably reach a moment when he could say with certainty, " Euston must be, and indubitably is, the station for Bletchley." But the method of exclusion would in this case be very cumbrous.

But while negation is explicitly employed only in order to increase knowledge or to facilitate the increase of knowledge by the rejection of false suggestion, yet the principle on which it rests is all-pervasive, being the principle of difference or distinction. In order to be at all, a thing must be something ; to be without being anything is obviously to be nothing : *Sein = nicht sein.*

And in being something (*e.g.* red), an object inevitably is not something else (*e.g.* yellow).

It is important, though by now so evident as hardly to deserve mention, that this Difference is always within a system or unity of some sort, and that explicit negation must therefore always have reference to some intelligible " world of discourse." Thus " not red " implies that the object is (or is supposed to be) coloured, so that to say, " The present system of inheritance is not red," is to talk nonsense.

We have now considered the main forms of the Judgment as the unit of thought. But it has become clear that as it is the unit, so it is the whole of thought. For the Judgment in its various forms is always the articulation of a system, the realisation of the concrete universal or unity as a whole of parts or as a principle operative in divers modes. And Inference is essentially nothing more than this ; it is the apprehension of the relation between two or more of the differences inherent in some one universal or system.

For it is clear by now that a universal—so far as it is of any real use in thought—is not an abstract quality but a concrete principle or whole. When we begin to think about any subject, our universals are still very abstract. Indeed, at this stage it is true that the extension and intension of terms, as we use them, vary inversely. The white wooden triangle is more concrete than the universal " Triangle," for the latter term means only a plane figure bounded by three straight lines. But as we study triangularity its meaning increases ; we find that it exists in three modes—equilateral, isosceles, scalene ; that, whatever its shape, its internal angles are equal to two right angles, etc. And while it lacks whiteness and woodenness no doubt, it is far more rich in geometrical significance than the particular white wooden triangle. It is only in regard to irrelevant qualities that the particular is more concrete than the universal ; in regard to what is relevant, the universal, when we understand it, is concrete and the particular relatively abstract.

To increase our knowledge of relevant facts is therefore the same thing as developing our apprehension of the concrete universal. It needs all its different elements for its full expression. But as the system or concrete universal grows before our mind we perceive new relations between its different elements; and *this is Inference.* It is not a new form of thought ; it is an incident in the progress of the Judgment to that perfect Disjunction which is the form of omniscience. We speak sometimes of "drawing" a conclusion ; but, strictly speaking, we perceive it. By putting together two premisses we construct a system in which we *see* the relation between the Subject and Predicate of our "conclusion." This is so in the syllogism, where the essential matter is the apprehension of the Major and Minor Premisses in one act of thought. It is equally so in the well-known instance already cited : If A is ten miles north of B, B ten miles west of C, C ten miles south of D, then A is ten miles west of D. Clearly what happens here is this : we put together the various facts given us, and *perceive* that they constitute a system (a square in this case) in which the previously unknown relation of A to D is a manifest element.

The conclusion of an inference is then that element in a concrete universal which we are at the moment interested in emphasising. Inference does for the concrete universal what the most elementary judgment does for a fact of perception ; it analyses one element out from the whole and then remakes the synthesis precisely in order to lay stress on this particular element in the synthetic or concrete whole from which it starts.

A good illustration of this is given by the principle of causation. We are generally content to regard the antecedent which we call the cause as actually itself producing the effect. But it is clear that " causation in time can only be understood as the manifestation of an underlying system itself not temporal." [1]  In practice, when we ask for the cause, *e.g.*, of some accident, we mean that one of the conditioning antecedents which was preventable.   But the whole cause, from which the effect *necessarily* follows, is the totality of its conditions. At some point in the continuous stream of events we make a cross section ; we treat what follows that section as the effect and what precedes as cause : or rather (inasmuch as we are not ever thinking of the whole course of the Universe at all) we select what interests us in the consequent and call it effect, and similarly select what interests us in the antecedent as being preventable, or unexpected, within the same system,[2] and call it cause.   But in each case we are really doing no more than emphasising the relation between two differences or particulars within a known system or concrete universal.  A judgment affirming causal relation is a case of inference—the intuition of the connexion of elements within an intellectual system.

Let us revert to our instance of the Royal Commission.   It begins with endless facts on one side, and an abstract universal—Unemployment, Vagrancy, Railway Nationalisation—on the other.   At the end, if it is successful, it has correlated the facts, and thereby made the universal concrete, so that to the reader of the Report the term Unemployment, for instance, means no longer merely a being out of work but a whole system of conditions which is itself part of the larger system called the Industrial Organisation of the country, or the like.  Certain elements in this concrete whole are singled out as capable of improvement by practicable means.   These are the "recommendations" brought forward by the Commissioners as the "conclusions" of their investigation.

---

[1] Bosanquet, *The Value and Destiny of the Individual*, p. 301.  Cf. the same author's discussion of the causal relation of Day and Night in his *Logic*, vol. i. p. 275.

[2] It is to secure that it is within the same system that we apply such methods as Mill formulates : they carry us no further than that.

This is the invariable nature of thought. The Will
to Know urges the mind to wider and wider apprehension; it is the impulse towards totality in the intellectual
sphere; logic is simply the method of this impulse;
and if we attend to real thinking and not to debating,
we shall find that while the details of the method are
dictated by the subject-matter, so that logic cannot
legislate for any science, yet its essential principle is
always the same: the ever fuller apprehension of the
concrete universal which is the same thing as the ever
wider grasp and closer correlation of the facts of experience. "A man's mind must be continually expanding
and shrinking between the whole human horizon and
and the horizon of an object glass." If a man is able
εἰς ἓν καὶ ἐπὶ πολλὰ ὁρᾶν, he has the divine capacity for
Truth.

# CHAPTER VI

## THE METHOD OF INTELLECT AND THE
## PROVINCE OF TRUTH

"Truth is one aspect of experience, and is therefore made imperfect and limited by what it fails to include. So far as it is absolute, it does, however, give the general type and character of all that possibly can be true or real. And the universe in this general character is known completely. It is not known, and it never can be known, in all its details.

"Absolute truth is error only if you expect from it more than mere general knowledge. It is abstract and fails to supply its own subordinate details. It is one-sided and cannot give bodily all sides of the Whole. But on the other side nothing, so far as it goes, can fall outside it. It is utterly all-inclusive and contains beforehand all that could ever be set against it. For nothing can be set against it which does not become intellectual and itself enter as a vassal into the kingdom of truth. Thus, even when you go beyond it, you can never advance outside it. . . .

"Truth is the whole world in one aspect, an aspect supreme in philosophy, and yet even in philosophy conscious of its own incompleteness."—BRADLEY.

IF our consideration of the Judgment has been success-ful, we are now acquainted with the essential quality and method of the intellect. We may summarise it in this way: contradiction is at once its enemy and its stimulus. It finds incoherence in its apprehension at any given time and reorganises its content to remove that incoherence. Contradiction is what it cannot think; and yet contradiction is what makes it think. So by the perpetual discovery of new contradiction it is forced on to a more and more systematic apprehension.

Perhaps this is most easily seen in the vast move-ments of the logic of a civilisation. At first we see the tribe or clan whose communistic organisation allows little or no initiative to the individual. Then we find a consciousness of this "contradiction"; for it is not only a strain in feeling but a contradiction in thought, inasmuch as the community exists for the good life of its citizens and is found to be checking that good life in certain ways. Gradually, with many subordinate oscillations, the thought of the citizens moves from the communist to the individualist position. But here a new contradiction arises, for it seems possible that the strife of unfettered competition may ruin many individuals and even disrupt the community itself. Consequently a new tendency towards centrality appears, under the name of Socialism or Collectivism, which aims at state control precisely for the sake of individual freedom. This tendency will probably develop, with subordinate oscillations, for five or ten centuries, until it is found to " contradict " some interest which it exists to safeguard, and so will again be thrown back by a new individualism. We shall find, when we come to consider The Problem of Evil,[1] that the same principle holds good of moral development. We have, moreover, already seen how close may be the relation between theoretical logic and political organisation in any period.[2] Feudalism and subsumptive Logic belong to one another ; so do Democracy and the modern Logic. And the transition from Feudal to Democratic political theory (through Hobbes who kept the pyramidal form, Locke who compromised it, and Rousseau who reached the modern doctrine in general and failed to apply it in particular) is a fair sample of the dialectical movement which is the vital process of all thought. Perhaps it is as well to remark, lest we be accused of making too much of tendencies and too little of individuals, that the supreme and lonely genius of Spinoza had already reached a full apprehension of the modern doctrine of the state.

This close connexion of political fact with theory in what seems to most people its most abstract form—for Logic is the theory of Theory—is no accident or freak; it

[1] Pt. IV. Chap. XX.　　　　[2] Chap. I. pp. 17, 18.

is due to the fact emphasised in the passage quoted from *Appearance and Reality* at the head of this chapter. So soon as any part of experience becomes matter of reflection it enters the sphere of intellect, and must be handled by the principles of the intellect. It is futile to protest against this in the name of Pragmatism or Vitalism or Activism or any other -ism. "Truth is one aspect of experience"—of all experience. And while it is only one, it is not to be supposed that we can gain any advantage by trying to escape from it in any way ; we may supplement it, but we cannot do without it. Art is other than science ; but there is a science of art, and its name is criticism. Conduct is other than science ; but there is a science of conduct, and its name is ethics. Religion is more than science ; but there is a science of religion, and its name is theology. Truth is an all-pervasive aspect of the real world ; in no department may the claims of the intellect be ignored or flouted, nor the admissibility of its method denied.

Having said so much we may safely, perhaps, go on to speak of the one-sidedness of the intellect without being supposed to underestimate its authority. We said in Chapter III.[1] that science inevitably begins with a two-sided abstraction. It is bound to ignore the mental image which accompanies and makes possible the apprehension of the content ; and thereby it ignores the particularity of .the facts with which it deals. Scientific truth, then, is a system of contents—or, as we may express it, a nexus of relations ; but we cannot suppose that Reality is a nexus of relations, for a relation at least implies related terms. A relation in which nothing is related is bare nothing. But a term cannot be altogether constituted by its relations. This has sometimes been suggested by the language of some philosophers, and perhaps believed by them. But it is impossible. Such a belief must rest on the root fallacy of Determinism—a term generally reserved for ethics,

[1] Pp. 37, 38 ; 41, 42.

but really a logical term.   In fact, the main objection
to Determinism is logical.   Determinism, the theory
that everything is constituted by its relations to other
things—that it consists, in fact, of these relations—is
seen to be fallacious so soon as its application is
universally extended.   It tells us that in a system
A B C, A is only A in virtue of its relations to B and
C ; B and C determine it as A.   And that seems easy ;
but why is B, B ?   It must be determined as B by A
and C.   And similarly C by A and B.   If, then, each
term is nothing till its external relations constitute it,
we are confronted with the spectacle of nothing at all
developing internal differentiation by the interaction of
its non-existent parts.   We may echo the question
which Coleridge asks about the self-differentiation of
Schelling's Absolute—*Unde haec nihili in nihila tam
portentosa transnihilatio* ?   Nor does this matter become
any better by being put into the Time-series, though we
may veil some of the difficulties by so doing ; for an
individual to be entirely determined by its past, or by
its present, environment, or by both, is utterly impossible.
For as its present environment is only other individuals,
so is its past environment ; and what determined them ?
To regard this process as strictly infinite is really to
give up the game ; it is only a way of saying that you
never do reach a positive which may commence turning
nothing into something.   Infinite Time, the only escape
for the pure Determinist, seems to be the assertion of
an infinite undifferentiated substance ; and an undifferentiated substance is for this purpose the same
as nothing at all.   It is logically the same, for bare
being (*sein*), which is not a something, is indistinguish-
able from not being (*nicht sein*) ; and it is the same in
effect, for there is still no means of getting the differentiation started.   But if we allow the differentiation as a
fact, we are giving up pure external Determinism.
We are now in the position of saying that in the
system A B C, A is determined as A by B and C ; but

it must have been something in its own right first, and
that too of such a kind as to make the determination as
A possible to it—*a*. Thus if we abolish, or suppose
abolished, B and C, A will not disappear but will
become *a*. A hand cut off from the body, to use the
old illustration, is no longer a hand in the full sense ;
but it is not become nothing. We are led, then, to the
position that the system A B C is the synthesis of *a*, *β*,
and *γ*. That is to say, A is not isolable, because the
attempt to isolate it reduces it at once to *a*; and so
with B and C. Of course the actual distinction between
*a* and A must be determined specifically in each case ;
but the distinction is real, and this is the fact represented
by the scientific method of reducing all individuals to
their relations. An individual is what it is in virtue of
its relations ; that is true ; but we are not justified in
concluding that apart from its relations it is nothing at
all. All of this will call for revision later on ; but we
may say at once that the effort of science to reduce
everything to relations can only be provisionally fruit-
ful. Science has to treat every particular instance as *a*
case, a specimen of a species, not as *this* case ; but yet
each case is just itself, so that for full apprehension we
must, in Spinoza's language, proceed from *cognitio secundi
generis* to *scientia intuitiva*. The generic character of
scientific knowledge requires the individuality of things,
from which it abstracts in order to make sense of itself.

The intellect is, of course, quite able to form the
conception of particularity and attend to the particularity
of existent things ; but particularity is itself a generic
term, and is not *a* particular.

The intellect is ready enough to assert that particular
and universal are different aspects of an identity ; and
some writers always seem quite happy as soon as they
have pointed out that two opposites are complementary
aspects of an identity. But this is a mere formality.
The problem here is for the mind to realise the identity
of universal and particular ; and I submit that the mind

cannot do it *qua* scientific intelligence.  It only sees
that it "must" be done "somehow"; but it cannot
display the *how*.  This is why the word "somehow"
occurs so very often in some metaphysical works, and
why some philosophers talk of *merging* the different
aspects in their unity.  I believe all this occurs because
they try to make the intellect solve problems which it
sets by being the intellect—*i.e.* by treating things in the
scientific way; and we can only solve these problems
by moving on to another method altogether—in this
case the artistic.  In perception where an adequate
percept is forthcoming, and in artistic imagination
where an adequate image is created, the problem is
solved, though it did not admit of intellectual solution.
The characters, for instance, in a drama are both types
and individuals; they have universal significance, though
they are utterly particular.  There is no need to emphasise the universal significance of artistic creations; and
their particularity is clear enough; when the characters
in a drama are *mere* types we at once condemn the
piece from the dramatic point of view.  We require
that they should be living and individual.  Now I have
already said that it is clear that Truth cannot be a
complete system in itself because it has got to make a
complete unity with other modes of personal life.[1]
Here then, as it seems to me, we reach an ultimate
dualism which scientific thought as such cannot solve,
but which finds solution when thought passes into
imagination.

Of course it is not intended to make a strict and rigid
distinction between intellect and imagination.  The
movement of the mind in these two functions is
sufficiently distinct to make the use of separate names
advantageous; but it is still one mind at work.

The goal of the intellect is the apprehension of the
whole universe as a nexus of relations.  No doubt the
ideal is unattainable by a human mind within the period

[1] Chap. II. pp. 34, 35.

of a human life on this planet ; but it cannot be un-attainable in principle. And the judgment in which such an apprehension is realised will be a non-temporal statement or grasp of an object known to be successive. This non-temporal grasp of the successive is reached in every department of science in whatever degree the mind has mastered the subject-matter. But at present the temporal character is not altogether overcome. For while we are still at the intellectual or scientific stage, the mind is characterised by unrest and motion. This is the essence of "intellection" or science, that it asks "Why?" perpetually ; as soon as it is answered it asks "Why?" again. And when, having rounded off some relatively complete whole or system, it contemplates the result, the mind is passing from the intellectual and scientific to the imaginative and artistic function.

In Mathematics we are emancipated from Time by the way of sheer escape ; we are free from it because our material, being an object of thought only, is itself non-temporal. All Science seeks to approximate to Mathematics, but its material is the temporal and changing world. Its achievement is reached when it presents a complete nexus of relations which gives the unchanging ground or law of the changes in the real world—a timeless formula of the temporal. It thus delivers us from mere transitoriness by giving us the permanent law of the transitory.

Thus the goal of the intellect is a Truth which emancipates from the control of Time, but never gives that actual mastery over Time which, as we shall see, is conferred by imagination.

# CHAPTER VII

## RELATIVITY AND INDIVIDUALITY

"No kind of relation could be assumed as subsisting between things, acting upon them, conditioning, preparing, favouring or hindering their reciprocal action; but reciprocal action itself, the passion and action of things, must take the place of relation."—LOTZE.

THE scientific intellect, ignoring the particularity of things, grasps the world as a nexus of relations. But a relation, by itself, is just nothing at all; it is irredeemably adjectival, and must have substantives *between* which it exists. Again, the smallest consideration shows that in fact there is nothing *between* the two substantives, and the relation is seen to be a character of the substances said to be related. Similarly a law of nature is a mere generalisation of the way in which individual things behave.

We are here on the fringe of innumerable controversies; but they do not affect our purpose. It is easy to see that the abstraction made by the intellect in its search for pure content has set well-defined limits to the scope of its enquiry. It is a perfectly legitimate, indeed a necessary, function of Mind, but by itself it can never give to Mind its final satisfaction.

In fact, the whole machinery by which the intellect works is incapable of leading to a full grasp of Reality. As we have already seen, it works with Terms and Relations. But these never exhaust the significance of the whole within which both exist. The musical critic analyses a symphony into themes and the relations

73

between them in the whole ; and yet the whole is more
than the themes and their relations. In some cases the
terms in the relation are modified by the relation in
which they stand ; in others there is no such modification. But in all cases we begin with the continuous
Whole of presented experience, and we get the terms
of our reflective thought by analysis of that experience ;
we do not reflectively build up our world by adding
one term to another. Our analysis will follow lines
suggested by our interest in making it ; and at any
point where we stop we shall have Terms and Relations.

The Intellect, then, obtains its individual Terms and
their Relations in this way. We begin with the whole
continuous given Reality : in order to deal with it we
have to analyse it, to isolate the elements with which
we are to deal. This isolation must, of course, remove
those elements from their setting in the rest of Reality.
Whether the removal of this contact has any further
consequences must be specially determined in each
case. (The removal may, of course, be either actual,
as in physical experiment, or ideal, as in any case of
selective attention.) Thus if we remove Plato's philosophy altogether from its relations to Greek thought
and civilisation, we shall certainly miss a great deal of
his actual meaning, for much of what he says derives
its meaning from that relation. Or, on the other hand,
we may presumably remove the lack of sunshine during
the summers of 1912 and 1913 from its relation of
simultaneity with Mr. Asquith's Premiership without
affecting its nature at all in any other respect. The
two are connected, in so far as in the metaphysical ideal
they would be seen to cohere in a single system ; but
it is at least possible that there is no more direct connexion than that ; the bare relation of simultaneity is,
of course, a fact, but it may have no determining influence
on the two simultaneous events. If so, it may be said
that in such a case the relation is in the whole which
the related elements make up, and yet not in any of

those elements.    But let us take another instance where
we seem to have the same sort of relation—a musical
chord ; take the common chord of C major—CEG.
That chord is no doubt an individual fact.    But it is
quite vital to its nature that all the three notes com-
posing it should remain in the chord what they were
outside it ; if they are altered, it becomes a different
chord.    If, for instance, E becomes E♭, the chord is
that of C minor and not of C major ; if it approximates
to E♭, it is out of tune.    Each note is in the chord what
it was outside    Yet the chord is a single new fact :
" Taking three sounds, I frame, not a fourth sound,
but a star."    And the reason is that in the chord there
are three relations—C to E, E to G, and C to G—and
the further relation of these relations to one another,
which are not in the separate notes, but are in the
whole chord.    When the chord is analysed into the
separate notes—*i.e.* when these are played separately—
these relations disappear ; but the notes remain what
they were.    The whole is thus more than the sum of
any parts that can be reached by analysis ; yet those
parts are present, unaltered, in the whole.    The point
which I want to emphasise in this connexion is that
there are some relations whose removal makes no
difference to the related term other than this removal
itself ; in all other respects the term out of that relation
is just what it is in it.    Such relations, then, may fairly
be said to involve no modification of the related terms ;
the weight of a book in its place upon the shelf is the
same as its weight in the hand.

But not all relations are of this character.    Some
relations modify their terms through and through ; and
the higher we go in the scale of being, the more do we
find this to be the case.    Mere mechanical objects are
not capable of entering into really intimate relations :
the brick that is built into a wall thereby enters into
new relations ; but its colour and its weight remain
what they were.    The new relation does not affect the

old relations—or at any rate not all of them. I suppose it is true that the atom, or the electron, or whatever we call the last result of physical analysis, in so far as it is regarded as really existent, must be held to be totally unaffected by any relation into which it enters except in the manner specified by that relation. But as we rise in the scale, the dependence of any individual on its relations becomes greater and greater : the dependence of the plant on the soil is greater than that of the stone. And at last, in the animal organism we find that the most important characteristics are given by relation. A hand is still something when it is cut off ; for anatomy it may even be still a hand. But for all purposes which the hand itself should serve it is not a hand at all. This process reaches its climax, so far as we can tell, in human beings. The individual man derives very nearly all his characteristics from his environment ; take from him all his social relations, and he is at once changed out of all recognition.

Yet this does not contradict our previous argument. It is still true that the individual cannot be dissolved into relations. Rather the fact is that Reality is a continuous system which we analyse along the lines suggested by our interest from time to time, and that the results of this analysis are always individual members of the system, each containing its own original and underived contribution to the whole, which would remain extant even though everything but it were abolished, but determined in character, to a smaller or greater degree, by the other members of the system. Its relations to those other members may be purely external, as in the simultaneity of two totally disparate events ; or they may be internal, or intimate, as in the relation of an individual man to the civilisation into which he is born, and under which he is brought up. In neither case is it constituted by its relations, as I hope that we have sufficiently shown :[1] in the former case it is not

[1] Chap. VI. pp. 69, 70.

even modified ; in the latter it is.   The whole can never
be actually dissected into its parts, because in the process
the external relations vanish, and the modifications of
the parts are changed.   Yet the parts are really there
in the whole, for each is an original and underived
element ;  in entering the whole it may be modified,
but it cannot become something quite different—it can
only become actually what it always was potentially.

I have been saying that we arrive at finite individuals
by analysing a given continuous Reality, and that we
analyse on principles suggested by our interest from
time to time.   But this does not mean that the ascrip-
tion of individuality is determined by our caprice, or
indeed by us at all.   In that analysis we discover it, we
do not make it.   We determine what principles of division we shall apply, but after that we have no control
over the result.   Suppose that there are upon a hanging
bookshelf four books on philosophy, three bound in
red and one in green ; and three books on history, two
bound in red and one in green.   If our interest is with
the weight of the whole, we treat shelf and books as a
single individual—analysing it out of the whole room
where it hangs ; if our interest is with the subject-
matter of the books, there are two individuals—a group
of four and a group of three ; if our interest is with the
colours, there are again two individuals—a red group of
five books and a green group of two books ; if our interest is in reading the books, inasmuch as we can only
attend to one at a time, the separate books are individuals.   In each case our analysis only discovers
what is actual fact without it ; the last result, the individuality of the separate books, is no more real than
the other individualities, but is more important, because
it is relevant to the essential purpose of the books.   It
is, of course, logically quite legitimate to analyse a
book into pages, and the pages into square inches, and
even into molecules and atoms.   The analysis into
pages seems sane, and the analysis of the pages into

atoms seems sane, because each is valuable for a rational purpose ; the analysis of a page into square inches seems insane—and yet it is not logically invalid. There is no reason why a man should not count the square inches contained in the page of a book if he likes ; but it is for liking it that we call him insane. The process is logical, but is not rational. Logically, those square inches are perfectly individual. But we do not attend to their individuality because they are not differentiated by any function relative to the purpose of the page or the book. *Individuality*, then, is *discovered by analysis*, that analysis being guided by interest ; but individuality is not determined by either analysis or interest ; it is *determined by function*.

But not only is the individuality so discovered real in itself ; the degrees of individuality differ also in things themselves. We may say that it is more fitting to call a man an individual than his foot, because for normal human purposes the analysis that reveals the whole man is more important than the analysis that reveals the foot as an individual. But there is more in it than this. Individuality is discovered by analysis ; but it is determined by function, and some functions are dependent on, and therefore secondary to, others, as in any organic whole the part is dependent on and secondary and subservient to the whole ; this would not be true in the case of stones in a heap, but it is so in the case of the limbs of a body.

In the sense we have adopted, individual means amongst other things irreplaceable ; the individual is this unique case of a universal. But irreplaceable may be used in the barely logical sense of necessary to the coherence of a system ; or it may mean irreplaceable in the realisation of a purpose ; the two are not really distinct, for in postulating the coherence of the system of Truth or Reality we are formulating a Purpose—the Purpose that our own experience shall become coherent with the coherence ascribed to ultimate Reality. But this purpose has to be realised piecemeal through the accomplishment of many minor purposes. And so we may legitimately test, not indeed the uniqueness, but the richness of any individual by considering the number and comprehensiveness of the purposes for which it is irreplaceable ; and then it is at once clear that the self-conscious ethical spirit has an individuality of far greater fulness than any other known to us. Even the social system, of which the individual man forms a part, is less completely individual in many ways ; for it has no sensations, except those of the individuals who compose it, and these are strictly confined in each case to the particular individual in question. The nation is an individual for political purposes, but those very political purposes must be formed and held by separate persons, and it is therefore self-contradictory to merge the citizen in the State, or the individual believer in the Church. Inasmuch as man is social, the State and the Church must be maintained even at great cost ; but it must not be forgotten that the happiness or character they aim at producing can only be actualised by their individual members, and the individuality of the State is subservient to that of the citizens, because its function is subservient. Individuality is therefore ascribed to persons with more right than to anything else. And yet no being is so dependent as man on his environment. Indeed, paradoxical as it may at first appear, it is just those whom we call the greatest individuals who owe most to their surroundings. The original contribution which every man brings into the world is a capacity or capacities ; that is, it is always something which may or may not become something else, as circumstances determine ; and the greater the number of these capacities, the greater is the man's dependence. The stone is capable of motion and rest, and is scarcely affected by its environment except in the matter of motion and rest. But the infant who is capable of being a great statesman or a great artist depends for his character almost wholly on his environment. There may be a capacity for scholarship, for painting, for music, for finance—all latent in one child ; if his environment develops these capacities he becomes a great man ; if not, he remains, it may be, a casual labourer, warped in sentiment and sluggish in mind. Or the case may be like that of Plato's youth, with the gifts that might make him a philosopher-king all perverted by false education. The greater the natural gifts, the more dependent is the man on environment. The ideal genius would be a man with a capacity corresponding to every function of the universe ; and for the development of those capacities he would be dependent on all existence. The great individual is not one who is independent of his environment, but one whose environment—or horizon—is so wide that he is *relatively* independent of isolated occurrences. The man who is dependent on the whole universe will not fear what flesh can do unto him, and he seems independent of circumstance because he is almost independent of those few and trivial circumstances on which most people depend altogether. He is conditioned just as completely as other men, and in far more ways. He is responsive to the whole universe ; the whole universe is focused in him. And he alone fully realises the whole ideal of individuality. For he alone contains his significance within himself.

And yet he above all others derives his significance from outside. So entirely does the machinery of Terms and Relations fail us at the critical point. At the most elementary stage it works fairly well, as long, that is, as we are dealing with purely mechanical objects. But in proportion as the individual object is higher in the scale, the relations into which it enters affect it more radically, till at last we reach the stage where the completest development of individuality coincides with the completest receptivity of influence.

For full understanding of such an individual, still more of several such individuals in mutual interaction, the scientific method is of little use. It is not to be ignored, but it must be supplemented. The dramatist tells us more truth about men than the moralist, or the psychologist, or the sociologist, or the criminologist. For the Imagination does not move between Terms and Relations, but contemplates the whole fact of which they are the dissection. The analysis of the intellect is useful, but only provided we return from it to the contemplation of the Whole.

# CHAPTER VIII

## KNOWLEDGE AND PERSONALITY : THE SOCIETY OF INTELLECTS

"The representative centre of any range of externality can only represent it in a way of its own."—BOSANQUET.

ACTUAL knowledge is not only the work of Mind but of this mind and that mind. Every mind is a separate focus of the universe ; according to its capacity it apprehends the world about it, and according to its instinct for totality (or will to know) it tries to increase its range and hold together in a united system all that it can experience. We conceived at the end of the last chapter a mind whose range was that of the whole universe. Such a mind would be in possession of all truth.

And yet it would focus it in its own way. For its apprehension must always be coloured by the history preceding and conditioning it. No amount of development of my mind can make irrelevant the circumstances of my birth and early training, the ease or difficulty with which various departments of knowledge have been, or hereafter shall be, mastered.[1] If not the knowledge itself, yet its preciousness is vitally affected by the mode of its attainment. And here as elsewhere there are values of great excellence, which are yet not compatible with one another, and must be realised, if at all, in different subjects.

[1] I am here (to my sorrow) in direct conflict with Dr. Bosanquet, *The Value and Destiny of the Individual*, pp. 282-289.

We have introduced the Category of Value; and that carries us on at once to a new stage of the enquiry. We now need to make a distinction, somewhat parallel to that drawn by Locke between Primary and Secondary Qualities. Without entering on the controversy between Realism and Idealism,[1] we can see that there are certain propositions which are true (if at all) for all minds, and some which are only true for certain minds; or perhaps it is more accurate to say that certain aspects of reality are only actualised in the experience of certain minds. Thus the qualities which can be mathematically estimated are identical for all intelligences; but there are other qualities, equally real, which vary from one person to another. The colour of a red and green object has a totally different æsthetic value for a man with normal sight from that which it has for a colour-blind man; the very words "red" and "green" have different meanings for the two men. But the statements of optical science as regards "wave-lengths" in the ethereal undulations and so forth have the same meaning for all minds which attach any meaning to them at all.

It is to be noticed that the variable element is always to some degree adjectival; it is a product of the qualities which are mathematically determinable and therefore constant in the sense of identical for all intelligences. But these "secondary" qualities, to use Locke's term, are perfectly real, whether they are in the object or in the percipient, or are produced by the meeting together of these two;[2] these qualities are real, but certain persons can never apprehend them.

We have considered the most elementary case; but it is clear that there is a peculiar excellence in the easy grace of a character richly endowed by nature and developed by favourable conditions; there is another excellence in the grit and force of a character richly.

[1] To which, in my judgment, too much attention is usually paid as compared with other problems. No one is going to assert a complete disparity between mind and its objects or a complete dependence of either upon the other.

[2] Cf. Plato, *Theaetetus*, 156-7.

endowed by nature and developed through a persistent struggle with unfavourable conditions ; and there is yet another excellence in the steady worth of a character not richly endowed which is content to fulfil conscientiously the tasks for which it is fitted. These three types cannot be realised in the same person. Again each of these three types will be appreciative of different excellences and so bring to its completion a different function of Reality. In countless ways it appears that only through the diversity of personalities is the whole of Reality apprehended or its whole Truth known. For it seems impossible to deny that when a beautiful object is appreciated, it gains in quality itself. Whether or not a thing can fitly be called beautiful if no one can see it, I do not know ; but I am quite clear that, if no one can see it,[1] it does not matter whether it is beautiful or not. Its value begins when it is appreciated. Good must mean good for somebody ; apart from consciousness, value is non-existent.

And yet it seems impossible to say that the value is *in* the appreciating mind. It exists *for* it, and only so ; but it is *in* the object. So the object when appreciated becomes something which it was not until then. But if so, and if there are various values which cannot be all realised for the same consciousness, then the variety of intelligences is necessary for the full actualisation of the value of the world. The complete truth, therefore, if we include Value, is only grasped by the whole society of intelligences, and can never be fully grasped by one alone.

This phase of the subject cannot be ignored. For the value-judgment—even within the realm of Art—is still a judgment, an act of the intellect. It is possible to conceive a state of things where every one made the same value-judgments, but only if many of these are accepted from others on trust ; and there is a clear

---

[1] *I.e.* literally no one—no man or angel or God. I must confess that I simply attach no meaning whatever to Mr. G. E. Moore's position on this point, *Principia Ethica*, pp. 83-85.

difference between the judgment "This is beautiful," where it is a real analysis of experience, and "This is beautiful" where it is a repetition of the verdict of an expert : in the former case it means, "This gives me æsthetic pleasure," while in the latter. it means, at best, "This would give æsthetic pleasure to any one of sufficiently trained susceptibilities," and in this case the value is itself still potential and not actual.

But our value-judgments depend upon our characters —not just our moral character, but upon the whole psychic quality of our nature. This looks as if we were reduced to utter chaos, for it is clear that no one man can dictate what values another ought to find. But inasmuch as there is a particular character which every individual, as *this* member of the society of spirits, ought to make his own, so, by consequence, there are certain values which he ought to appreciate and thereby actualise.

So when we consider our experience as it is handled by knowledge, we find a world which is known and appreciated by the whole society of finite intelligences. The whole grasp of their collective experience cannot be held in one centre of consciousness however "Absolute" or "Infinite," because some of the elements are intrinsically incompatible. There cannot be one Mind which includes all of this. The Absolute Being (so far) appears precisely as the society of intelligences.

But why should we bring in the Absolute Being at this point at all ? We are bound to do so because the impulse of Self-Transcendence, of which the Will to Know is one manifestation, is always an impulse to the Whole ; it reveals itself alike in the sacrifice of love or loyalty and in the search of science ; it is the determination to get beyond one's mere particularity (though we can never leave it behind), and apprehend the Whole and our place in it and dependence on it ; "Love is the mainspring of logic." [1]  And this effort towards

---

[1] Bosanquet, *The Principle of Individuality and Value*, p. 341.  Cf. p. 243.

the Whole is stultified, and therefore all science is in principle stultified (for science is a phase of this effort), unless there is a Whole.

But this Whole or Absolute appears at this stage only as the physical world [1] and the perfected—or rather the mutually self-perfecting—society of spirits. And this is a real Whole. From the standpoint of the Will to Know we can demand no more. The intellect *working only upon the principles of its own procedure* will never lead to the Transcendent God of Religion, for its claims can be satisfied with less, and the further step is a leap in the dark such as Science may not take.

Let us, however, not underestimate what is implied in the Will to Know. The conception of the Universe coming to focus in a multitude of intelligences, and realising its own value [2] in their manifold appreciation of it, is not a notion which degrades our spiritual life; nor is it alien from the life of religion; for this Society of Spirits is the Communion of Saints, and the agency that builds it up is the Holy Church, which is that Communion as so far realised and active, and its spirit of self-transcendence and self-sacrifice (which are two names for one thing) is the Holy Spirit.

For the Society of Intelligences in which the truth and value of the world is grasped must be independent of the chances of Time. If the value realised by the heroes and artists of antiquity is simply perished, and other similar values come into being and again pass out of it almost daily, and if this flux is all that can be said to be at all, then our Society and the world of values make up no Whole at all, and again the effort towards the Whole is stultified. Somehow [3] that Whole must be Supra-temporal, and hold within itself all the values realised in all the ages.

---

[1] I put in these words to avoid begging the Idealist-Realist question.
[2] See next chapter.
[3] Cf. Chap. VI. p. 71. We shall begin to see how later on.

# CHAPTER IX

## TIME, VALUE, AND THE ABSOLUTE

Λέγωμεν δὴ δι' ἥντινα αἰτίαν γένεσιν καὶ τὸ πᾶν τόδε ὁ συνιστὰς συνέστησεν.
ἀγαθὸς ἦν, ἀγαθῷ δὲ οὐδεὶς περὶ οὐδενὸς οὐδέποτε ἐγγίγνεται φθόνος· τούτου
δ' ἐκτὸς ὢν πάντα ὅτι μάλιστα ἐβουλήθη γενέσθαι παραπλήσια ἑαυτῷ· ταύτην δὴ
γενέσεως καὶ κόσμου μάλιστ' ἄν τις ἀρχὴν κυριωτάτην παρ' ἀνδρῶν φρονίμων
ἀποδεχόμενος ὀρθότατα ἀποδέχοιτ' ἄν.—PLATO.

WE have said that "the intellect, working only upon
the principles of its own procedure," carries us to a
belief in a perfectly united Society of Intelligences, but
no further. And it may as well be said at once that
nothing which follows can invalidate that result ; it will
be supplemented but not abrogated.

But even at the point which we have already reached
it is possible to determine the ways in which such
supplementary process may be permissible.

At present we have a conception of the world as a
supra-temporal whole which "somehow" contains all
the facts and values actualised in all history. Such a
conception satisfies the scientific intellect. It is all-
inclusive and perfectly coherent. And though there is
an impulse to ask, "But why is it there at all ? and why
is it of this sort ? " Science must regard that impulse as
a temptation, a desire acting outside its proper sphere ;
for how can we get outside the world to judge it?
And how can there be any cause of the Whole ?

But within the Whole as the intellect apprehends it
there are elements favourable to an expansion of our
conception though they cannot be said to demand it.
Let us see what they are, so that we may know what

the intellect will allow us to accept if other functions of Mind suggest.

We have said that as the Universe comes to focus in the various centres of consciousness it realises its own value. But there must be potentially an exceeding value precisely in the unity of all these values, which, *ex hypothesi*, no finite mind can grasp. If therefore on other grounds we find ourselves led to the thought of an Infinite Mind, which is yet other than the finite minds and also other than the society of finite minds, this will supply something, which the scientific intellect cannot on the basis of its own procedure demand, but which it will welcome as the appropriate culmination of its own edifice.[1]

Now in all activity of the human mind, value (while always in one sense a mere adjective of fact) gives the reason for action; where the action is productive, it gives the reason for production, and therefore the *raison d'être* of the thing produced. In such cases, value is the explanation of fact. The thing is there because some one wanted it ; but what is wanted is not the mathematical properties of the thing, but the good which depends on appreciation for its existence. If, then, on other grounds we find ourselves led to the thought that the world as a whole exists for the sake of its Value, and that the Mind which appreciates the Whole is also Creative Mind or Will (as the human mind is creative when it sets out to build its palaces of Science, Art, Civilisation, and Religion), this too will be welcomed by the intellect as adding to its scheme a final completion.

For we found the intellect anxious to ask why the world is here at all. The question for the moment was rejected as a temptation. Totality had been reached, and the legitimate impulse of Intellect had reached its goal. But if from some other department of Mind's activity an answer is suggested, the intellect (if not

---

[1] The First Person begins to be surmised behind the Third.

impeded by "intellectualist" dogmatism) will gladly accept it. And Mind does accept as final an explanation in terms of Purpose and Will; for this (and, so far as our experience goes, this alone) combines efficient and final causation. "Why is this canvas covered with paint?" "Because I painted it." "Why did you do that?" "Because I hoped to create a thing of beauty for the delight of myself and others." If, then, we find any ground for saying that the world is the product of an Infinite Will, created for the sake of its Value,[1] the intellect, which could not *from any consideration of its own procedure* reach any such result, will none the less accept this doctrine as altogether agreeable to itself.

And further, if it appears that the Value of the Whole, and therefore the Content of the Infinite Will, can be adequately symbolised in terms appreciable by the human mind,[2] so that the human mind may thereby, in some degree at least, enter into the joy of the Eternal, that too will be welcomed by the intellect as the very crown of its endeavour, exceeding the utmost limits of its hopes.

Let us summarise our results so far.

The rationality of the Universe is the primary certainty. This certainty is, no doubt, an act of faith, but all other certainty depends upon it. I have no right to say that $\therefore 2 + 2 = 4$, $\therefore$ 2 apples + 2 apples = 4 apples, except on the supposition that my principles of reasoning are valid of the real world.

Truth is a universal aspect of experience, and there is nothing, therefore, which can claim exemption from the criticism and analysis of the scientific intellect.

But Truth is only one aspect of experience, and must not be treated as if it were the whole. The intellect is not the only function of Mind.

---

[1] The Problem of Evil is here crying out for attention, as in John i. 3. But, like St. John, we ignore it for the present. See Chap. XX.

[2] The Second Person is surmised beside the First and Third.

Truth emancipates from Time, but does not give mastery over Time. In itself it gives only a timeless formula of the successive (except in mathematics whose subject-matter is even below succession in the scale of reality). But herein it gives promise of a real apprehension of the successive, wherein the Mind would rise above succession altogether and contemplate it as with a bird's-eye view.

The intellect is an unending restlessness of Mind, asking Why? and again Why?

It recognises the fact of value, and the further fact that values, while real only for the appreciating mind, cannot all be real for the same mind.

It therefore demands the existence of a Society of Minds in which, as a supra-temporal Whole, all values may be realised.

Beyond that it regards nothing as requisite for the validity of its own method, but it will accept certain further positions if other functions of Mind suggest them :

A real experience perfecting the emancipation from Time effected by Truth into the very mastery and possession of the successive ;

The existence of an Infinite Mind realising the value precisely of the whole of the values realised in the experience of the collective society of Intellects ;

The recognition of this Infinite Mind as Eternal Will, purposing the Universe for the Value which it will realise therein ;

The adequate symbolic representation of this Infinite and Eternal—" the express image of His Person "—by contemplation of which the human mind may be rapt into the joy for which the world was made.

# BOOK I—*continued*

## PART II

### ART

# CHAPTER X

## THE NATURE AND SIGNIFICANCE OF ART

Επὶ τὸ πολὺ πέλαγος τετραμμένος τοῦ καλοῦ καὶ θεωρῶν.
'Ενταῦθα τοῦ βίου . . . εἴπερ που ἄλλοθι, βιωτὸν ἀνθρώπῳ, θεωμένῳ αὐτὸ
τὸ καλόν.—PLATO.

WE have already said that the activity of art is
complementary to that of science. In reality, as given
to us at the most elementary stage of apprehension,
there are always two aspects or functions—the particular
and universal. Science for its own purpose attends
almost entirely to the universal function ; this is because
the scientific method of understanding is to relate any
given object to the rest of the universe ; it asks Why ?
and to the answer asks Why ? again. Everything is
explained by its reference to environment and context.
For this reason a scientific theory may become out of
date, as the Ptolemaic astronomy has, and so lose all
but a historic interest. A change in the understanding
of the context may lead to a change in the explanation
of any given fact. The artistic method of understanding is the exact opposite of this ; it concentrates
attention upon the particular fact which at the moment
excites interest, and helps us to understand it by helping
us to see it better than we had seen it before; it holds
us contemplating it until we grasp its whole detail.
The work of art is therefore never out of date. If it
was successful it actually presented some object, and it
then has for ever whatever value it has at all. Shakespeare's world is richer and more complex than Homer's,

93

but Homer is not out of date. Whereas science is mental restlessness, art is essentially mental repose ; it is indeed an activity of repose, but repose is the dominant note. If we consider such a thing as a sunset, the scientist will explain it by general laws concerning the refraction of light and so forth, which will help us to understand how such a thing occurs ; but the poet or the painter, with more vivid apprehension, will speak of it in such a way that by sympathy with him we come to see what he has seen and to realise the sunset in and for itself. The nature of the imaginative activity by means of which this is accomplished and the experience which it occasions must now be considered.

Mr. Balfour concluded his delightful Romanes Lecture with the following suggestions as to the nature of the æsthetic experience :

I regard it as the highest element, the highest sub-class in that whole class of emotions—a much larger class of emotions —which do not suggest or lead to action. You enjoy a picture, you enjoy a poem, you enjoy a symphony, but your enjoyment does not go beyond this ; it never prompts any policy, any course of action ; it does not drive you into the practical world at all. A great many feelings which answer to that description hardly rise to the level of what we call æsthetic emotion. We keep that name, rightly I think, for the highest classes of the species, and if we are wise we do not attempt any too nice or precise distinction between these higher classes and others lower in the same scale. But the pleasure we derive from what is neat, from what is dexterous, from the presentation of anything which seems to us to be suitable—these are genuine pleasures. They belong to the same great species as æsthetic emotions, though in my terminology they are lower in the same scale. But there is another class, and, let us admit it, a much greater class of emotions which do lead to action, which are sharply distinguished from the æsthetic class in its wider aspect. This other class extends over the whole area of conscious life ; it may perhaps even go below conscious life. They may lose themselves, these emotions, at the lower end of the scale, in the mere reaction, the mere muscular reaction or nervous irritability and sensibility. At the higher end of the scale they may rise to the greatest feelings of which human

nature is capable ; rise to love celestial and terrestrial ; the love
of God, humanity, country, family ; love in all its innumerable
aspects.   These are at the upper end of the scale, and with all
the pedigree behind them,—which like the pedigree of every
great thing either in human institutions or in human nature
is very unworthy of its final progeny.   If therefore you have
in mind these two great classes of emotion ; at the head of one,
a great class of æsthetic emotions ; at the head of the other, a
class of these loftiest feelings of love and devotion, why should
you quarrel because you find no adequate philosophy of the
æsthetic emotions, when we live in fair contentment without
being able to have any philosophy of even the highest and the
greatest of the practical emotions ?

    \*       \*       \*       \*       \*

These two great departments of human emotion and human
feeling, each graded from the lowest to the highest, stand side
by side, both of them recalcitrant, as I think at present, to any
logical or philosophical treatment.   If you ask me whether I
am finally content with such a state of things I frankly admit
that I am not.   If you ask me how I propose to escape from
it, I can only say that I see no escape at present, except in
something which may deserve, as a term either of praise or of
reproach, the description of mysticism.[1]

Various reflections are at once suggested by the conception of two parallel series of emotions here outlined ;
chiefly perhaps this, that in the term which he uses as
the climax and culmination of one series he has a principle of unity by which, if he chose, he could draw the
two series together.   For love, whether terrestrial or
celestial, is not only practical ; it always contains a
strong æsthetic element.   Duty is the climax of the
purely practical emotions or impulses, as Beauty is of
the purely contemplative.   In Love, the practical or
the contemplative may be the more prominent, but both
must be there.   If I have passed through respect to real
love of a person whose physical features are in themselves not beautiful, these features will none the less be
for me the symbol and expression of the person I have
learnt to love.   In short, beauty may generate love,

---

[1] *Questionings on Criticism and Beauty*, pp. 21-23.   The lecture was subsequently
rewritten under the title *Criticism and Beauty*.

but also love may discover beauty, not by adoring its object but, as we sometimes say, by seeing it with new eyes.   Cupid is not blind ; nor does he wear rose-coloured spectacles.   When the lover finds beauty where others find none, both are right; they are looking at different objects: the indifferent see the physical form ; the lover, as in a glass darkly, sees the animating soul, and that a soul that perhaps can only be revealed to love.

> Lo, the moon's self !
> Here in London, yonder late in Florence,
> Still we find her face, the thrice-transfigured.
> Curving on a sky imbrued with colour,
> Drifted over Fiesole by twilight,
> Came she, our new crescent of a hair's-breadth.
> Full she flared it, lamping Samminiato,
> Rounder 'twixt the cypresses and rounder,
> Perfect till the nightingales applauded.
> Now, a piece of her old self, impoverished,
> Hard to greet, she traverses the houseroofs,
> Hurries with unhandsome thrift of silver,
> Goes dispiritedly, glad to finish.
>
> What, there's nothing in the moon noteworthy?
> Nay : for if that moon could love a mortal,
> Use, to charm him (so to fit a fancy),
> All her magic ('tis the old sweet mythos),
> She would turn a new side to her mortal,
> Side unseen of herdsman, huntsman, steersman—
> Blank to Zoroaster on his terrace,
> Blind to Galileo on his turret,
> Dumb to Homer, dumb to Keats—him, even !
> Think, the wonder of the moonstruck mortal—
> When she turns round, comes again in heaven,
> Opens out anew for worse or better !
> Proves she like some portent of an iceberg
> Swimming full upon the ship it founders,
> Hungry with huge teeth of splintered crystals ?
> Proves she as the paved work of a sapphire
> Seen by Moses when he climbed the mountain ?
> Moses, Aaron, Nadab and Abihu
> Climbed and saw the very God, the Highest,
> Stand upon the paved work of a sapphire.
> Like the bodied heaven in his clearness
> Shone the stone, the sapphire of that paved work,
> When they ate and drank and saw God also !

What were seen ?   None knows, none ever shall know.
Only this is sure—the sight were other,
Not the moon's same side, born late in Florence,
Dying now impoverished in London.
God be thanked, the meanest of His creatures
Boasts two soul-sides, one to face the world with,
One to show a woman when he loves her !

This I say of me, but think of you, Love !
This to you—yourself my moon of poets !
Ah, but that's the world's side, there's the wonder,
Thus they see you, praise you, think they know you !
There, in turn I stand with them and praise you—
Out of my own self, I dare to phrase it.
But the best is when I glide from out them,
Cross a step or two of dubious twilight,
Come out on the other side, the novel
Silent silver lights and darks undreamed of,
Where I hush and bless myself with silence.

Love surely is æsthetic at least as much as it is practical.   But, at any rate, we may agree with Mr. Balfour
that the æsthetic emotion is quite non-practical in the
sense that while it, and it alone, possesses us, the will
and every kind of desire is quiescent.   The perception
of beauty may indeed stir up all manner of impulses ;
but in itself it is merely contemplative.   All writers,
I think, agree on this ; Schopenhauer even regards
the contemplation of beauty as the nearest approach
permitted to living man to that complete annihilation
of the will which, with Buddhism, he regards as the
true goal of life.   So long as the æsthetic emotion, and
it alone, possesses us, we are content, we even long, to
gaze and gaze.   The past and the future vanish ; space
itself is forgotten ; whether or not mysticism is, as Mr.
Balfour fears, the only possible philosophy of art, it is
beyond all question that the æsthetic experience is a
purely mystical experience ; that is to say, it is the
direct and immediate apprehension of an absolutely
satisfying object.

No one has ever grasped and expressed the nature
of this experience with so great a vividness as Robert

H

Browning ; two poems are enough to illustrate the abolition of time and space in the artistic experience ; the first is *Abt Vogler*, which describes the musician's memory of the sounds he has just called forth, and of how, while the music lasted, the pride of his soul was in sight.

In sight ?   Not half ! for it seemed, it was certain, to match man's birth,
    Nature in turn conceived, obeying an impulse as I ;
And the emulous heaven yearned down, made effort to reach the earth,
    As the earth had done her best, in my passion, to scale the sky :
Novel splendours burst forth, grew familiar and dwelt with mine,
    Not a point nor peak but found and fixed its wandering star ;
Meteor-moons, balls of blaze : and they did not pale nor pine,
    For earth had attained to heaven, there was no more near nor far.

Nay more ; for there wanted not who walked in the glare and glow,
    Presences plain in the place ; or, fresh from the Protoplast,
Furnished for ages to come, when a kindlier wind should blow,
    Lured now to begin and live, in a house to their liking at last ;
Or else the wonderful Dead who have passed through the body and gone,
    But were back once more to breathe in an old world worth their new :
What never had been, was now ; what was, as it shall be anon ;
    And what is,—shall I say, matched both ? for I was made perfect too.

The other poem that I will quote is a love-poem which treats the emotion of love in a purely mystical and æsthetic manner—it is the little gem called *Now*.

    Out of your whole life give but a moment !
    All of your life that has gone before,
    All to come after it,—so you ignore,
    So you make perfect the present,—condense,
    In a rapture of rage, for perfection's endowment,
    Thought and feeling and soul and sense—
    Merged in a moment which gives me at last
    You around me for once, you beneath me, above me—
    Me—sure that despite of time future, time past,—
    This tick of our life-time's one moment you love me !

How long such suspension may linger ?   Ah, Sweet—
The moment eternal—just that and no more—
When ecstasy's utmost we clutch at the core
While cheeks burn, arms open, eyes shut and lips meet !

"The moment eternal"—that is the essence of the æsthetic emotion.   It is a moment, for in it there is no duration ; and it is eternal for exactly the same reason. The occurrence of this experience in our life that creeps in its petty pace from day to day is a paradox ; here is an essentially timeless experience which begins and ends ; but we must return to that problem when the nature of the experience is more clearly before us.

There is no doubt some impudence, and some imprudence, in trying to understand this experience more fully ; we may spoil our capacity for enjoying it in the future.   Professor Bradley, speaking of the Spirit of Poetry, magnificently applied the words of Marcellus about the ghost in *Hamlet* :

> We do it wrong, being so majestical,
> To offer it the show of violence,
> For it is as the air invulnerable
> And our vain blows malicious mockery.

With this we must all sympathise ; and if any one is altogether content with that, let him rest content and not think about æsthetics ; but if any one itches to understand, let him proceed, taking the inevitable risk.

Benedetto Croce, in his quite admirable *Æsthetic*,[1] has done good service by defining the limits of Æsthetic more clearly, so far as I know, than any previous writer.   At two points he seems to me to attain this clearness at the cost of definite error ; but it is useful to start with a sharp and crisp definition, even though we may wish to modify it later.   Croce's leading points,

---

[1] Translated by Douglas Ainslie (Macmillan).   If I have rightly understood this work, I am in full agreement with it, except on the points mentioned later on, and must express the indebtedness of nearly all that follows to its lucidity of statement and sureness of grasp.   In many places I have simply adopted Croce's expressions and illustrations.

then, are these : Æsthetic is concerned only with expression ; and all intuition is expression.

All art is expression ; and the primary æsthetic question is simply this : Do these words, these lines and colours, express anything at all ? Until this question is answered, artistic criticism has no interest in the value of the thing expressed ; and so far at least the maxim of the independence of art is sound. So far there is no difference of opinion. But many people think that artistic expression differs in its very nature from other expressions ; they never succeed in telling us wherein this difference consists, and take refuge, with Mr. Balfour, in mysticism. I wish to deny altogether any essential difference between artistic and other expressions. But if we follow Croce in this, we must follow him in his further contention that all intuition is expression, and that we only possess fully such thoughts and images as we express—that is, make clear and distinct to ourselves ; for whether our expression is one that others can understand and appreciate is a secondary matter. Art is primarily a matter of experience ; it is an experience which is also its own expression. No doubt we often claim to possess important ideas which we cannot formulate ; but the fact is that on those occasions we only know that an important idea is needed as the solution of our confusion ; we know the intellectual function it is to exercise, but we do not know what it is. This we discover in discovering the expression ; the two discoveries are identical. Our expression may be for ourselves alone ; expression that communicates knowledge is a further matter altogether, which we must consider later. In the case of spatial form, however, this difference does not exist ; if a man says he knows the shape of Great Britain, but, when he comes to draw it, puts Edinburgh due north of Portsmouth, or even of London, whereas it is due north of Cardiff, he can only mean that he would recognise a map of Great Britain if he saw one, not that he carries an

exact map of it in his head.   If 1 have such a map in
my head, I can draw it—not very precisely perhaps,
but with substantial accuracy ; and here the expression
must be just as adequate for others as it is to me.   This
is so in the case of all our primary qualities ; "two
inches" means the same to every one who attaches any
meaning to the words at all.   But where any emotions
are involved, this is not so.   As the Cheshire Cat
pointed out to Alice, the noise by which a dog expresses
anger is very like the cat's expression of pleasure, and
the two animals certainly use their tails in very diverse
ways.   So, too, a phrase which seems infinitely suggestive
to one may be almost barren to another ; this is due to
a lack of sympathy : another man's expression can
never create in me the experience of which it is a part
unless he respects the ordinary significance of words
and I am capable of the experience ; but so far as I am
capable of the experience, I am identical with him in
artistic power.   Let me quote Croce's statement of this
point :

The individual A is seeking the expression of an impression,
which he feels or has a presentiment of, but has not yet
expressed.   Behold him trying various words and phrases,
which may give the sought-for expression, which must exist,
but which he does not know.   He tries the combination M,
but rejects it as unsuitable, inexpressive, incomplete, ugly ; he
tries the combination N, with a like result.   HE DOES NOT
SEE ANYTHING, OR HE DOES NOT SEE CLEARLY.   The expression
still flies from him.   After other vain attempts, during which
he sometimes approaches, sometimes leaves the sign that offers
itself, all of a sudden (almost as though formed spontaneously
of itself) he creates the sought-for expression, and LUX FACTA
EST.   He enjoys for an instant æsthetic pleasure or the
pleasure of the beautiful.   The ugly, with its correlative dis-
pleasure, was the æsthetic activity, which had not succeeded
in conquering the obstacle ; the beautiful is the expressive
activity, which now displays itself triumphant.

We have taken this example from the domain of speech, as
being nearer and more accessible, and because we all talk,
though we do not all draw or paint.   Now if another individual,

whom we shall term B, desire to judge this expression and decide whether it be beautiful or ugly, he MUST OF NECESSITY PLACE HIMSELF AT A's POINT OF VIEW, and go through the whole process again, with the help of the physical sign, supplied to him by A.　If A has seen clearly, then B (who has placed himself at A's point of view) will also see clearly, and will find this expression beautiful.　If A has not seen clearly, then B also will not see clearly, and will find the expression more or less ugly, JUST AS A DID.

. . . . . . .

It is clear from the preceding theorem that the judicial activity, which criticises and recognises the beautiful, is identical with that which produces it.　The only difference lies in the diversity of circumstances, since in the one case it is a question of æsthetic production, in the other of reproduction. The judicial activity is called TASTE ; the productive activity is called GENIUS : genius and taste are therefore substantially IDENTICAL.

. . . . . . .

To posit a substantial difference between genius and taste, between artistic production and reproduction, would render communication and judgment alike inconceivable.　How could we judge what remained extraneous to us ?　How could that which is produced by a given activity be judged by a different activity ?　The critic will be a small genius, the artist a great genius ; the one will have the strength of ten, the other of a hundred ; the former, in order to raise himself to the altitude of the latter, will have need of his assistance ; but the nature of both must be the same.　In order to judge Dante, we must raise ourselves to his level : let it be well understood that empirically we are not Dante, nor Dante we ; but in that moment of judgment and contemplation, our spirit is one with that of the poet, and in that moment we and he are one single thing.　In this identity alone resides the possibility that our little souls can unite with the great souls, and become great with them, in the universality of the spirit.[1]

Expression, then, is the first element in the æsthetic fact ; Croce would say the only element, and I shall discuss that view in a moment ; but beyond question it is the first and indispensable element, and good expression is simply expression that really does express

[1] Croce, *op. cit.* pp. 194-199.

—that is, which is itself the experience of the artist. Of such cases Emerson's fine phrase is an accurate account : "The word is one with that it tells of." There are no rules of good style. "Effectiveness of assertion is the Alpha and Omega of style."[1] Elegance is all right when appropriate ; it can be more vicious than any bareness. Only he can have style who has something to say ; for style is precisely the right way of saying things. If any one wants to write Latin Oratory such as would please an ancient Roman if he could hear it, he must study the stylistic habits of the Roman Orators : the composition of Latin Oratory is quite harmless, and if he likes it he had better do it ; but do not let him suppose that it has any æsthetic value, unless it may be said to add generally to the amenities of life, like a military band at a garden party. There would only be æsthetic value in such composition if the rhythms that were expressive to the old Romans were also expressive to us.

I am far from asserting that the study of ancient forms is valueless ; intellectually it is of the greatest interest ; but I emphatically deny that the imitation of ancient forms has any æsthetic value, unless those forms are as effective expressions to us as they were to those who created them. On the other hand, it is worth while to spend almost endless time and trouble in recovering the general psychical conditions which made the ancient forms expressive ; as an antecedent and preparatory study no antiquarianism is amiss, if at the end we feel what Sophocles felt when he wrote the *Oedipus Coloneus*, or what any chance Roman felt as he read Catullus's Elegy on his brother. This is the great and inalienable privilege of criticism—to put us in the environment from which the artist's experience sprang. We do not want to be told whether the figures are in or out of drawing ; if we do not detect an error, we can enjoy the more. Ruskin was quite right when, to

---

[1] G. Bernard Shaw, *Man and Superman* : Epistle Dedicatory, p. xxxv.

enable us to appreciate Bellini, he wrote a vivid history of Venice in her days of splendour.

Style is expression; and for this reason "slang" may be excellent style, provided, of course, that it is appropriately used; it may be good style but cannot be "in the grand style." If a new word is able to "catch on," it thereby proves its right to a place in the language. Objection to the style of an orator, if it is not a silly squeamishness, must be due either to the fact that he does not express his meaning, or that his meaning is one that ought not to be expressed. From the point of view of style or expression the only kind of slang which is objectionable is the use of great words for little matters; and the objection here is twofold—they do not really express what is intended, and they are made useless for the occasions that require them. The ruin of the word "awful" is a case in point. They do not really express; their "slang" use is like all bad art. It is good art to call a spade a spade; indeed this is the fundamental quality of art; but it is bad art to call it a "damned shovel"—for the simple reason that it is nothing of the kind. For purposes of communication this sort of thing may be necessary. I once heard a working man say rather querulously: "One never knows whether you University men mean what you say; you have such calm countenances." There are some people who always understand less than is said; they are not sensitive to verbal or pictorial or musical expression, and the truth must be exaggerated if it is to be conveyed at all. That is why we all like bad art at first; if the symptoms of emotion are not overdone, we do not detect them at all; great art, therefore, seems cold and lifeless, while Doré and Gounod seem to express the quintessence of pathos and longing. After some practice in reading the works of the painters and musicians, we find that Doré's women are not really crying, as we thought, but have recently put some rouge into their eyes by accident, while Gounod's religious music is not the outpouring of a soul with strong crying unto God, but the screams and whimperings of undisciplined sentimentalism.

Art is expression; what then does it express? Itself. There is no other expression. Most of our language is so inartistic that we think different sets of words will serve as expression of the same thought or feeling; that is because none of them really express it; they are mere labels. "Death" is the name for an experience we must all endure; it has other names— decease, demise, passing away, and so on. But these are labels, sufficient for many practical purposes, but wholly inexpressive of the gigantic fact they stand for; to find that fact expressed we must go to the artists— to Watts, or Michael Angelo, or Beethoven, or Shakespeare. But it is not only our language that is inartistic. Our imaginations are normally so feeble that unless we can discover a conceptual meaning in a poem or picture, we are inclined to say that it has no meaning at all. When a man says, "But what does it all mean?" he is very often requiring what can never be given—a statement of the artist's meaning in the terms of the understanding; he is assuming that the poet or other artist always begins with an idea or notion, which he then embodies in a decorative presentation; thus he may suppose that a man paints a picture of a girl with bowed back and blindfolded eyes, sitting upon the globe of the world and listening to the note of the one string left unbroken in her lyre, because he thinks Hope the dominating force in life, though perpetually on the verge of extinction. And where no such conceptual meaning is present, we think there is no meaning at all: if there is no doctrine we think there is no reality. Very often, of course, we may find doctrine in a picture, but not always; and certainly no great artist thinks of his meaning first and packs it into a picture afterwards. Moreover, much art is in its nature incapable of such expression of notions; music, for example, does not tell us truths ; it presents us with beauty, which is in itself neither true nor false, though it has a definite relation to Truth and Falsehood, and has always the logical structure of Truth, as we shall find later on. Even in poetry, though here the use of words must almost inevitably suggest a skeleton of conceptual meaning, it is often quite impossible to paraphrase. Professor Bradley has amused us by a paraphrase of Hamlet's line—

> To be or not to be, that is the question,

into the words, "What is just now occupying my attention is the comparative disadvantages of continuing to live and putting an end to myself." The absurdity is clear ; yet this meaning is no doubt present in the original. As Professor Bradley says, for the practical or scientific purposes of the coroner the paraphrase may be said to mean the same thing as the original, but not for the sympathies of a human being. Other lines defy paraphrase altogether. Take a celebrated instance— the last two lines of the third act of Shelley's *Prometheus Unbound* :

> The loftiest star of unascended heaven
> Pinnacled dim in the intense inane.

It is impossible to produce a paraphrase of that ; it has a quite definite meaning, but its meaning is just itself. Or if any one finds those two lines, without their context, inexpressive, let me quote the last three stanzas of *The Cloud* :

> That orbèd maiden with white fire laden,
>> Whom mortals call the moon,
> Glides glimmering o'er my fleece-like floor,
>> By the midnight breezes strewn ;
> And wherever the beat of her unseen feet,
>> Which only the angels hear,
> May have broken the woof of my tent's thin roof,
>> The stars peep behind her and peer ;

And I laugh to see them whirl and flee,
　　Like a swarm of golden bees,
When I widen the rent in my wind-built tent,
　　Till the calm rivers, lakes, and seas,
Like strips of the sky fallen through me on high,
　　Are each paved with the moon and these.

I bind the sun's throne with a burning zone,
　　And the moon's with a girdle of pearl ;
The volcanoes are dim, and the stars reel and swim,
　　When the whirlwinds my banner unfurl.
From cape to cape, with a bridge-like shape,
　　Over a torrent sea,
Sunbeam-proof, I hang like a roof,
　　The mountains its columns be.
The triumphal arch through which I march
　　With hurricane, fire, and snow,
When the powers of the air are chained to my chair,
　　Is the million-coloured bow ;
The sphere-fire above its soft colours wove,
　　While the moist earth was laughing below.

I am the daughter of earth and water,
　　And the nursling of the sky ;
I pass through the pores of the ocean and shores ;
　　I change, but I cannot die.
For after the rain when with never a stain,
　　The pavilion of heaven is bare,
And the winds and sunbeams with their convex gleams,
　　Build up the blue dome of air,
I silently laugh at my own cenotaph,
　　And out of the caverns of rain,
Like a child from the womb, like a ghost from the tomb,
　　I arise and unbuild it again.

It is plainly impossible to paraphrase that passage.
But it must be added that the test is entirely empirical.
All that can be said is that most of us, with practice,
find the same words or forms or melodies to be expressive.　When we meet with a genuine expression of
any emotion we recognise it.　There is no external
criterion discoverable.　No one can say why the bronze
Charioteer at Delphi is absolutely perfect ; but no one
is likely to deny it.

So far we have simply been following the lead of

Croce's two main doctrines—that Art consists in expression, and that all intuition is expression. And before we pass on a word or two more must be said on the latter point. It is sometimes suggested that whereas Science deals with facts, Art carries us away into realms of fancy. This is a misrepresentation of a truth to which we must attend in a moment ; just now we must observe that the first requisite of the artist is to attend to his actual impressions without being biased by his scientific knowledge. This is very difficult ; most of our conscious perceptions are so highly inferential that we find it hard to attend to the basis of the inference alone. Thus if a child is set to draw a cube he is very likely to show four or even five sides at once in the drawing, though only three are visible. I remember watching a lady sketch Helvellyn as seen from southwest at sunset ; she was quite correctly colouring the mountain a deep purple, but her little daughter, having been up Helvellyn the day before, objected vigorously. " Why do you make it that colour ? " she asked, " it's green, it's all grass." It is just the same with perspective ; I know the ceiling of my room is level, and find it very hard to recover the original impression of it as coming a long way down in the corner opposite my table ; I know the sides of a road are parallel, and my attempt to draw a road makes it look like an ever-widening waste that turns at last into a great desert of mud and gravel. No doubt there are technical devices to be employed here ; but the great difficulty and the prime necessity is to recover the true impression which our scientific knowledge of the world so utterly obscures. If I am to express something, I must first have a complete apprehension or intuition of it in its individuality —an apprehension which is itself the expression I am seeking.

But here I must leave Croce. For he insists that this apprehension is the only æsthetic fact there is. He regards what he calls the externalisation of this as

secondary and relatively unimportant ;[1] and he refuses
to see the value of what is expressed as an æsthetic fact
at all : he refers the discussion of this to Psychology.[2]
The former leads him to the assertion that the artist
always possesses his meaning, or expresses it to himself,
before he externalises it, and the latter is a denial of
degrees of Beauty.   But it is simply not true that an
artist always knows what he is going to say before he
says it.   Painters and poets no doubt have different
methods ;  but some at least have composed in the
manner magnificently attributed by Chesterton to
Watts.   " Standing before a dark canvas upon some
quiet evening, he has made lines and something has
happened.   In such an hour the strange and splendid
phrase of the Psalm he has literally fulfilled.   He has
gone on because of the word of meekness and truth and
of righteousness ;  and his right hand has taught him
terrible things." [3]   With regard to the poets we may
quote a passage which both handles this point and
admirably sums up what I have attempted to say so far.
" Pure poetry is not the decoration of a preconceived
and clearly defined matter : it springs from the creative
impulse of a vague imaginative mass pressing for
development and definition.   If the poet already knew
exactly what he meant to say, why should he write the
poem ?   The poem would, in fact, already be written.
For only its completion can reveal, even to him, exactly
what he wanted.   When he began, and while he was at
work, he did not possess his meaning ;  it possessed him.
It was not a fully formed soul asking for a body ;  it
was an inchoate soul in the inchoate body of perhaps
two or three vague ideas and a few scattered phrases.
The growing of this body into its full stature and perfect shape was the same thing as the gradual self-defini-
tion of the meaning.   And this is the reason why such
poems strike us as creations, not manufactures, and have

---

[1] Croce, *op. cit.* pp. 156-158, 182 ff.          [2] Pp. 142-152.
[3] Chesterton, *Watts*, p. 169.

the magical effect which mere decoration cannot produce. This is also the reason why, if we insist on asking for the meaning of such a poem, we can only be answered, ' It means itself.' " [1]

Croce's exclusion of everything but expressiveness is a more serious matter ; it leads him to the paradox that there are no degrees of Beauty. " The beautiful does not possess degrees, for there is no conceiving a more beautiful, that is, an expressive that is more expressive, an adequate that is more than adequate. Ugliness, on the other hand, does possess degrees, from the rather ugly (or almost beautiful) to the extremely ugly." [2] He admits æsthetic grades, but only calls perfection of expression " Beauty." This may be permitted in the interest of clearness ; but quite plainly one perfect expression has more value than another if its range and significance is wider and deeper. Ariel's song in *The Tempest* is beautiful in Croce's sense ; it is a perfect expression ; but its value is not equal to that of *King Lear* ; and to refer this difference to some other science than Æsthetic is to dissect a living whole into lifeless fragments. Croce's main doctrine is that æsthetic meaning and æsthetic expression are the same ; and if so, the value of the meaning is part of the æsthetic fact.[3]

An accurate grasp of a geometrical figure would be for Croce an intuition which was also expression ; [4] but it is not artistic. The truth I take to be this. Science gives us facts and (by its method of external relations) the truth concerning facts ; Art gives us facts and (by concentrated apprehension of the facts in their

---

[1] Bradley, *Poetry for Poetry's Sake*, pp. 28-29.

[2] Croce, *op. cit.* p. 130.

[3] His error is parallel to that of Hedonism, which separates Pleasure from pleasant activities, and then treats all pleasures as alike.

[4] Cf. his discussion of this on pp. 174-5, where " bodies which possess geometrical forms " are said to be " ugly or beautiful, like every natural fact, according to the ideal connexions in which they are placed." But what are these " ideal connexions "? If they are the apprehension of other facts, the statement seems meaningless ; if they are " values," then the value of the " meaning " is brought back into the æsthetic sphere.

entirely) the value inherent in facts. Like all distinctions in the spiritual world, this must be taken broadly; there is no accurate line of demarcation; but Euclid is scientific in aim and temper, while Shelley is artistic in aim and temper. To Euclid it is fatal that his conclusion should be proved false, or his chain of reasoning unsound; to our appreciation of Shelley it is a matter of very little importance whether or not we agree with his objections to orthodox theology or monarchical government. It is sometimes claimed as a mark of Tennyson's superiority that *In Memoriam* was written before the publication of *The Origin of Species*. That may show that he was intellectually alert, but plainly it has nothing to do with the value of the poem. Homer is not immortal because he observed that the Pleiades do or do not set in the ocean. The greater part of poetry's subject matter is as old as humanity: it is the things which "go with hunger and thirst and love and the facing of death." The one thing we want to know is this: has the poet really presented his fact, or has he only talked about it? If the motives and passions are those which we recognise as our own, expressed fully and as we could not express them, that is enough. No doubt all conclusions and abstract theories have an emotional value, and are thus capable of artistic treatment; but this treatment will reveal their value and not their truth.

The function of the artist, then, is not only to give the "expression of impressions," [1] but so to express as to reveal value. That is why he must first go back to the actual impressions which objects make upon us; his process is not that of science, and he must go behind all scientific procedure to the original data of sensation, and work over the material on his own principles from the outset. No doubt a work of art may contain scientific truths or moral maxims, but they are subordinate to the general emotional value to

[1] Croce, *op. cit.* p. 21.

which they contribute ; [1] just as a scientific work may contain artistic passages, but only in subordination to its conceptual purpose. No doubt, too, the value revealed in any object by the artist must be accepted not as imaginary, but as the real value, which we should have detected there ourselves had we the artist's faculty. And for this reason Art and Philosophy must meet, as we shall see, when each is brought to its full development.

It is in order to reveal the true value of the objects it handles that Art must lay all our volitional activities to rest. Volition is the effort to reach an ideal as yet unrealised ; but so far as the artist succeeds, the ideal is realised. Also, in order that we may attend to the beauty before us and appreciate it in and for itself, it must be isolated from the other facts of experience and concentrate our attention upon itself alone. But not only must there be no movement of the mind from the work of art to anything outside it, there must be no movement of the mind within its limits. An intuition is of necessity one and individual, and the connexion of different intuitions is of necessity conceptual ; a work of art, therefore, in which we pass from one impression to another and link them all up in our minds is really a scientific treatise whose several paragraphs or sections are artistically presented. This is the fundamental law of unity. A work of art must produce a single impression. " In works of art that are failures, the beautiful is present as unity and the ugly as multiplicity." [2] A good instance of this failure is Botticelli's large picture of the *Coronation of the Virgin* in the Academia at Florence ; the picture consists of two halves—above there is the main subject, encircled with dancing Angels, and below, separated by a great stretch of sky, the figures of four adoring Saints. The connexion between the upper and lower halves of the picture is purely conceptual ; one knows that the Saints

---

[1] Cf. Croce, *op. cit.* p. 4.        [2] Croce, *op. cit.* p. 129.

are adoring the figures in the scene above ; but one merely knows that, of course, this must be so, one does not see that it is so. I very much fear that a similar criticism must be made of another picture by the same artist—the great *Enthroned Madonna* which hangs immediately opposite the *Prima Vera*. This picture seems to me to contain more beauty than any I know ; the yearning pathos of the Virgin, the astonished pity of the Angels, the rapt contemplation and deep meditation of the two ecclesiastical Saints, the silent, pondering wonder of St. Michael—all these are depicted in a manner beyond praise. Yet somehow as a whole the great picture is not a complete success ; though it contains so much beauty, it is not altogether beautiful. And I believe that this is because it produces no single impression ; the connexion between the figures is logical, not intuitive. Let me mention one other picture by the same painter—the round *Magnificat Madonna* in the Uffizzi. Here there are not perhaps so many figures of astounding beauty, but the picture is a single whole ; one may study it point by point, and appreciate it the better in consequence ; but its impression is single and its meaning is one and indivisible. We may notice that the Child is reading His Mother's song, moving His finger along the words ; He has reached the word " humilitatem," and pausing there has thrown back His head to look up in her face, as though to say, " Ah ! that was it ; we know about that " ; and she leans over Him, and is quite unconscious that from behind her the Angels are lowering a crown upon her head. And, no doubt, it helps our appreciation of the picture to notice such points separately ; but as we sit in front of that picture, it seems that nothing else exists but the Divine Humility and the Crown which quite unconsciously it wears. But I am attempting the impossible : if anybody wants to know what the greatest picture in the world is like, he must go to Florence and look at it.

I

I suppose that this effect of unity is technically achieved through "grouping," and an arrangement of the lines which compels the eye to travel from any point in the picture to some other kindred point, so that we move spontaneously from point to point within the picture, and never have to think out connecting links. In music it is achieved through the manipulation of the endlessly repeated "subject" and of the rhythm; in poetry through a balance of rhythms and rhymes. Among musicians Chopin strikes me as one whose compositions are patchworks of beautiful pieces, but very often fail to be altogether beautiful precisely because they are incoherent and lack unity.

Dramatic unity is a complex form of the same fact. Here each character may be admirably drawn, and yet the whole play remain inexpressive ; all the characters must so act on each other as to give the impression of a single living society. Even in an almost one-part play like *Hamlet* the total effect is that of a social life, in which no doubt one person was more interesting than all the others put together, but which would not have been the same had a single character been removed ; and this total effect is moreover an impression of the value of a very rich experience, with thoughts and ambitions and disappointments and actions all stored within it. The artistic value of the play is not the value of any one of these, nor the sum of all their values, but the value of their unity in the artistic experience.

It is from a failure to grasp this point that Browning's Dramatic Monologues—the greatest artistic creations in recent poetry—have sometimes failed to secure full appreciation. Let me refer to one of the greatest—*Bishop Blougram's Apology*. The subject handled in the Monologue is Christian Apologetics. But that is not the subject of the poem. The subject of the poem is Bishop Blougram, a modern, realistic, and partially sceptical ecclesiastic, revealing as much of his mind as he thinks fit to "Gigadibs, the literary man." This canting journalist demanded perfect honesty and no humbug; and the Bishop sums up his position and meets it :

> So, drawing comfortable breath again,
> You weigh and find, whatever more or less
> I boast of my ideal realised
> Is nothing in the balance when opposed
> To your ideal, your grand simple life,
> Of which you will not realise one jot.
> I am much, you are nothing ; you would be all,
> I would be merely much : you beat me there.
>
> No, friend, you do not beat me : hearken why !
> The common problem, yours, mine, every one's,
> Is not to fancy what were fair in life
> Provided it could be—but, finding first
> What may be, then find how to make it fair
> Up to our means : a very different thing !
> No abstract intellectual plan of life
> Quite irrespective of life's plainest laws,
> But one, a man, who is man and nothing more,
> May lead within a world which (by your leave)
> Is Rome or London, not Fool's-paradise.

Well, any donkey can say "Pure Prose !" It is not that, because, as Coleridge said, "The opposite of prose is not poetry but verse, and the opposite of poetry is not prose but science." But this passage is nearer science than poetry, and this is what is meant. The fact to be presented is not what Blougram really felt, which would require poetry, but his tone towards Gigadibs. The metre is merely formal—only endless iambi cut into lengths, with five to a length. That exactly expresses the fact requiring expression— Blougram's contempt for and lack of interest in his guest. But a little later he comes to something which he cares about so much that even before Gigadibs he will show his emotion. The suggestion has been made that since doubt is inevitable we should give up faith and take to deliberate and absolute unbelief. Blougram says, "Very well; try it. Can you live on in undisturbed denial of religious doctrines? Not a bit of it."

> Just when we are safest, there's a sunset touch,
> A fancy from a flower-bell, some one's death,
> A chorus-ending from Euripides—
> And that's enough for fifty hopes and fears
> As old and new at once as nature's self,
> To rap and knock and enter in our soul,
> Take hands and dance there, a fantastic ring,
> Round the ancient idol, on his base again—
> The grand Perhaps! We look on helplessly.

Here we have poetry; but it is no more artistic than the "prose" before. In both cases the style expresses exactly the emotion of the man who is the subject of the poem. Let me quote another passage, where the great artist turns not from "prose" to poetry, but from poetry to prose, on realising suddenly that he is casting his pearls before a pig.

> Pure faith indeed—you know not what you ask!
> Naked belief in God the Omnipotent,
> Omniscient, Omnipresent, sears too much
> The sense of conscious creatures to be borne.
> It were the seeing him, no flesh shall dare.
> Some think, Creation's meant to show him forth:
> I say it is meant to hide him all it can,
> And that's what all the blessed evil's for.
> Its use in Time is to environ us,
> Our breath, our drop of dew, with shield enough
> Against that sight till we can bear its stress.
> Under a vertical sun, the exposed brain
> And lidless eye and disemprisoned heart
> Less certainly would wither up at once
> Than mind, confronted with the truth of Him.
> But time and earth case-harden us to live;
> The feeblest sense is trusted most; the child
> Feels God a moment, ichors o'er the place,
> Plays on and grows to be a man like us.
> With me, faith means perpetual unbelief
> Kept quiet like the snake 'neath Michael's foot
> Who stands calm just because he feels it writhe.

> Or, if that's too ambitious—here's my box—
> I need the excitation of a pinch
> Threatening the torpor of the inside-nose
> Nigh on the imminent sneeze that never comes.
> "Leave it in peace" advise the simple folk :
> Make it aware of peace by itching-fits,
> Say I—let doubt occasion still more faith !

One feels at once the Bishop's sudden shyness at talking in any high vein to the shallow-pated journalist. Prose and poetry alike are justified, because the aim of the poem is not to express emotions, as a lyric poem does, still less to defend the Christian faith, as a treatise might set out to do, but to exhibit the character of Bishop Blougram as it would be seen in such a conversation, and to reveal its value ; in this aim it triumphantly succeeds.

I am impelled by sheer love of it to give another instance of Browning's abrupt introduction of the sublime—a passage from *Aristophanes' Apology.*

> So, swift to supper, Poet !   No mistake,
> This play ; nor, like the unflavoured " Grasshoppers,"
> Salt without thyme !   Right merrily we supped,
> Till—something happened.
>
>                    Out it shall at last !
> Mirth drew to ending, for the cup was crowned
> To the Triumphant !   " Kleonclapper erst,
> Now, plier of a scourge Euripides
> Fairly turns tail from, flying Attike
> For Makedonia's rocks and frosts and bears,
> Where, furry grown, he growls to match the squeak
> Of girl-voiced, crocus-vested Agathon !.
> Ha ha, he he ! "   When, suddenly a knock—
> Sharp, solitary, cold, authoritative.
>
> " Babaiax !   Sokrates a-passing by,
> A-peering in for Aristullos' sake,
> To put a question touching comic law ? "
> No !   Enters an old pale-swathed majesty,
> Makes slow mute passage through two ranks as mute
> (Strattis stood up with all the rest, the sneak !)
> Grey brow still bent on ground, upraised at length
> When, our priest reached, full front the vision paused.

"Priest !"—the deep tone succeeded the fixed gaze—
"Thou carest that thy god have spectacle
Decent and seemly ; wherefore I announce
That, since Euripides is dead to-day,
My Choros, at the Greater Feast next month,
Shall, clothed in black, appear ungarlanded ! "

Then the grey brow sank low, and Sophokles
Re-swathed him, sweeping doorward : mutely passed
'Twixt rows as mute, to mingle possibly
With certain gods who convoy age to port ;
And night resumed him.

By the simple device of maintaining a formal identity
of metre and yet changing the rhythm almost indefinitely Browning is able to reduce to artistic unity
the most incongruous elements.

Whenever such unity is achieved, we have the sense
of absolute freedom. The artist has then overcome all
obstacles and made his material the vehicle of his meaning. As moral freedom is reached through obedience
to law, so the freedom of art is won where all the
elements in the artistic expression combine through the
precision of its form to make up a single whole. Ease
of style is reached by careful polish, not by headlong
dash. It is the same in the motion of perfect dancing ;
just because the rhythm is perfect, it seems that there
is no set rhythm at all. Freedom in art as elsewhere
means the combination of many elements to produce a
single total effect.

But the unity of a work of art is not only internal.
Not only must its own effect be single ; it must be all-
engrossing. If our attention keeps wandering to other
matters, the general effect upon our minds is one of
multiplicity. The impression of the picture itself or
the poem itself may be one and indivisible ; but if the
picture or the poem is set in a whole environment of
other impressions, the total effect upon the mind is one
of multiplicity, and therefore of either confusion or
logical and not artistic connexion. The work of art
must focus all our attention upon itself.

I sometimes think that the whole Nature of Art is best realised when we ask why pictures should be put into frames. The aim is to assist just that concentration of the mind upon the æsthetic object which constitutes contemplation. We put something abruptly irrelevant, though not discordant, round the picture so as to keep the attention from wandering to other objects. Buildings such as towers or spires are more " beautiful " when " framed in trees " or seen through an archway, because in such a setting the object in question receives a more concentrated attention, and we actually see it more perfectly. The frame comes to the assistance of the system of the grouping or the arrangement of architectural " lines," which make the object a unity in itself and keep the attention moving within its limits. In music the same unity, both internal and external, is reached by the regularity of the rhythm and the intertwining of the melodies ; in poetry by the interaction of images, rhythm and (often) rhyme. It should be noticed that rhyme, far from being " the invention of a barbarous age to set off wretched matter and lame metre," is a most potent force in numbing desire or restlessness and leaving us purely contemplative ; its repetitions, particularly when somewhat complicated as in the Spenserian stanza, give the poem an effect of turning in upon itself, and thus help to exclude all other themes from the field of attention. Milton's phrase about "wretched matter " has, however, this amount of justification, that rhyme is particularly appropriate in a poem dealing with slight subjects ; Shelley's poem, *The Cloud*, depends almost entirely on its exquisite rhymes and their see-saw effect. We could not attend with pleasure to the " matter " of the poem even through the  hree stanzas quoted above, if it were not for the fascination of the rhymes. Where the subject is in itself of absorbing interest, as in Epic or Drama, we do not need this assistance in fixing the attention, so that rhyme is unnecessary and at once seems artificial and vexatious. Even the rhythm in such cases should be as elastic and flexible as possible, " blank verse," or its parallels in other languages, being the most appropriate.

No doubt rhythmic forms and rhyme, once introduced, have a further value as part of the expression in each case ; some rhythms at once suggest certain types of emotion. But the question why this or that movement or gesture or rhythm should accompany this or that emotion is one that Æsthetic cannot investigate ; the question why amusement should find expression in laughter does not belong to Æsthetic, which merely notes the fact that the connexion exists and that therefore laughter is the true expression of that emotion.

We find, then, that these factors in the expression have the effect of making the whole expression still more effective through their power of assisting concentration upon it. In demanding such concentration, the work of art implicitly claims to offer a complete satisfaction. It is here, of course, that the mystical character of the work of art is most apparent, and it is here that the meaning, as well as the expression, becomes æsthetically important ; for if our whole attention is to be held, there must be no opposition from any part of our nature. As Professor Bradley has pointed out, in a poem or tale of any length we demand the exhibition of certain moral principles ; a long poem cannot be taken as the expression of a passing mood, and though we might pardon, for instance, the utter pessimism of a short lyric, utter pessimism is intolerable in a Tragedy. And it is æsthetically bad ; for if as we watch we are in an attitude of protest, our experience is plainly not purely æsthetic. If we are to be in the æsthetic attitude, our whole nature must be satisfied ; it is for this reason that Art and Philosophy must at last unite ; we must like what is said as well as the way it is said ; in fact, the meaning is here more important than the style, for to find sentiments one wishes to repudiate expressed in an elegant manner is quite peculiarly vexatious. And here the leading question seems to be, Are we in sympathy with the artist ?   He may depict vice if he likes ; he may depict it so as to make us sympathise ; but he must not depict either vice or virtue in such a way as to make us angry with him.   This, for example, is my trouble with Tennyson ;   I am in an attitude of permanent opposition to his moral judgments.   When in a poem of unquestionable beauty—*Guinevere*—he shows every symptom of approbation for Arthur as he stands over his wife and talks like an Archdeacon, I am reduced to something approaching frenzy.   Browning, of course, would either have made him hug her, or else would have shown his own indignation.   To create a Pharisee may be well enough, but to hold him up to admiration is an insult to any Christian reader. Browning and Tennyson have both expressed their natures very perfectly in their poems ; so far, there is little to choose between them.   But one of them is to me uniquely attractive, and the other is distinctly the reverse.   Incidentally, moreover, Browning created scores of " Men and Women "—all of them interesting and attractive, though not all admirable ; Tennyson never created a character at all.   Arthur is Tennyson virtuous ; Launcelot is Tennyson less virtuous, but, as Guinevere discovered, better company, though still uninteresting.   Elaine is presumably his ideal of womanhood ;   she is a dead doll.   In short, to one of these poets I am naturally in an æsthetic attitude ;   to the other not.

This æsthetic attitude must be induced in us by the artist ; we cannot force ourselves into it.   For in the artistic experience the will must be wholly quiescent. That experience is of its very essence experience of attainment ;  and volition is therefore out of place.   But there are degrees of attainment, or at least of satisfaction.   A poem may be perfect and thus satisfactory in itself ;  it still remains to ask—how much of my nature is satisfied ?   Here we find the reason for the revived

appreciation of the pre-Raphaelites. We have been
rapidly recovering the experience of the great epoch of
Catholicism, and are consequently in sympathy with
Fra Angelico and the two Lippis from the outset, so
that we can again hear what they are saying. Despite
some lack of technique they have something to say
which we wish to hear. Raphael has a better voice,
but we are not interested in most of what he says with
it. For myself, there are only two Madonnas by
Raphael which I wish to see again—the *Granduca* at
Florence and the *Sistine* at Dresden. His women are
more like real women than, say, "Cimabue's"; but
"Cimabue" gives a poor likeness of an interesting
woman, though good enough, of course, to show that
she is interesting; Raphael usually gives us a good
likeness of a nugatory woman. The Madonna in Santa
Maria Novella used to move all Florentines to worship;
no one can ever have felt a touch of reverence for *La
Belle Jardinière* however much he may admire its technical skill or enjoy its prettiness. "Cimabue" is a
great artist—that is, an artist handling great themes
with sufficient skill to convey his meaning; but he is
not a good artist. Raphael is always a good artist, but
not always a great one.

No doubt the inclusion of this sympathetic element
introduces vagueness and ruins precision. But as
Aristotle reminds us, we must not require more exactness in the treatment than the subject-matter permits.
If we introduce any value other than adequacy of expression we make it impossible to give a definition of
the beautiful by which taste may be guided; for one
age will find beautiful what the next thinks insipid or
even unpleasing—as indeed actually occurs. But this
is determined by the general spiritual character of the
successive ages; and when we say that a work of art
"expresses itself," we must remember that this "self"
varies from age to age. Value is only realised in relation to consciousness; and that relation may be affected

by the subjective as well as by the objective term in the relation.   And it is through the variations on the subjective side that transitions from the classical to the romantic and the like are made possible.   There is no absolute division here ; but the romantic artist is one who reveals the value of momentous facts directly, while the classical artist reveals the value of order and of man's control of matter.   Michael Angelo's great figures are divine ; the Hermes of Praxiteles is not divine at all ; but the power that made it is.   Again to some people at all times, and to all people at some times, the prime necessity is to reveal the mere goodness of commonplace existence ; the landscape-painter makes us attend to the goodness of quite ordinary objects and therefore to see it for the first time.

> For, don't you mark, we're made so that we love
> First, when we see them painted, things we've passed
> Perhaps a hundred times, nor cared to see ?

Others, who realise by nature the goodness of mere living, find such art rather tiresome, and require that there shall be revealed the goodness of what seems terrible and of the ultimate forces.   Yet through all these varieties of human need, and therefore of what is important to man, the definition stands firm ; *beauty is adequate expression of the value of important fact or feeling*.   If the expression is not adequate we have no work of art at all ; if the thing expressed is tiresome to us we have a work of art without " charm " or power to grip the attention and satisfy the contemplating mind.

In any case, however, we may say that to achieve an all-engrossing interest is the object of all art, and it is no doubt sometimes due almost wholly to technical skill.   There is a great picture by Watts called *The All-Pervading*.   Its aim is to express infinity : and it succeeds.   It is not a very large canvas ; it depicts a single angel or spirit, seated and holding on his knees a crystal ball; above his head his wings are spread in great curves that almost meet. As one looks at it, it seems to become vaster and vaster and to spread itself around one on this side and on that. It is indeed the All-Pervading, and one recovers with a start to find that it is just a panel, not three feet across. But after all we do not find what the All-Pervading is. We have for the moment felt the immediate presence of Infinity, and that is all. The achievement is accomplished, as far as I can tell, through the attraction exercised upon the eye by two spots of light, the Spirit's eyes and the crystal ball. Each of these is, as it were, the focus of great curves—the drapery and wings of the spirit—spreading out in all directions at once, so that the eye feels drawn this way and that while held fixedly in the centre of the picture; from this outward strain comes the sense that the picture itself is gradually encompassing one as one looks at it.

But there are greater miracles than this. Sometimes the artist can so charm us with his skill, lulling us into reverie by melody and rhyme and rhythm, that for the moment the object presented is all there is.[1]

> Behold her, single in the field,
> Yon solitary Highland Lass !
> Reaping and singing by herself ;
> Stop here, or gently pass !
> Alone she cuts and binds the grain,
> And sings a melancholy strain ;
> O listen ! for the Vale profound
> Is overflowing with the sound.
>
> No Nightingale did ever chaunt
> More welcome notes to weary bands
> Of travellers in some shady haunt
> Among Arabian sands :
> A voice so thrilling ne'er was heard
> In spring-time from the Cuckoo-bird,
> Breaking the silence of the seas
> Among the farthest Hebrides.

---

[1] Professor Stewart has discussed the reverie of art in *The Myths of Plato*, pp. 382-395, and *Plato's Doctrine of Ideas*, Part II.

Will no one tell me what she sings ?—
Perhaps the plaintive numbers flow
For old, unhappy, far-off things,
And battles long ago ;
Or is it some more humble lay,
Familiar matter of to-day ?
Some natural sorrow, loss, or pain,
That has been, and may be again ?

Whate'er the theme, the Maiden sang
As if her song could have no ending ;
I saw her singing at her work,
And o'er the sickle bending ;—
I listened, motionless and still ;
And as I mounted up the hill
The music in my heart I bore,
Long after it was heard no more.

At the beginning of the poem the Highland Lass is " single in the field " ; a moment later she is single in the world. The secret of Arabian sands and of the farthest Hebrides speaks through her.

But this little masterpiece of Wordsworth is a short poem ; and if our attention is to be gripped for a longer period, the theme must be more complex. Many elements of our nature are quite unsatisfied by the reaping girl and her song ; they will rebel and distract us if the poet rivets our attention for too long upon so small a theme. For a moment, because our attention is held fast, she seems the Universe in herself ; the little poem is a microcosm ; but that can only be for a moment. If lasting satisfaction is to be given, and perfect Beauty attained, all life must be packed into one work of art. It is enough only to mention *King Lear* and Wagner's cosmic opera *Tristan und Isolde.* Where, as in Tragedy, elements that are normally terrible and horrible appear as constituents of the general beauty of the whole, we have the sublime.

In the presence of such transcendent Beauty, we realise the hope of mysticism. In a single impression we receive what absolutely satisfies us, and in that perfect satisfaction we ourselves are lost. Duration vanishes ; the "moment eternal" is come. The great drama proceeds ; the music surges through us ; we are not conscious of our own existence. We are simply the subjects of a mighty experience. We hear and see ; and when all is done, we consider and bow the head.

That is the Nature of Art. And its significance surely is twofold. First, it points to a perfect grasp of the entire Universe in all its extent of space and time by an Eternal Mind, such as we saw would be the appropriate culmination of that fabric of Truth which Intellect constructs.[1] There is no reason to attribute less validity to the method of Mind in Art than to that of Mind in Science. It is therefore strictly reasonable to postulate an Eternal Mind, other than the society of finite minds, to whom the whole history of that society, with all the universe beside, is present in the " moment eternal " of perfect intuition ; there is ground for postulating this, and *a priori* no ground for refusing to do so.

But, secondly, the significance of Art is also this —that the perfect expression of any element in being can for a moment stand for the whole Universe ; and that the perfect expression of a theme co-extensive with life can stand permanently for the whole Universe. It is because of this that a single object which thus arrests and fixes our attention can cause a timeless experience in the midst of time. For this timeless experience, at least in the case of music, poetry, and drama, is not reached by the exclusion of time but by inclusion of it and by apprehension of a whole succession in a single grasp. And it may be noticed that a great play is more appreciated when well known, because we understand each scene and every action not only in the light of its antecedent history, but also of its consequences. It was a true instinct which led the Greek dramatists to construct their own plots for comedies, but to adopt a well-known tale as the basis of their tragedies. For in the highest

---

[1] Chapter IX. p. 88.

æsthetic experience a whole stretch of time, future as well as past, is present to our consciousness at once. If we could grasp all history in a single apprehension that would be the culmination alike of science and of art. That is beyond the reach of finite mind, but if there is some one perfect expression of that principle of all history (and by the æsthetic law of unity there could not be more than one) then the contemplation of that would equally be the supreme artistic enjoyment as the fashioning of it would be the supreme artistic achievement.

Art aims at revealing the value of the world—not at discussion of it but at exhibition of it. And it does this by taking the fact whose value is to be revealed, and isolating it from the complex setting in which it is found in Nature, so that we may understand and appreciate it. This process of isolation involves unity both internal and external; for unless the work of art be one internally it will only suggest connexions and values, but will not reveal them; and unless it is one also by exclusion of all else from the field of consciousness, our experience as a whole is not purely æsthetic. The function of art is to reveal values by the creation of essential symbols—if by that phrase we may denote a symbol which is a perfect instance of what it symbolises. But in thus concentrating attention upon itself, it claims to be all-satisfying. In substantiation of that claim it gathers all the elements of life within its embrace. Perfect Beauty is thus attained; but the work of art is become a Sacrament and the æsthetic experience is passing into religion.

The Spirit of Art moves with undirected majesty through the world. Its "pathless march no mortal may control." From this group and from that it detaches him who must be its devotee. Royce has compared the Spirit of Mysticism to Coleridge's Ancient Mariner [1]; and beyond doubt the Spirit of

---

[1] *The World and the Individual*, vol. i. p. 85.

Beauty, mystical and magical, may be compared with
the strange figure who lives for ever in that most
wonderful poem.

> It is an ancient Marinere,
> And he stoppeth one of three.
> "By thy long grey beard and thy glittering eye,
> Now wherefore stopp'st thou me?"
>
> .    .    .
>
> He holds him with his glittering eye—
> The Wedding-Guest stood still,
> And listens like a three years' child;
> The Marinere hath his will.
>
> The Wedding-Guest sat on a stone:
> He cannot choose but hear;
> And thus spake on that ancient man,
> The bright-eyed Marinere.

He on whom Beauty has cast her spell is not his
own master, though in his bondage he finds freedom.
He must listen and gaze till his release is given.
However loud the hubbub of the world or however
enticing its interest he must gaze and listen—rapt in a
meditation which is perpetually passing into communion
with God. And we may imagine the Spirit of Art,
mystical and magical, speaking in the words of the
Mariner—

> I pass like night from land to land;
> I have strange power of speech;
> That moment that his face I see,
> I know the man that must hear me:
> To him my tale I teach.
>
> What loud uproar burst from that door!
> The wedding-guests are there:
> But in the garden-bower the bride
> And bride-maids singing are:
> And hark the little vesper bell
> Which biddeth me to prayer.

# CHAPTER XI

## THE MEANING OF TRAGEDY [1]

"Tragedy is the highest expression of the infinite value of human life."—
CHESTERTON.

"Our sweetest songs are those that tell of saddest thought."
SHELLEY.

"I form the light and create darkness : I make peace and create evil : I the
Lord do all these things."—ISAIAH.

I MAY sum up the result of the former chapter by saying
that the main function of art seems to me to be the
creation of what for lack of better words I may call
essential symbols ; by an essential symbol I mean a
symbol which is itself a perfect case of the principle it
symbolises. Perhaps it is worth while to illustrate this
by contrasting the symbolism of art with other forms
of symbolism. A word is a symbol of its meaning;
but derives all its interest from its meaning, which it
only expresses by a convention. No one seeing the
word Death would know what it means unless he
happens to know some English ; the symbol here is
quite arbitrary. Similarly, no one would know the
meaning of a picture representing a perfectly ordinary
old man with a scythe and an hour-glass, until he

---

[1] The speculations contained in this chapter are the result of some reflection
stimulated by three works of Professor A. C. Bradley—his Inaugural Lecture on
*Poetry for Poetry's Sake*, his article in the *Hibbert Journal* on "Hegel's Theory of
Tragedy," and above all his book on *Shakespearean Tragedy*. In the main, I am
endeavouring to take up the problem at the point where he leaves it in that book
and to apply his theory outside tragedy, and I am not at all sure that he would not
regard my whole method as unwarrantable ; in any case he is not to be held
responsible for my conclusions, though I shall borrow from him shamelessly on
the way.

looked in his catalogue and saw the word Death ;
though of course we have become so used to scythes
and hour-glasses that the combination of them in the
accoutrement of one old man might suggest the painter's
intention ; to any one not used to our accepted
hieroglyphics it would only suggest his lunacy. But
in contrast with the word and the inartistic allegory
let us put four pictures by G. F. Watts—*Time, Death,
and Judgment; Sic Transit; The Court of Death;* and
above all *Love and Death.* I am far from saying that
those masterpieces would suggest at once the word
Death ; but to me at any rate they do at once suggest
the gloom and mystery that hang over life, and culminate
in Death. In this sense then the word Death is a
formal and arbitrary symbol of a fact more essentially
symbolised by the curve of the back in the chief figure
in *Love and Death.* The word is a mere sign ; but
that curved back, with its dignity, its calm, its relent-
lessness, and its peace—that is, at least more nearly,
Death itself.

But the greatest painter is limited by the fact that
he cannot depict change ; the picture once painted is
the same for ever, unalterably. But all the realities of
life are processes, moving from point to point in an
ordered growth ; and here lies the great advantage of
the poet and the musician. In the symphony we may
have the burden of some great perplexity, the sharp
contrast of sorrow and mirth, the weaving of all threads
together in a single fabric. This is still clearer, though
no more true, in the case of the dramatist. Here life
itself is presented. And I return to my formula that
the function of Art is to create essential symbols. The
characters of a great play are symbols of the spiritual
forces that sway mankind ; but they are not arbitrary
or allegorical symbols ; they are individual cases of
what they symbolise. If they are not individual, they
are mere types ; and our interest in them is ethical and
not dramatic. So it is, for instance, in the morality

play, *Everyman*. The hero there has no real personal character; he is a mere type. And the interest with which we watch that play, absorbing as it is, is not strictly dramatic. On the other hand, if the characters are merely individuals, and their relations to each other fortuitous, we have no interest in them at all—or rather should have no interest in them, if there were any such; but there cannot be; a play or novel must be to some extent life-like, for life is all that the author has to draw from. But to be life-like is to represent the principles that actually govern life; and the more life-like a play is, and so the more truly individual its characters, the more light does it throw on life and its problems. Life itself, that is, human history as a whole, may be presumed to be the noblest drama of all; but it is at once so long and so complex that most of us can see no real and coherent significance in it at all, unless some man of genius has isolated some relatively complete whole and made us see its value. For, as Browning's Fra Lippo Lippi remarks in connexion with his pictures :

> We're made so that we love
> First, when we see them painted, things we've passed
> Perhaps a hundred times, nor cared to see ;
> And so they're better painted—better to us,
> Which is the same thing.  Art was given for that ;
> God uses us to help each other so,
> Lending our minds out.

Just so the dramatist. He takes some phase of life that we could not extricate from its setting in the complexities of the real world, and puts it bodily before our eyes, to see and to appreciate. And it is a symbol of life precisely by being itself, and because it is life-like. Othello is not a mere symbol ; but just because he is a real human being he is a better symbol of humanity in one of its phases. For this reason there is no way of saying what the good drama says, except by acting the whole of it over again. If we can say at the end, "This play shows us that it is imprudent to steal" or "that it is a mistake to treat one's wife as a doll," then it is a bad play. But if any one asks what Shakespeare meant by King Lear, we can only answer by reading the play to him and saying "He meant that." The play is not unmeaning ; but it is the only possible expression of its meaning. It is an essential symbol. What we learn from it cannot be adequately stated, for it gives us, not instruction, but illumination.

This being so, it ought to be possible to gather from a general consideration of any branch of art some general suggestions as to the problems of life as a whole. Now if we make an exception of music, few people are likely to deny that it is in tragedy that the artistic consciousness achieves its deepest and surest apprehension of reality. What, then, in general terms is Tragedy? It is not simply a tale of suffering : sordid horrors, grinding poverty, degraded misery— these do not, of themselves at any rate, constitute tragedy. Neither failure nor death is intrinsically tragic. We require a struggle and a conflict. But we have this in any melodrama, where the hero and the villain dog each other's steps, and the hero ultimately justifies righteousness by murdering the villain before the eyes of the audience. But that is not tragedy ; nor will it become tragedy if we alter the last scene, and let the villain complete his damnation by murdering the hero. The mere conflict of good and evil, embodied each in one character, is not tragic. There must be a conflict of good with good, and of right with right. This is, in general terms, the first main point in Hegel's theory of tragedy ; it may be insufficient, but it is true as far as it goes. Whenever the recognition of one right involves the violation of another, we have the material of tragedy. The fact that the preponderance of right is clearly on one side may diminish the tragic intensity, but does not destroy the tragic character.

Before going farther I should like to guard against a serious misunderstanding. When one speaks of the characters in a play as symbols, people are apt to suppose that one wishes to allegorise the play. I hope I need not say that I have no such design. Hamlet and Othello are symbols of humanity as a man's actions are symbols of his character ; only human history itself fully · embodies and . expresses the whole truth of humanity ; but that expression is of little use to us, for we cannot contemplate human history as a whole. English history is symbolic of the English character ; if we want to understand that character, we read the history which it has made. But if we would understand humanity as a whole, we cannot set ourselves to read all human history ; and if we did, we should only confuse our minds with endless uncorrelated facts ; its meaning would evade our grasp. We must come to the great masters whose inspired intuition has caught now one phase, now another, and set it before us ; and then, from our understanding of the various phases, we may construct some conception of the whole. There is a comic side to life, and even to death, for, as Mr. Bernard Shaw has reminded us, " Life does not cease to be funny when men die any more than it ceases to be serious when men laugh." And there is a serious and terrible side to death and to life—and this in its most terrible form is given us in tragedy. It is set before us ; we are not told about it, but we are bidden to behold it. If we treat Othello as the incarnation of jealousy, Iago as the incarnation of malignity, and Desdemona as the incarnation of submissiveness, we degrade the most perfect of all dramas to the level of a sermon ; it then tells us what Shakespeare thought about life, but does not exhibit life itself. And it becomes unreal ; jealous men exist, but jealousy is an unreal abstraction ; it exists nowhere but in our analytic heads. Othello is a jealous man with all the complexities of a man ; and just for this reason he can symbolise human jealousy, or rather jealous humanity, and show us what it is.   I think Hegel does not really do justice to the individuality of great tragic characters. He insists on it, of course, but having insisted on it seems to forget it again.   It is only by being themselves real and living that the characters can show us truth.   They must be life-like—not, of course, in the sense that they must resemble in their behaviour the actual men and women in the world ; one can see that behaviour any day without paying for a ticket or breathing the foul atmosphere of a theatre ; the characters must be life-like in the sense of showing the real spiritual tumult which people off the stage so studiously conceal. If by natural we mean possible in our own experience, then it is most unnatural for Cleopatra to say :

> Give me my robe ; put on my crown ; I have
> Immortal longings in me.

But it is most natural if by that we mean that it genuinely reveals the pride and high-souled greatness of the speaker.

And this leads me to make an addition to our former definition.   Tragedy, we said, is a conflict of good with good, and now we must add something and say, Tragedy is a conflict of good with good, worked out in characters of heroic mould.   It is this heroic mould which prevents Tragedy from being merely depressing.   In Professor Bradley's words, " No one ever closes the book with the feeling that man is a poor mean creature.   He may be wretched and he may be awful, but he is not small.   His lot may be heart-rending and mysterious but it is not contemptible. The most confirmed of cynics ceases to be a cynic while he reads these plays.   And with this greatness of the tragic hero is connected what I venture to describe as the centre of tragic impression.   This central feeling is the impression of waste." [1]   The conflict of good with

---

[1] *Shakespearean Tragedy*, p. 23.

good must involve waste ; and the heroic stature of the characters, in whom that waste is exhibited, forces it upon our attention and makes it terrible as well as pitiable.

Hegel's favourite example of his theory is the *Antigone*, where the claims of the State, represented at the opening of the play by Creon's edict, conflict with the claims of the family and of the dead, represented by the unburied body of Polyneices. Antigone must violate one or other of those claims ; and yet each claim is in itself right. Hence there is a conflict of right with right, and that too a conflict of rights more evenly balanced for the Greeks than it is for us ; we have kept the Greek reverence for the family, and added to it, but we have lost their feeling for the State and ought to remember this if we would appreciate the conflict of the *Antigone*. Hegel also works out his theory in connexion with the *Oresteia*. He urges that Clytemnestra represents the cause of vengeance for Iphigenia, as indeed she herself says in a passage where she even disclaims personal responsibility for the murder of Agamemnon ; Orestes, on the other hand, represents the cause of Agamemnon, and kills his mother as the murderess of his father. It is not in the least necessary, as I said, that there should be an equal amount of right on both sides ; the fact that to fulfil one the hero must violate another is all that is required. As a matter of fact, the *Oresteia* may be far closer to Hegel's ideal than he himself supposed ; if it is really connected with the struggle between the matriarchal type of civilisation, whose religion centred in Demeter, and the patriarchal type, whose religion centred in Zeus, it is far more of a conflict between rival claims than if its interest is entirely confined to the action of the play itself. Here again I must urge that I am not trying to treat the play as an allegory ; but if that conflict of civilisations and religions were still real to the Athenians, the significance of the play would be very much increased.

These two instances are very clear ; but the principle can be worked out elsewhere. Thus in the *Oedipus Tyrannus* we have the claim of the outraged moral code confronted by the claim of Oedipus' innocence. In *Bacchae* we have Dionysus' claim to divine honours confronted by Pentheus' claim to see to the well-being of his state. It is easy to give examples ; but one other play I will mention because in the main it is an exception—the *Oedipus Coloneus*. Here the only conflict of claims is, I think, in the scene where Oedipus curses Polyneices—paternal affection and patriotic justice being the rivals ; but then, too, I think that is the only part of the play that is strictly tragic ; for to me at least the death of Oedipus is rather a solution than a catastrophe, and the prevailing emotion produced by the play is not pity or terror but a sublime serenity and calm.

Hegel was inclined to regard Greek tragedy as tragedy at its purest—and the *Antigone* in particular was exalted in this way. It is true that the principle which he treats as the essential principle of tragedy is more *clearly* manifested there than, perhaps, anywhere else at all ; but not, I think, more fully, and it is Hegel himself who helps us to this correction. If one thing is certain about his whole philosophy, it is that he believed in the unity of the Good which none the less appears on both sides in the tragic conflict. That conflict is an internal strife, a strife within the Spirit itself ; it is proof of a fatal defect in the world that the good should thus be divided against itself. Now in the *Antigone* the two rival principles are embodied in two characters ; Antigone has no mental conflict, but identifies herself with the family as against the State from the first ; so it is too in the Oresteia. But the unity of this goodness which thus fights against itself is more clear when the conflict is altogether within the soul of the hero, or is at any rate reproduced there, as in Neoptolemus in the *Philoctetes*. It is in this respect

that Shakespeare makes the greatest advance upon the
Greeks ; if we take his four great tragedies we find him
dealing with this conflict in four distinct ways. In
*King Lear* the conflict is wholly external, and the hero
is not even one of the parties ; the forces of good and
evil fight over him, but he is the passive victim. In
*Macbeth* the conflict is between Macbeth and his
opponents, but is reproduced within the soul of
Macbeth, who is himself one of the conflicting parties.
In *Hamlet* the conflict in the hero's soul draws to itself
all the greater part of our attention, and overshadows
the external conflict. In *Othello* the conflict in the
hero's soul is simply everything. I do not think it a
mere coincidence that *Othello*, where the whole struggle
is internal, should be also dramatically the most perfect
of the four, and *King Lear*, where it is external, the
least perfect.

But it may be urged that the struggle here is not
one of good with good but of good with evil. In
*King Lear* this is true, if we confine our attention to
the conflict itself and ignore its origin. In *Macbeth* it
is not true at all, for in Lady Macbeth there is at least
one good quality — devotion to her husband — and
Macbeth himself is noble even in his uttermost degrada-
tion. In *Hamlet* and *Othello* the external conflict is
with evil, but the centre of interest is the internal
conflict, and in each case the conflict is a war of goodness with itself. This is rather an interesting point.
If we put aside *King Lear*, which requires separate
treatment on many grounds, we find that in the case
where the main struggle is between one set of characters
and another, the morally inferior characters are endowed
with a greatness and transcendence that are good in
themselves and do something to make up for the
moral inferiority. Macbeth and his wife are wicked ;
Malcolm and Macduff are good but small. As long
as we maintain the dramatic frame of mind, there can
be no doubt that the wicked pair commands more of

our admiration than the good pair. We can glorify God for creating a Macbeth, but who could glorify Him for creating a Malcolm? In this play, then, where the important conflict is external, the contending parties are both endowed with goodness, so that the death of Macbeth is not a mere relief, as from a fever, but the passing of a figure which for all its corruption is still noble. In *Othello* we find the opposite. Here the tragic conflict is internal, and the external force can therefore be represented as almost wholly evil, so that when Iago falls there is no sense of loss, and the play can conclude with the promise of his torture without our feeling one touch of sympathy for him. Between the two stands *Hamlet*; here the internal struggle is far more engrossing than the external, but the latter is part of the tragedy, and the King is not wholly vile; he displays both resource and dignity, and there is no reason to suppose that his feeling for Ophelia is hypocritical.

But it will be objected that though we have good on both sides here, there is no conflict of right with right. Hamlet's uncle has some good in him, but it is not the good in him that brings him into conflict with Hamlet. And this is true. The conflict of good with good, though not dramatically irrelevant, is none the less accidental; it is not a conflict of good with good arising from the nature of the good on each side, as is the case in the *Antigone*. If we are to find such a conflict it must be in the internal struggle.

In the case of Othello it is easy to detect this. It is just the intensity of his devotion that makes Iago's insinuations an agony. The more vitally a belief concerns us, the more sternly do we criticise its grounds to make doubt impossible. One sometimes hears people say of Othello, " He ought to have been able to trust her "; yes—if he had been like most people, affectionate and entirely sane, but then he would not have been worthy to be the hero of a tragedy. It is

not only that his whole being was devoted—that is so
in the case of many ordinary good men—but that he
was capable of an intensity of devotion that most of us
cannot rival.  This is what makes him so entirely
noble and transcendent ; and this is what conditions
his spiritual ruin.  The common phrase, "the defects
of his qualities," is a summary of the tragic fact,
as that fact is exhibited by Shakespeare.  And
Shakespeare's treatment of the tragic fact is at once
subtler and profounder than that of the Greeks, because
it shows more plainly the unity of the good which
fights against itself.

But, as I said, in *Othello* the matter is easy : so it is
in *Hamlet*, where the sensibility that has caused the
paralysis of will, and so causes seven unnecessary
deaths, is yet good in itself.  And it is part of its very
goodness that it should have these appalling consequences.  The good fights with itself.  So in *Macbeth*,
it is the hero's courage and splendid imagination that
make the temptations of ambition irresistible.

What of *King Lear* ?  It is dramatically the most
faulty of the sacred four, as I have said.  I am convinced that Professor Bradley is right in regarding it
as a play to read rather than to see.  The opposing
characters are more nearly types than in the other
plays.  The conflict of good and evil is more direct
and more purely moral than elsewhere ; Edgar and
Kent seem faultless, while Goneril, and Regan are more
terrible than Iago, and Edmund is more contemptible—
all the characters are very simple, as if each were the
organ of some cosmic force.  The entire interest is
transcendent ; we witness the convulsions of a universe.
Dante wrote a Divine Comedy ; this is the Divine
Tragedy.  But as a poem it stands at the head of all
achievements of the human spirit, and it is certainly
a tragic poem ; a theory of tragedy which leaves it
out is self-condemned.  Yet where is the conflict of
good with good ?  Lear is a tragic figure, but in him

there is no conflict. He is passive, and achieves
tragic stature by the immenseness of his sensibility.
Ingratitude is always painful, but few men are capable
of suffering as Lear suffered. Yet in him there is no
conflict. Outside there is a conflict—but that is of
good with evil, not of good with good ; and, except
Goneril, the characters do not at first seem to be of
tragic stature—Kent and Edgar are the salt of the
earth, but they are not tragic. It seems that our
theory must go. Let us look closer. In this poem,
Hell is loose ; but who loosed it ? And the answer
is—Cordelia. Hers is a short part, only just over a
hundred lines, and careful reading is necessary if we
are to grasp its significance. But she is tragic ; she is
own sister to Goneril. Cordelia is not "sweet" ; she
is a woman to the marrow, but a proud strong woman,
with the firmness and the exaltation of Antigone.
Think how, in all the tension of that opening scene,
she meets Burgundy's refusal to marry her without her
dowry :

> Peace be with Burgundy !
> Since that respects of fortune are his love
> I shall not be his wife.

Think how she meets defeat :

> For thee, oppressed King, I am cast down,
> Myself could else outfrown false fortune's frown.

Think of her last words—following at once on those
lines—"Shall we not see these daughters and these
sisters ? " Of course she was tender ; but firmness
and tenderness are not incompatible ; it is often the
soft hearts that are cruel. She had been the Fool's
friend ; when Lear asks for the Fool, a Knight answers,
"Since my young lady's going into France, sir, the
fool hath much pined away." But at the critical
moment she failed. Her virtue rose in rebellion
against her sisters' hypocritical protestations, and she
could show her father no sign of love or demand.

Some critics have found this unnatural; but only, I think, because they assume that she was "sweet." It is not unnatural, but it is very terrible. If she could not speak, she might have gone and pressed his hand. But just because she was the great-souled woman, she could do nothing at that moment. And her failure is the source of all the horrors. Lear would never have been outraged in the houses of his other daughters if Cordelia could have spoken then, for he would have lived with her :

> I loved her most, and thought to set my rest
> On her kind nursery.

The purely evil forces would have been powerless if goodness had not failed, and failed by reason of that quality which was its excellence.

The actuality of the conflict of good with itself as an element in tragedy may now, I hope, be admitted. That it is an essential element is seen at once if we try to remove it. Thus let us take *King Lear*, where the failure of goodness is only exhibited at the opening of the play ; and let us follow Nahum Tate so far as to write, not a happy ending, but a happy opening ; let us suppose that Lear himself had shown no wilfulness, but had abdicated in favour of his two daughters, Cordelia having gone to France with her husband ; and then let the whole play stand as at present from the close of the first scene onwards. It is no longer a tragedy ; the beauty of the words might cast a spell on us, but the plot is become revolting—a mere tale of unprovoked outrage ; such things may happen, we say, but they do not express the real meaning of the world. For the fact is that in a drama, or any imaginative work of considerable length, we demand an exhibition of some kind of justice ;[1] a long poem or tale cannot be taken as the expression of a mere passing mood ; if its object is to call attention to

---

[1] Cf. *Shakespearean Tragedy*, p. 279.

existing facts, as in the case of Mr. Upton Sinclair's novel, *The Jungle*, mere horror may be justified, because the writer's purpose is not artistic ; but in a work of art we demand a basis of justice ; for its function is to symbolise reality, and we refuse to regard reality as unjust.　I do not mean, of course, that Lear and Cordelia *deserved* their agony ; certainly they received far more than double for all their sins ; yet the catastrophe was the recoil upon themselves of the consequences of their own failures.　Even in the case of Othello the tragedy is the recoil upon himself of the consequences of the defect inherent in his virtue. But it is not the case with Antigone ; here the catastrophe in which she is involved is due to no failing in herself, and I confess that this seems to me a fault in this play and in Greek tragedy generally ; if it were not that Antigone made her decision with her eyes open and knowing what it would bring upon her, the catastrophe would be intolerable ; even as it is it makes me a little rebellious ; and the combination of innocence and helplessness in the hero of the *Oedipus Tyrannus* makes that play, to me, in this respect frankly disgusting ; I even suspect that Sophocles himself was dissatisfied and wrote the *Oedipus Coloneus* to put matters straight, for taken together the two form a noble drama.　No doubt, when we are in its actual presence, the *Oedipus Tyrannus* charms by the beauty of its language ; but this does not justify it.　We never assent to that catastrophe, and only bear it because the poet lays us under his anæsthetic spell. I deeply regret to add that the same must be said of *The Cenci*—Shelley's "superb achievement" as Browning rightly called it.

This difference between Greek and Shakespearean tragedy is rooted in another—their difference in the treatment of the supreme Power, which in Tragedy we may call Fate.　The Greeks recognised the power and the right of an external Fate, as embodied in the utterance of an oracle ; and it acts upon the characters from without. But in Shakespeare Fate acts mainly through the characters from within. I do not mean that Shakespeare made no use of opportune accidents ; Desdemona's dropping of her handkerchief, the meeting of Hamlet's ship with the pirates, the lateness of Edmund's messenger, are all accidents without which the catastrophe would be averted. But external fate never determines everything as in the case of the *Oedipus Tyrannus.* Fate brings the characters together, but once they are brought together they are their own destiny. Given Othello, Desdemona, and Iago, with their characters, the tragedy ensues as a logical deduction ; the accident of the handkerchief determines its course, and perhaps makes the catastrophe more terrible than it could otherwise have been—but it does not create the tragedy, which springs direct from the persons and their collocation. Hence the sense of personal freedom and therefore of responsibility is stronger and more invariable in Shakespeare than in the Greek tragedians, and I think we may say that Shakespeare's apprehension of freedom satisfies us as true and sufficient. But this freedom is the freedom of members of a system, and it is encompassed in the darkness of almost total ignorance. The men and women act of their own responsibility and deliberately, but they do not understand their acts ; think of them all, Lear and Cordelia, Macbeth and his wife, Hamlet, his mother and his uncle, Othello and Iago—each acts to satisfy some desire, righteous, innocent and guilty, and his act involves his destruction. The sense of a fate brooding over the world and luring all to the appointed end is even stronger, I think, in Shakespeare, where the Fate works through the free choice of the characters, than among the Greeks where it works upon them from without ; for in the latter case it seems comparatively accidental and arbitrary, but in the former the people are their own fate, and it is because they are

they, that the tragedy arises.  Fate is thus made less
arbitrary but even more inexorable ; it is the law of
the world of which the men and women are members ;
they both make it and obey it ; they cannot escape it,
for it is themselves ; nor can they modify it, for that
would involve themselves becoming other people.  They
are free, for the origin of their actions is themselves ;
they are bound hand and foot, for from themselves
there is no flight.

Such is moral freedom as exhibited in tragedy, not
libertarianism but self-dependence.  And what is the
Fate that broods over the whole—the law of this tragic
world ?  It is precisely the Good, which in the tragedy
fights against itself.  This tragic world purges itself of
evil, not by conquest without loss, as Messiah scatters
the rebel hosts in *Paradise Lost*, but by loss of its very
best.  The catastrophe that destroys Goneril and Regan
engulfs also Lear and Cordelia ; Othello's life is wrecked
and cut short in the convulsions by which the Spirit
rids itself of Iago.

What then is the light thrown by tragedy upon the
problem of evil ?  Evil is the occasion of the whole ;
the conflict of Good with itself is evil.  But there is
a positive evil beside this—the force which, taking
advantage of the defect in Good, brings havoc on the
world ; the ingratitude of Goneril and Regan ; Iago's
joy in the sense of personal power ; the ambition,
hypocrisy, and bestiality of Claudius.  This evil is the
real and active enemy of the Good which is the law
of the tragic world ; it breaks up that law and reduces
its world to chaos.  It is essentially blind and irrational
and is intelligible only in the sense that we recognise it
as a factor of our real world and of our own selves.  In
the end of the tragedy it is purged out.  Iago alone of
Shakespeare's villains in these four plays is still alive at
the end of the last act, and the last words of that act
are the decree that he shall die by torture.  Evil, then,
is the source of havoc, thus proving its antagonism to

the order of the tragic world, and hence the goodness of that order; and in the end it perishes. Tragedy, then, is, so far, the triumph of good over the evil to which it gives occasion by its own defect.

But the triumph is imperfect; it is won at a terrible cost. Where, as in *Macbeth*, the hero himself is mainly evil, we feel that the cost is greater than the gain. The world is indeed rid of a pest; but if Macbeth was terrible, he was at least great, and the men who remain to us are small. This impression is, I think, stronger in Macbeth than in the other plays, because the union of wickedness and greatness in the one character forces it upon our notice. Yet it is quite as real elsewhere; Hamlet, Othello, Cordelia—all must perish in the destruction of their enemies. · If the impression of waste is less strong in these plays, I think it is because we see the impossibility of Hamlet and Claudius continuing to exist together; and Hamlet cannot live on when Claudius is killed, because then the seven violent deaths caused by his delay would be unavenged; *he* let the evil loose—he did not make it evil, but he gave it its operative power—and he must be involved in its doom. So, too, with Cordelia and Othello. But Macbeth might go on living, the good and bad in him together, for does not his sheer greatness more than counter-balance his wickedness? No; to ask the question is to answer it; but we are prompted to ask it here, and not, I think, in the other plays. Tragedy is a triumph —spoilt; Good wins, as we won at Trafalgar, with a loss that makes victory a defeat.

Yet the total effect is not depressing; we are at the end neither crushed nor rebellious. I think this is mainly due to a vague half-conscious sense that a deep stern justice governs the whole. This is the second main point of Hegel's theory; "above bare Fear and tragic Sympathy stands the sense of Atonement, which the tragedy affords by displaying to us the eternal justice." [1]

[1] *Aesthetik*, p. 532.

L

But I think Hegel is guilty of a very bad over-statement. He says,[1] "The last impression is, not unhappiness and suffering, but the satisfaction of the spirit, only in so far as the necessity of what happens to the individuals can appear in the end as absolute reasonableness." This is all of a piece with his statement[2] that he prefers a happy ending. Of course he had a thesis to maintain—the thesis, namely, that evil is a moment in the perfection of the Absolute Idea. But to apply his theory to tragedy he has to run counter to experience. It is significant that he says nothing about evil in tragedy except in so far as the self-opposition of good is evil. But tragedy at its best contains substantive, positive evil. To put the matter in Hegel's terminology—Tragedy is not nearly so affirmative as he tried to make out ; his error was forced upon him by his whole philosophy ; for he could not deny the deep significance of tragedy. To allow that significance, while leaving tragedy its apparently negative conclusion, would have been inconsistent with his type of Absolutism. So tragedy had to be somewhat moulded ; it had to exhibit eternal justice. But it doesn't do all that ; only melodrama does all that. The deaths of Antigone and Haemon, the deaths of Lear and Cordelia, do not display the eternal justice ; the necessity never appears as absolute reasonableness. But the great artist, in the secret manner of art, forces us to assent, in spite of our regret and complete failure to comprehend. There is no direct consciousness of justice, but a vague half-conscious sense of something that is not injustice in the Power that rules the world. Not, of course, that Othello and Cordelia only had what they deserved—the bare conception of desert is inadmissible in this connexion ; we do not judge—we hear and see, consider and bow the head. But we bow the head in assent—sorrowful, involuntary assent —for the sufferers we think of at the end are not

---

[1] *Aesthetik*, p. 533, 4.        [2] *Ibid.* p. 574.

innocent; it was they that opened the floodgates, and we cannot be rebellious if the flood is too strong for them.

Sorrowful, involuntary assent; yes — but subtly mingled with this there is a sense of exaltation, of solemn, tremendous joy. I know that here we come more than ever within the region of personal and, very likely, idiosyncratic impressions. As far as I can interpret my own impression, this exaltation is not prominent, and yet suffuses the tone of the whole. Perhaps it is largely due to the feeling that no external calamity really weighs at all in the scale against the spiritual transcendence of Othello or Cordelia. But I find the feeling strongest in the case of *Hamlet* and *King Lear*, and weakest in that of *Othello*; and it can be no coincidence that in the two former plays we have close to the end a suggestion that the hero's story does not close with his death. Hamlet breaks off his last speech to murmur " The rest is silence "; but Horatio does not accept that :

> Now cracks a noble heart. Good-night, sweet Prince,
> And flights of angels sing thee to thy rest.

No doubt Horatio is a commonplace sane person, who might be expected to believe in immortality; but the fact that Shakespeare put the words into the mouth of a suitable person is no evidence that he regarded them as unimportant. Of course this passage does not prove Shakespeare's belief in immortality, or even suggest it; my point is that the occurrence of these words colours the whole conclusion of the play—as with the faintest touch of light in the utter gloom, a glimmer that may be the herald of a new dawn. Professor Bradley suggests that this may be permitted here by Shakespeare because Hamlet alone of all the heroes is in gloom from the very opening of the play. I should feel this argument more strongly in the case of the similar passage in *King Lear*. After the King is dead, Albany invites Kent to take a share in the government of the kingdom, and Kent replies :

> I have a journey, sir, shortly to go ;
> My master calls me, I must not say No.

Surely this is more than a mere refusal to survive his master, which is all that Professor Bradley sees in the lines ; I am clear that to me at any rate the lines have an immense value—not that the light they bring into the gloom is bright, for it is barely discernible, but they make all the difference between total and just not total darkness.

But I cannot accept Professor Bradley's justification of Horatio's address to the dead Hamlet—it seems too accidental ; there is evidence that Hamlet's early life was singularly happy—not like that of Cordelia, with Goneril and Regan for elder sisters ; and the mere accident that the play does not commence—*i.e.* that we do not happen to come across Hamlet—till the gloom is settled on him could hardly of itself justify the suggested extension of the interest beyond the limits of the action. Hamlet is in gloom throughout the play, but we do not feel that his has been a peculiarly unhappy life taken on the whole. Yet both Horatio's speech and Kent's are undeniably justified. I suggest that the justification is to be found in the cosmic character of these two plays. In this respect they differ from *Othello*. *Othello* is the most purely human of the plays. There is something fateful in the advance of Iago, but I can detect little sense of a brooding fate operating through the characters to reach an end that none of them dreams of. There is less of mystery in this play ; less of the sense that the characters, however real and living, are our points of contact with a reality vast and solemn which speaks through them but is more than they. I believe it is this sense—strong in *Hamlet* and overpowering in *King Lear*—which makes those faint suggestions of immortality admissible. For

Macbeth we dare not desire immortality—he himself has jumped the life to come.  But for Hamlet and Lear and Cordelia we may desire it, and its suggestion is admissible because throughout the play we have been conscious of great hidden forces ; the interest was never really confined to the action on the stage, and so no unity is broken by the suggestion that it continues after the curtain falls.

I am tempted to support this suggestion by reference to a modern play of far inferior merit—Browning's *A Blot in the 'Scutcheon.*  That play is a true tragedy ; there is a conflict of rights.  Lord Tresham is wholly governed by his care for the honour of his family ; his sister Mildred and Lord Mertoun love each other with deep and pure affection, and are engaged.  Tresham catches Mertoun on his way to a nocturnal visit to Mildred, challenges him to fight, and kills him.  As Mertoun dies he bids Tresham take his last message of love to Mildred.  Tresham goes to Mildred to obey, and this dialogue follows :

TRESH.    He bade me tell you . . .
MIL.                                    What I do forbid
          Your utterance of ! so much that you may tell
          And will not, how you murdered him . . . but no !
          You'll tell me that he loved me, never more
          Than bleeding out his life there :  must I say
          "Indeed" to that ?   Enough !   I pardon you !

TRESH.    You cannot, Mildred ! for the harsh words, yes :
          Of this last deed Another's Judge—whose doom
          I wait in doubt, despondency, and fear.

MIL.      Oh, true !   There's nought for me to pardon !   True !
          You loose my soul of all its cares at once.
          Death makes me sure of him for ever !   You
          Tell me his last words ?   He shall tell me them
          And take my answer, not in words, but reading
          Himself the heart I had to read him late.

Now this direct appeal to immortality jars on me, and I am compelled to regard it as a dramatic flaw.  And

so far as I can discover the nature of the jar here, it
is in the sudden extension of the interest beyond the
limits of the action—those limits being otherwise carefully respected in this case.

If the function of Tragedy is in any degree what I
take it to be, this point cannot be dismissed as a mere
matter of technical construction.  All essential matters
of technique are essential to the work of art which
contains them.  If, then, I am right in my suggestion
that the thought of Immortality is æsthetically admissible
in dramas, where the individual characters are throughout regarded as representatives of a spiritual order which
they symbolise but do not exhaust, it is legitimate to
infer that no man is immortal by right of his individuality, but as he is a member of the whole spiritual
world ; or in Pauline language, that it is not as
ourselves but as sons of God that we are heirs of
eternal life.  So Plato represents the Creator as
conferring on finite spirits the immortality which He
alone possesses by necessity and right.

Such, then, seems to me the contribution made by
Tragedy to the problem of immortality ; its contribution to the problem of evil we have already seen.  Evil
is a real and positive force—not only a defect of goodness ; it gains its opportunity through a defect of goodness ; it is in the end purged away from the world, but
in its process it both enhances the value of, and accom-
plishes the partial destruction of, the good.  It is worth
while that Goneril should exist, that the full potential
splendours of Cordelia's spirit may be realised ; yet
Goneril remains a monster, and Cordelia perishes in the
general ruin.

We speak of the problem of evil, but not so frequently of the problem of good.  Yet there is a
problem of good, and tragedy presents it.  For we find
that human good at least is of such a nature that it
may be divided and war against itself, or else may have
some defect, which is of the same stuff with its virtue

and yet makes it serve the cause of evil at a critical moment.

As to the relations of good and evil, tragedy reveals them as utter opposites ; they are not different aspects of one thing in any intelligible sense—only, in fact, so far as both exist and are thus different aspects of the total Reality.   In their strife good is in this sense victorious, that it partially survives ; at the end of the tragedy much good has perished, but all the evil ; and the good that has perished has fallen a victim to the forces let loose by its own self-opposition or defect. In this sense and to this extent the philosophy of tragedy is ethical and optimistic.   Further, we have seen that precisely when tragedy is most itself, that is, when it is most clearly an essential symbol of human life, it may legitimately hint that its hero's career does not end with death, and that the glorious good whose destruction we have witnessed is not really lost to the Cosmos.   But this can only be a hint ; for the subject lies beyond the province of tragedy.   It is the function of art, as we saw, to extricate some single fact from the complexities in which it is entangled in the real world, and to set it clearly before us that we may appreciate its significance and estimate its meaning.   Tragedy does this with the fact I have endeavoured to describe ; it may hint at other facts, but to do more than hint would be to desert the tragic function, and destroy the unity of aim which gives the drama its artistic, that is its interpretative, value.

This, then, is the philosophy of tragedy.   Good by its self-opposition and essential defect gives occasion to its enemy, evil ; in the struggle evil is destroyed, but much glorious good—all of good that *is* glorious— perishes with it.   As we behold, we rejoice in the immeasurable greatness of man ; we feel terror at the evil and pity for the good ; and we accept without protest, but not without lament, the destruction of so much good by the evil to which it gave opportunity.

Man is so great in and through the struggle, and good so glorious, that we would not have the evil simply abolished ; for that would be to abolish the struggle, and with it much of the greatness and the glory. The world revealed in tragedy is a noble world, and better than any we can conceive—yet it is terrible and pitiable and sad beyond belief. We would not alter it ; yet we cannot be content with it. This is the Philosophy of Tragedy ; and if it is not the last word of human philosophy, at least we know that no philosophy can by any possibility be true which does not contain it, or which diminishes in any degree whatsoever the depths of its exalted sad solemnity.

# CHAPTER XII

## INTELLECT, IMAGINATION, AND WILL

Διάνοια δ' αὐτὴ οὐθὲν κινεῖ.—ARISTOTLE.

And so the Word had breath, and wrought
With human hands the creed of creeds
In loveliness of perfect deeds
More strong than all poetic thought.
TENNYSON.

WE have hitherto been regarding the imaginative function of the mind as something wholly distinct from the intellectual, but we have now to add that there is no sharp line between the two, but only a difference of emphasis. Moreover, the intellect becomes imaginative when it is itself sufficiently concentrated and intense; and (as we shall see) it is through thus becoming imaginative that it may gain its hold upon Impulse and so constitute Will.

But this does not mean that we were mistaken in describing the two phases as almost antithetic to each other. For the *normal* life of intellect is abstract [1] and restless while the *normal* life of imagination is concrete and contemplative. To use again the old illustration, Boy and Man are words with quite distinct meanings, though there is no moment at which any particular individual passes from one stage to the other. And in the case before us the matter is all the more important, as the imaginative movement of mind will seriously interfere with the intellectual if it is introduced too

[1] In the sense that it is concerned with *meaning* to the exclusion of *fact* or *image*.

153

soon, and will also be vain and futile if it is initiated
without intellectual preparation, for then it is valuable
and indeed tolerable only as a graceful relaxation.
Beauty we defined as " the adequate expression of important truth or fact "; and we have now to add that
beauty must always exhibit the logical structure of
Truth—totality and internal necessity.

It is of course plain that in a work of art no one
part determines the other parts ; we do not find here
that determination of events by temporal antecedents
which natural science seeks to establish in its causal
laws. No one who has read only the first line of
Milton's *Sonnet on his Blindness*—" When I consider
how my light is spent "—can possibly infer that a little
later the poet will say, " His state is kingly "; but
when he has read the whole sonnet he will see how each
word must be just what it is and where it is. The
meaning, only fully expressed by the whole poem, none
the less controls every syllable of the expression with as
great rigidity as can be found in any geometrical
demonstration. Art is, in structure, Logic *in excelsis*.
This point has been so well made by Dr. Bosanquet [1]
that I must ask leave to quote him at length :

All logical process is the reshaping of a world of content
by its own universal spirit. There is no repetition—not so
much as the recurrent application of a word—which is devoid
of this creative element ; and in creative production *par excellence*
we have only the same thing at its fullest.

And as we learn to deal with greater shapes of art, and
as æsthetic insight and experience increase, the penetrative
imagination reveals itself as the higher form of the creative.
And we feel that not the invention of novelty, but the logic
which lays bare the heart and structure of things, and in doing
so purifies and intensifies the feeling which current appearances
are too confused and contradictory to evoke, is the true secret
of art. No doubt we should fail to predict the incarnation
which a painter's or a poet's thought will assume ; if we could
predict it, we should ourself be he. But this is not because we
are too rational, but because we are not rational enough. The

---

[1] *The Principle of Individuality and Value*, pp. 332, 333.

"fundamental brainwork" is lacking to us; as is a special capacity for the *infinitely delicate logic*[1] of expression, by which the passionate thought, already in itself too great for us, is embodied in a million ramifications of detail, constituting a tissue of precise determination in which alone the thought in question with its passion could find utterance—could become itself. If we say that the process is not rational, because it is largely unconscious, we are committing a serious confusion. The process itself is an intense and exquisitely adjusted and organised consciousness to a great extent obviously and plainly logical. But it is not, of course, another and a different consciousness watching and analysing the first while it proceeds. And in this sense, we are apt to forget, all logical process without exception is unconscious. You cannot make the working function of a syllogism into its major premiss: you cannot predict its conclusion *ab extra* by a watching and inactive consciousness. The spirit of logic, when at work, deals with what is before the mind and reshapes it; but it is not itself a part of what is before the mind. And in this, though remote in degree, it shows its kinship with the creative imagination which at its best and greatest, as we have urged, turns markedly towards the penetrative. If it is "creative," it is so because profound penetration reveals positive treasures beyond the scope of the average mind; not because it deviates into paths of arbitrary fantasy. In short, then, all logical activity is a world of content reshaping itself by its own spirit and laws in presence of new suggestions; a syllogism is in principle nothing less, and a Parthenon or "Paradise Lost" is in principle nothing more.

What is thus so eloquently said in insistence upon the continuity of the scientific and artistic functions of mind I can only echo, merely repeating that this does not affect the distinction which we drew; intellect as a rule is content with the skeleton and persists in pushing enquiry further, while imagination clothes the skeleton with flesh and then contemplates its finished work until satiety overtakes it. Each would find fulfilment only in the full apprehension of the structure of the universe adequately embodied and expressed.

We have now to see how it is through passing out

[1] The italics are mine.

of its normal self into imagination that intellect is able to gain control of impulse and so constitute will. And here we are at once confronted with one of the supreme difficulties of philosophical exposition, which arises from the fact that we are aiming at the apprehension in one grasp of many interlocking systems, so that to follow the true order of enquiry will always involve a great amount of cross-reference, recapitulation, and the like. Thus, for example, it would be well to determine what we mean by the will, or by volition, before discussing how the will is affected by the apprehensions of the intellect or the intuitions of imagination. But there is also a convenience in dealing at once with this great function of imagination while the nature of the operations called by that name is still fresh in our minds. This will involve some anticipation now of results only reached in subsequent discussion, and some recapitulation then of what is suggested here. But we shall be enabled to keep the whole discussion of imagination together, and perhaps this gain outweighs the attendant disadvantages.

The most familiar problem in the practical moral life is that of carrying out in actual practice what we know to be right. For the science of ethics more interest may attach to the occasions when our difficulty is that of determining what course is right ; but those occasions are less frequent in the lives of most men than the times when, knowing what we ought to do, we shrink from doing it.

Aristotle's celebrated discussion of this problem, provided it is taken as a kind of diagram rather than an exact description of the psychical state in question, contains the clue to its solution. Taking as an instance a simple desire (the desire for sweet things), which runs contrary to a general plan (of avoiding unwholesome things), he shows that any particular sweet object may be referred to either of two general propositions. The general plan suggests " Sweet things are unwholesome " ;

the desire of the moment suggests "Sweet things are pleasant." Both of these are true. Everything therefore depends on the question to which of these the particular instance — "This is sweet" — should be referred. And inasmuch as "Sweet things are pleasant" has a direct appeal to appetite while "Sweet things are unwholesome" has not, the former will carry the day unless some further step is taken.[1]

Now the man who acts from an impulse has not actually got syllogisms of any kind before his mind ; but it is quite true that what is before his mind can be schematised in this way. We have, then, to ask what determines the reference of the particular instance, "This is sweet," to one rather than the other of the two propositions ; or if, as was said, the proposition which has an inherent appeal to impulse will win if other things are equal, what is it that makes other things unequal in the case of the self-controlled man ?

Another passage of Aristotle's comes to our aid.[2] The true end is the good ; and the end for any given man at a particular time is what seems good to him— τὸ φαινόμενον ἀγαθόν, the appearing good. But what seems good, or what "the appearing good" is, depends on character, which again depends on nature and training. But he holds a man responsible for what appears good, for the φαντασία. And though Aristotle carries the implied suggestion no further, and indeed seems unconscious of the implication, we may follow the hint he gives in the following way.

The apparent good is not only that which seems good, but also the good which appears, which takes shape before the senses or in the imagination. And one thing at least which Aristotle's weak-willed man may do is to summon impulse or appetite to the side of the general plan of life by calling up a picture of the precise evil which will result from imprudent indulgence —the actual pain of gout or whatever it may be.

---

[1] *Eth. Nic.* 1147 a 24-b 19.       [2] *Eth. Nic.* 1113 a 20.

Certainly if I met a man, whom I knew to be given to excessive drinking, standing apparently in hesitation at the door of a public-house, I should not dilate on the evils of indulgence, but should try to call up a picture which would appeal ; I should not say, " Indulgence is sure to bring its penalty," but rather, " Remember your wife and children."

We may take an illustration from a wholly different type of moral problem. Every one agrees that no man should appoint another to a post of great responsibility on any grounds except that of his fitness for the post. But very respectable citizens are liable to appoint a man " because it will please his old father," or for some other wholly irrelevant consideration. And the failure is due to lack of imagination. On one side there is the pleasure of the well-known old man clearly envisaged ; on the other there is an arid principle. But if the arid principle is translated into the actual distress of many families through financial incompetence on the part of the old man's son, or of death and bereavement due to military incapacity, or of whatever definite evil is likely to result in the particular instance, the man responsible for the appointment will no longer be ready to buy an old friend's pleasure at the cost of so great a risk.

Nor is it only in the avoidance of wrong that the imagination can supply the requisite stimulus to the will. Art does not derive its æsthetic merit from its practical utility ; but it may, in certain instances, derive great practical utility from its æsthetic merit. Tyrtaeus by his songs put heroism into the Spartan soldiers, and many another poet has done the same. No doubt it is true that, inasmuch as Art demands of us contemplation, it is only works of art on a small scale and of minor æsthetic value that lead to direct action. A song with a strong chorus may have such an effect, though hardly a great play or poem. And if a play or poem does stir us to action, it thereby creates a restlessness which interferes with contemplation, and in so doing renounces all attempt to reach the greatest æsthetic heights. Still it is true that the activity of imagination, in clothing an idea in form and rhythm, may vastly enhance the practical effectiveness of that idea.

In short, it may be said that a purely intellectual idea, a mere scientific formula, has no power to awake desire and so stimulate action. Intellect cannot control appetite. At any given moment a man's end, his "apparent good," is fixed for him by his character at that moment. By thinking, he may be brought to see that two objects which he has set before himself are incompatible, and so he may be led to choose between them and abandon one of them. Or again, he may, by thinking out in detail one of his aims or habits, find that it is not what he supposed, and that on a fuller understanding it becomes repellent instead of attractive. But intellect has no direct control over action. If by reason Hume meant what we are calling intellect, he was right when he said that reason is and ought to be the slave of the passions. Its normal function is to think out the means to an end already chosen. In the cases where the true principle is intellectually or scientifically grasped, but there is lacking any desire to act according to it, imagination must come to the aid of intellect and give body to the right principle, so that it may have attractive power. Imagination is normally the link between intellect and will.

But there is a particular act of will for which this use of the imagination is indispensable—the act of worship. And, though here again we must anticipate, it seems well to say what has to be said at this point. Most of us would find it very hard, if not entirely impossible, to worship any such Deity as philosophy can lead us to, unless the Mind which was thinking in the philosophic process has called into play its imaginative function also. How much exactly Aristotle meant by his celebrated statement that God moves the world as an object of love [1] is doubtful ; but that God as defined by Aristotle should actually be an object of love to the whole creation or to anything in it passes belief.  Let any one who doubts try to love the Unmoved Mover, or the First Cause, or the Absolute wherein all contradictions are resolved.  The Jew was forbidden to make any likeness of the incomparable and transcendent God ; but the most religious souls in Israel resorted to the boldest anthropomorphism, as the most casual reader or the prophetic books will learn.

Now it is just here that we need most of all to keep in remembrance the essential unity of the Mind which operates now as Intellect, now as Imagination.  As we have seen, the imaginative function only raises to adequacy the image-element always present in any act of thought whatsoever ; it is the thinking out in minute detail of what intellect apprehends in outline ; so that its difference from intellect is by no means absolute, though its emphasis is on the image rather than the meaning, while the emphasis of intellect is on the meaning rather than the image.  And if imagination is the raising of the image-element to adequacy, there must first be a meaning to which it may be adequate, otherwise it degenerates into fantasy, which is the making of images with no regard to realities ; when images thus made are of a kind to stimulate emotion and consequently also activity, they lead men's whole conduct astray.  It is thus that men follow the will-o'-the-wisps of superstition.

But if the giving free rein to imagination leads thus to foolishness or fanaticism, it is also true, as we saw, that without it the emotional functions will never be called into play at all.  What we require, if we can find it, is some embodiment or presentation of Universal Truth which may awaken and lead into captivity to itself the whole emotional nature of men.  It is not only that it may "enter in at lowly doors," but that it

---

[1] *Metaph.* Λ 7.

may be potent in the heart of any man alive, that we desiderate " Truth embodied in a tale."

We have already seen that the æsthetic experience at its highest is on the point of passing into worship. We may here recall what was then said by quoting the closing lines of Coleridge's poem written to Wordsworth after hearing him read a great part of *The Prelude* :

> Scarce conscious, and yet conscious of its close
> I sat, my being blended in one thought
> (Thought was it ? or aspiration ? or resolve ?)
> Absorbed, yet hanging still upon the sound—
> And when I rose, I found myself in prayer.

We have also seen that Intellect and Imagination, Science and Art, would reach their culmination in the apprehension and contemplation of the supreme principle of the universe adequately embodied or incarnate, if such embodiment or incarnation is anywhere to be found ; and we have seen that this expression can only be judged adequate if it contains within itself the full solemnity of Tragedy, which, however much transcended, must be in no way mitigated or annulled by what claims to express the truth about this world and the life it nourishes.

M

# BOOK I—*continued*

## PART III
### CONDUCT

# CHAPTER XIII

## WILL AND PURPOSE

Διὸ ἢ ὀρεκτικὸς νοῦς ἡ προαίρεσις ἢ ὄρεξις διανοητική, καὶ ἡ τοιαύτη ἀρχὴ ἄνθρωπος.—ARISTOTLE.

WE have already mentioned the element of Impulse, whose introduction carries us across the line which divides the Theoretical from the Practical. It is at work in the creation of knowledge and beauty, but only in a highly specialised form. The will to know contains an impulsive element; so does artistic creation; for impulse is necessary to any activity whatsoever; out we have been able to assume the existence of just that impulse which is relevant in each case. We have now to consider the psychic life in which all manner of impulses find their place side by side with Mind, and which Mind has to organise into a harmonious whole by its own methods.

We have seen that pure Determinism breaks down logically;[1] we have also seen that individuality, while discovered by analysis, is determined by function,[2] and, moreover, that the completest development of individuality coincides with the completest receptivity of influence.[3] But to that statement something must now be added.

We have spoken many times of value, and have now to consider the various kinds of value. The inanimate Thing is aware of no value; but the lowest form of sensitive organism is aware of the value of certain

---

[1] Chapter VI.      [2] Chapter VII.      [3] *Ibid.*

feelings ; and where there is no memory or anticipation
there can be no capacity to appreciate other kinds of
value.   But where memory and anticipation exist, it
becomes possible for the consciousness concerned to
compare itself with its actual past and ideal future ;
it becomes possible to have, over and above the
immediate desires, a purpose which may be pursued
though desires have to be suppressed one after another
in its attainment.

This purpose may be wholly unconscious.   A man
may live for a long time by principles which he could
not formulate and of which he has never consciously
thought at all.   Most of us must at some time
or another have discovered such principles by the
very fact that suggestions made by other people, or
impulses arising in our own nature, have conflicted
with them.   Probably a very large proportion of the
real purpose of a man's life remains permanently
unknown to him.   Here as elsewhere there is great
danger in trying to live only by that which has come
into explicit consciousness ; to do this is almost inevitably to make life shallow and rob it of its most
profound significance ; and yet it is also true that to
bring into full consciousness what has been subconscious
is always in itself a gain.   In that outer region, which
lies beyond our power of observation, there are many
elements, bad as well as good, and to depend upon
it for the direction of our life is to be in a highly
precarious condition.   Consequently our aim must be
to try to include within the field of consciousness as
much as is possible of the wealth stored in our subconscious nature, and yet at the same time never to
suppose that our consciousness has grasped the deepest
springs of our action.   Here, as in the case of thought,
it is only the conscious purpose with which the
philosopher can deal ; so long as anything lies outside
the range of consciousness it plainly cannot become
the subject-matter of reflection ; and so we are bound

to deal with the purpose of life so far as it becomes explicit, only remembering that this is in no case the whole of it. The relation of the conscious and the unconscious parts of our purpose must occupy us when we come to the discussion of education.

Will is not a separate entity ;[1] the tendency to regard it as such seems to arise from the failure, not of intellect but of imagination, to apprehend activity apart from something which acts ; imagination is, of its very nature, always materialistic, and has imposed upon thought an unreal demand for substances which may support attributes and activities. This demand in psychology led to a belief in "faculties" as actually constitutive parts of a substantial soul ; and as Purpose is certainly different from any one of our chaotic impulses and ideas, a Will was invented to be the organ of Purpose. It was then asked how this will is determined, and whether it is free. The absurdity of the latter question is sufficiently exposed in Locke's celebrated chapter on "Power," where he points out that it is sensible to ask "Is man free ?" or "Has man a will ? "—for these mean the same thing ; but to ask "Is the will free ? " is nonsense, for it only means "Has the power to choose got power to choose ?" Locke thus reminds us that the fact before us is Choice ; it is actual concrete cases of choice that we are concerned with ; and for the explanation of choice I believe we cannot improve on Aristotle's account of προαίρεσις as ὄρεξις διανοητική or νοῦς ὀρεκτικός—the union of Appetition and Intellect; while for a statement of the ideal in this regard we cannot improve on Plato's ἕνα γενέσθαι ἐκ πολλῶν—out of many to become one.

Our actual practice in early education supplies us with some valuable guidance here. As soon as the child's physical life is fairly well established we begin

---

[1] Here, and for the next few paragraphs, I am covering the same ground, often in the same language, as in *The Nature of Personality*, Lect. III.

to say that for a short time every day the child shall attend to some one thing. At first the child is a mass of chaotic interests and impulses whose notice is attracted and fixed altogether by external occurrences; if by Will we mean the capacity to form a Purpose the child has no will at all; he may show great determination in struggling for whatever he wants, but this is vigorous appetition, not will; it is the material out of which strength of will may be made, but as yet it is not strong will nor even will at all. The first thing to be done is to create a power of concentration, of attending to some one thing whatever it may be. And so we insist that for a period every day he shall not allow himself to be distracted by anything. That period is called lessons. It scarcely matters at this stage what subject is taught. It should be as attractive as possible, so that attention may be concentrated easily. The vital matter is that the child should learn "attention" or "concentration" in general. Gradually the period is extended, and the whole system of regulations, called "discipline," is developed, till "lessons" and "discipline," together cover nearly the whole of life; then the external pressure is relaxed again, and the individual is set free in the sense that he is now left to the guidance of the habits which discipline has created in him; and the educator may say, "I have created a will in you; at first you were a mere mass of impulses; I have co-ordinated and systematised those impulses, and I have developed your power of thought alike in calculating means to ends and in comparing together the various ends open to you, so that now you have a real will and purpose of your own; I have forced you into freedom; now go and exercise that freedom."

These impulses are in themselves neither good nor bad; they are the material out of which virtue and vice are made. But, if left to themselves, they will (as the doctrine of Original Sin reminds us) issue in a life which is vicious, at least in the sense of being the opposite of virtuous ; how far such a life would be guilty is a further question, and to speak of guilt in such a connexion would seem to be absurd ; the savage is not guilty for being uncivilised, and every man would be uncivilised if society did not civilise him. The impulses of human nature all have a place in the economy of the ideal human life, but they can only be made elements in such a life by much effort. If left undisciplined they will not make up a single moral life at all ; the man will remain a chaos of impulses.; and he cannot himself conduct this discipline at first (though as it moulds him he becomes able to co-operate with it and to conduct it altogether at last), because at first he is just the chaos of impulses. Society educates and disciplines him. By enforcing concentration of atten- tion, by restraining through fear or otherwise the excessive activity of any one impulse, and so on, it co- ordinates him and makes him for practical purposes one agent instead of many, or in other words makes him truly free. Of course when once the process is fairly begun, the child, as we have said, co-operates with it ; and from the reaction of certain forms of conduct on his own self-respect, as this grows under the educative influences, he is led to take an ever greater share in the moulding of his own character.

This is the true freedom of man, when his whole nature controls all its own constituent parts. Its root is the merely formal freedom which we found to be the inalienable property of any individual object whatso- ever. As we rise in the scale of being this freedom or individuality begins to count for more and more ; in the case of a purely mechanical object it may be ignored in practice ; the difference between two billiard balls, for instance, is negligible ; each will move in the same way in answer to the same stimulus. But two plants will respond quite differently to the same environment, and among the higher animals it becomes impossible to predict how one of them will behave in any given circumstance, except on the basis of individual knowledge. This process reaches its culmination (so far as our experience goes) in civilised man, so that a knowledge of men in general becomes almost a contradiction. We all know how disastrously shallow is the insight of the sort of person who is said to "understand men," and how fallacious is his guidance.

This kind of freedom is a fact ; it is not a treasure. It enables and indeed requires a man to feel with regard to any action—"Something that was mine and mine alone went to the doing of that act." It thus carries with it some measure of responsibility, but it is no particularly excellent possession ; for the man may feel that just because the source of some evil action is himself, there is no escape.[1] "O wretched man that I am, who shall deliver me from the body of this death?" Go where he will, into whatever environment, the impulse to that action goes with him. True freedom is not only or chiefly a freedom from external control, but from internal compulsion ; it is found, not when a man says, "I did it, and no one else," but when a man says, "I did it, and I am glad I did it, and if opportunity arises I will do it again." Only such a man is really free or really directing his own life. The man who has no purpose in life, or having one yet perpetually acts in direct opposition to it, is in bondage to a part of himself. Plato justly compares him to a state governed by a tyrant, where one member of the community imposes his will by force on the whole community, that will not being for the common good. So in the case of the man we are considering, a single element in the soul forces upon the whole man an action not good for the man as a whole. Hence it is at once apparent that discipline or external restraint, far from necessarily diminishing freedom, may be the means of increasing it ; this, of course, applies to wise

---

[1] Cf. The "freedom" of tragic characters remarked upon in Chap. XI. p. 144.

legislation and is one of the tests of the wisdom of legislation. The goal is that, as in ideal Democracy all the citizens together constitute the sovereign which each individually obeys, so in the fully developed personality all the impulses under the controlling supervision of Mind constitute a Soul or Self which all obey ; and the truly free man or the man of strong will is not the man who may do anything at any moment, but the man who has some great purpose which he follows despite all impulses and all obstacles.

But in our experience this ideal of perfect self-determination does not exist. Not only do we depend very largely on our environment, but we have not complete control of ourselves. We have no purpose in life wide enough to include the satisfaction of all our impulses and strong enough to check each from undue indulgence. Consequently our purpose, so far as it is active at all, is very often apparent chiefly in restriction upon appetite. Will, so far, seems to appear in the inhibition of this or that impulse or instinct. Since our character is, throughout our lives, in process of formation, the co-ordination of the various inherited instincts and impulses remains incomplete, and any one of them may rush us into an action directly contrary to our general purpose in life, an action that we regret as soon as it is done, and sometimes even while we are doing it. We may know it is wrong, even that it is self-destructive, but rather than pluck out our right eye, rather even than close it, we fling our whole body into Hell. Of course we are responsible for our act, but it is not an act of real freedom. It may be defiant in manner, but it is not an act of strength. The man of strong will, as was said before, is not the man who may do anything, but precisely the man who can be depended on : in fact strength of will reveals itself in certain splendid incapacities, as when it is said of a man accused of taking bribes, " He could not do it." People with no will at all like to attribute the variegations of their conduct to their freedom ; one day a man *chooses* to be respectable, another day he *chooses* to be dissolute. But such choice is at best a mere rhythmic occurrence of various impulses or the mechanical response to various environments, or both. The man of strong will is the man who is the same from day to day and in all circumstances, not turned from his purpose by outward obstacles or inward passions. True freedom manifests itself in constancy and stability of character.

It is clear that the attention of Purpose is fixed upon the Future, and if Purpose is the chief distinguishing characteristic of human personality it is clear that for men the Future is of more importance than the Past. And indeed this appears to be the case, since occurrences in the future may change the character of events in the past, which, as mere facts, are, of course, unalterable ; we quite commonly say, " I am glad now of what seemed at the time to be a terrible misfortune," or similar words.

The Past is plainly in one sense unalterable ; it has happened and to all eternity it will have happened. But the value of the Past is not irrevocably fixed ; it remains to be determined by the Future. Let me illustrate this point from that part of our experience which, as we saw, is deliberately occasioned with a view to certain effects, namely Art. The Artist, we said, isolates some relatively independent fact and concentrates our attention upon it ; when he presents a temporal succession, as the dramatist and the musician do, he fixes our attention in this way upon a period of time which we can grasp in a single experience. Now consider two plays, each in three acts, one proceeding from a cheerful opening, through a neutral phase, to a gloomy close ; the other proceeding from a gloomy opening, through a neutral phase, to a cheerful close. It is by no means the case that in each play the first and last acts cancel each other, making a neutral effect on the

whole : on the contrary, the former play is peculiarly
depressing, more so than a play which is gloomy
throughout ; and the latter peculiarly exhilarating,
more so than a play which is cheerful throughout.
Yet this second play would have been depressing if it
had stopped at the end of the first act.    The emotional
value, therefore, of that first act is quite different in
isolation from its value when the two latter acts are
added : at its own close it has a quite definite value,
but at the end of the play it has another value ; yet,
though an element in tragedy or comedy, it is still **in**
itself just what it was.    The value, then, of any event **in**
time is not fixed until the series of which it is a member
is over, perhaps, therefore, not to all eternity.    But now
we may pass on to a cognate point.    The genius of
the Greeks seems, as we saw,[1] to have led to a rule that
in Comedy, that is where only superficial matters are in
question, or where serious matters are superficially
treated, the dramatist is to make his own plot ; but in
Tragedy the plot was always something well known.
And indeed it is necessary to our appreciation of
Antigone's great action that we should know, as we
watch, not only what consequences she anticipated, but
what consequences would actually ensue.    In any great
drama our appreciation is increased by knowledge of
the story, because we see each incident in the light, not
only of the Past, but of Past and Future together.

This gives us some valuable hints as to the nature
of Personality in its relation to the time-process.    Those
events in the Past which seem to require obliteration
cannot indeed be made unreal, but their value, though
not their occurrence, can be changed.    They may become
the occasions of some spiritual state of great value which
could not have been reached without them.    Till the
power is known that can so transform them, they
remain mere blots : and the man, in whose experience
they are, feels the weight of an irremovable burden.

[1] Chapter X. p. 126.

But if there is known to him some transforming power his despair vanishes. It is clear that we are here on the borders of the doctrine of the Atonement : and we cannot embark on such a topic as a digression. The point is that they do not cease to be evil, but their very evil becomes an element in good.

If all this is true, it follows that the more fully Purposive we are—that is, the more complete our Personality—so much the more will the Future preponderate over the Past in our interest. The later in time has upon the earlier a far greater influence than the earlier upon the later. And if we may rightly assume that in man we have a fuller manifestation of ultimate Reality than in any of the less developed forms of existence, it will follow that not only for man, but in the nature of things, the future has this preponderance of importance over the past, and that, while only the whole of Reality contains the full explanation of any part of it, yet, as Lord Haldane has said, explanation is to be sought in a system of Ends rather than of Causes.[1]

But so we are brought back into the successiveness of the temporal. In the higher achievements of the intellect we had reached a position to which Time was indifferent ; and in the " moment eternal " of the artistic experience we won a real mastery over Time. But now, as it seems, we are back in the flux. Is Conduct, and all the moral effort of men, something less than Knowledge or Art? Or if Conduct is the main business of life, is it only in his bye-products that man reaches his fullest apprehension of the real ?

The answer seems to be in the recollection that we have passed from the theoretical to the practical. In the spheres of Knowledge and of Art, while, of course, the mind is active, its activity consists in concentrated attention upon what is already there. Man's Knowledge is indeed in one sense a creation, but it is a creation of

[1] *The Pathway to Reality*, vol. i. pp. 298, 299.

a copy, and its perfection is not something self-contained, but consists in its relation to the world which is there independently of it. Similarly in the artistic experience, a man stands over against a work of art and contemplates it. He is active passively, if the phrase may be allowed. He can contemplate a drama or a symphony in such a way as to grasp its whole succession in a timeless and relatively eternal intuition, precisely because he is himself outside it. But in Conduct he becomes an actor on the stage himself, and that too not an actor who has learnt a previously written part, but one who is working out the plot of an unknown drama by his own thoughts and deeds. The actor who impersonates Macbeth in the early scenes of the tragedy must know that the murder of Duncan will be the death of his own soul; but it is vital to the significance of the tragedy that Macbeth himself knows nothing of the kind. And in Conduct one is no more the critic in his study (which is the scientific intellect), nor the spectator in the auditorium (which is the appreciative imagination), nor the author of the play (which is the constructive imagination), but an actor in a play not yet composed, and of whose leading idea the different actors have wholly different conceptions. But there is a guiding idea; for the Society of Intelligences and Wills cannot be like an omnibus, full of chance passengers related to each other in no way except their momentary juxtaposition, unless the universe is chaotic, which no one is able to believe.

There must then be a principle of unity in the vast drama which is called human history; and by a right apprehension of this principle of unity a man can make his life part of an artistic or perfect whole, with relative completeness and perfection in itself. And some men in old age seem to be able to regard their own life in much the same way as the spectator regards the drama, and to find similar satisfaction, and, indeed, fuller satisfaction, not because it is their own achievement which they contemplate (for this stage is in fact only reached when egoism is dead), but because the life of history has a fuller reality than the life of drama. To the onlooker life may be perfect in a few years :

> It is not growing like a tree
> In bulk, doth make man better be ;
> Nor standing long an oak, three hundred year,
> To fall a log at last, dry, bald, and sere :
> A lily of the day
> Is fairer far in May,
> Although it fall and die that night—
> It was the plant and flower of Light.
> In small proportions we just beauties see ;
> And in short measures life may perfect be.

But it seems unlikely that the person so spoken of should feel this satisfaction, at least before his death. It is only the old man, who has followed a course in harmony with the world's plan through a full period of human existence, who can speak in his own name :

> Grow old along with me !
> The best is yet to be,
> The last of life, for which the first was made :
> Our times are in His hand
> Who saith, " A whole I planned,
> Youth shows but half ; trust God ; see all nor be afraid ! "

Such a man seems to be on the point of achieving a timeless or eternal apprehension even of that succession which his own life constitutes. But it must at once be pointed out that it is only when regarded from the end that it has this quality. A good biography of a great man shows us every stage of his life as an element in a complete whole. The life is one though its episodes are many. But its unity is of such a kind that the latter stages are not fixed by the preceding. The unity is only real when it is complete. The half shown by Youth does not reveal or determine the remaining half. There are real choices, not the mere evolution of a given material. *Sub specie temporis cuiusdam*—regarded in the light of any time less than the whole—there is a real indeterminism ; *sub specie temporis totius,* the life is one and a coherent whole. This is a more complete conquest of the successive than is represented by science or art, just because of this real indeterminism which is overcome, but is only overcome when the process is complete. A man whose life is given to a purpose lofty enough to claim the allegiance of all his faculties and rich enough to exercise them all is the nearest approach in human experience to the realisation of eternity.

We have here a principle in virtue of whose presence any relative Whole is self-explanatory. Such a life as is suggested above is not merely coherent, but united by a principle to which the mind assents. Will as thus exhibited is just such a principle as we saw that Intellect would welcome as supplying a need which it could by analysis of its own procedure never supply. But as seen in man the unity is only apparent when the process is complete ; if we are to find an explanation of the world that is really adequate we must have recourse not only to the thought of an Immanent Will but also, in the way that our discussion of the significance of Art has indicated,[1] to the thought of a Mind which in a perfect intuition grasps that very process which as Will it is engaged in working out. But this enquiry will concern us later.

[1] Chapter X. p. 126.

N

# CHAPTER XIV

## GOOD AND MORAL GOOD

Πειρατέον τύπῳ γε παραλαβεῖν αὐτὸ τί ποτ' ἐστὶ καὶ τίνος τῶν ἐπιστημῶν
ἢ δυνάμεων. δόξειε δ' ἂν τῆς κυριωτάτης καὶ μάλιστα ἀρχιτεκτονικῆς. τοιαύτη
δ' ἡ πολιτικὴ φαίνεται.—ARISTOTLE.

VALUE is an wholly irreducible aspect or function of
Reality. The terms that express its various modes—
Good and Bad and what lie between these—cannot be
translated into the terms of any other category ; they
are not unintelligible, but they are untranslatable ;
and if any one attaches no meaning to them, no kind
of argument can enlighten him. It is therefore impossible to argue *a priori* to the Goodness of anything
whatever, unless indeed we can show that the Good is
the determining principle of all existence ; for in that
case, of course, we can argue from the mere existence
of a thing to its goodness in its own time and place.
But then we should be compelled to include utility in
our conception of goodness, if only to avoid manifest
absurdity (for who would call the existing phase of
European civilisation, for example, good in itself ?) ;
and utility is not really goodness at all. The things
generally called good fall into three obvious classes—
those that are good in themselves, those whose results
are good, and those which, being good in themselves,
have good results.[1] Of these only the first class are
genuinely good, and the last so far as it falls within the
first. The second are not good, but a means of

[1] Plato, *Republic*, ii. 357 B-D.

producing what is good. If, for example, we say that
Pain may be good as a discipline, we are not really
attributing any goodness to Pain ; we are asserting
that the results of the discipline may be so good as to
be worth the cost of the pain by which they are reached,
so that the process and result together contain a greater
balance of good over evil than the absence of process
and result ; but in the pain itself there is no Good.
But if we cannot argue *a priori* to the Goodness of
anything, it follows that we can appreciate the Good
only by direct experience. The intention of the term
Good may be known *a priori*, but its extension only by
experience ; we can only tell what things are good by
experience of those things. So far the Empiricists are
right; and Plato too was right, when by way of commend-
ing Justice he merely exhibited it in the life of the State
and the Individual. There can be no argument about
intrinsic value ; one approves or not, and there's an end.
The tastes may be trained and so may the moral sense ;
but the method of such training is always submission
to authority. If I revel in Doré's pictures or Gounod's
music, it is no use for a superior person to tell me I
don't ; but he may say, " You like that now because,
being unused to the language in which artists and
musicians express themselves, you can find no emotion
where it is not crude and obvious ; if, however, you will
look at Fra Angelico or listen to Beethoven you will
come to enjoy them in course of time far more than
you now enjoy Doré and Gounod " ; and then perhaps
I may take his advice ; the great masters seem cold
and uninteresting at first, but slowly one learns their
language, and then, intuitively, appreciates their excellence. So it is with all forms of Value ; it is known
by intuition alone, though the faculties of intuition may
be trained. Our chief needs in this connexion are
clearness of thought and honesty ; clearness of thought,
to be sure that we do not confuse means with ends,
and honesty to be sure that we do not pretend to find

Goodness where in fact we find none. But an objective standard is not to be found ; we can get no nearer to it than a general consent, or the verdict of Aristotle's φρόνιμος. And if an individual differs from the world at large, or from the expert, it is always possible that he may be right. As Mr. F. H. Bradley has argued— "Our sense of value, and in the end for every man his own sense of value, is ultimate and final. And, since there is no court of appeal, it is idle even to inquire if this sense is fallible." [1]

Now we have already seen [2] that not all values can be realised in any single consciousness. Locke's "Primary Qualities" are the same for all percipients, but his "Secondary Qualities" are different for different persons, and this is true of all values. But it does not follow that values depend on accidents, or that every man has a right to rest content with his instinctive value-judgments at any moment. For every man is a member of the human society, and it may well be that there is a specific type of character which he ought to acquire and with it, as a necessary consequence, a particular set of value-judgments. For what seems good to us is determined by our own condition ; to the sick man what is normally a poison becomes a medicine ; to the vulgar man severe beauty is insipid ; to the licentious man temperance is contemptible. Yet, while denying that all men ought at last to realise the same values, we may still assert that these men are wrong in the value-judgments which they form. For though there is no one right experience for all men in these matters, there is the right experience for each individual man ; and it is determined by the precise place which he holds in the general structure of society. As this member of the Society of Spirits, I have a particular destiny to fulfil. And just as I may be mistaken on a question of fact—where my peculiarities do not affect

---

[1] *Mind*, N.S., 66, p. 230 ; *Essays on Truth and Reality*, p. 132.
[2] Chap. VIII. p. 83.

the nature of the fact—so I may be mistaken on a
question of value, where my peculiarities do affect both
the judgments I pronounce from time to time and the
judgments I ought to pronounce. Now these right-
value judgments are in their own way facts ; but they
are contingent facts—contingent upon the perfection of
Society and all its members. And whereas the truths
of the mathematical sciences can, so far as their nature
goes, be all realised by one mind, the full truth about
the world of value can only be realised by the whole
Society of Spirits, each doing his own part.[1]   An
Omniscient Mind would of course know what value-
judgments any given person ought to be forming ; but
the value only becomes fully real when the judgment is
formed—and thus it is only by the entire Society that
the whole truth of the world of values is apprehensible.

What has been said applies to all Values ; and we
see that even in the general discussion of Value we have
the principle of Society in evidence—the principle by
which various co-operating agents constitute a single
whole with a life which, though collective, is one. And
now what is the differentia of Moral Value? If we
look at the terms peculiar to the moral sphere—" Duty,"
" Obligation," " Ought "—we find that they always
express a relation between an individual agent or group
of agents and other similar beings. If some catastrophe
swept all conscious beings out of existence with the
exception of a single man, would he still be under any
sort of obligation ? Not to other men, for *ex hypothesi*
there are none ; nor to God, for He too, as a conscious
being, is excluded by the hypothesis. Can he be under
obligation to himself? The phrases " Duty to self,"
"You owe it to yourself," certainly occur. But under
what circumstances ? Either when a man has earned
some reward, which he is foregoing—and then we do
not regard it as his duty to take it, but only as a right
the waiving of which is morally admirable rather than

---

[1] Chap. VIII. pp. 84-85.

evil; or else such a phrase occurs when a man is contemplating a course of action in some one's interest by which he will diminish his own usefulness—such as giving up a holiday when it is much needed; and here we do regard it as his duty to take the holiday and maintain his usefulness—a duty not to himself but to Society. Duty is a term never applied strictly to the isolated individual. Kant, as we all know, tried to evolve a Categorical Imperative out of the autonomous will of the individual; but when it appeared it took the form "Act at all times from a maxim fit for universal law," where the word "universal" introduces the reference to society in unmistakable form. Indeed Kant's fundamental argument to prove that only the Good Will is absolutely good rests on a surreptitious reference to the admitted interests of society. And so it must always be. The isolated individual may be wise or foolish; he cannot be moral or immoral. The Atheistic Debauchee upon a Desert Island is not liable to moral censure. It is then our membership in society that makes us capable of morality, and it is consciousness of that membership that endows us with a moral sense. This is the condition of the possibility of obligation—of any sense of "ought"—and of the particular form of Good which is distinguished as Moral Good or Right. And if this is so, it becomes a matter of quite primary importance for the purpose of ethics that we should find out what we mean by Society and by the individual's membership in it.

Let us then consider the general Nature of Society, and let us begin with the obvious and uncontroversial facts about it. Plainly a Society is a collection of persons united by some non-physical bond; this bond may be economic as in a Joint Stock Company; or it may be scientific, as in the British Association; or political, as in the Liberal or Conservative parties; or social, in the narrower sense, as in a group of friends. Or of course it may be united by several such bonds at

once.    But when we look at these more closely it
appears that every one of them is a determination of
the human will.    The real bond of union in a Company
or a Trade Union is not any economic fact or facts,
but the purpose of the members that certain economic
conditions shall continue to exist or cease to exist or
begin to exist.    In each case the members are united
by a common purpose, which may be fairly simple, as
in the case of a scientific society, or highly complex,
as in the case of a nation.    The essential basis of a
society is community of purpose.

Just as in the individual, the purpose by which his
life is determined may lie outside the field of consciousness, so in an even greater degree may the purpose
which constitutes the nation.    It has been remarked
that the Greek City State had already done its practical
work when its significance was drawn out into full
light by Plato and Aristotle, and the great nations
which have attempted the problem of applying on a
vastly greater scale the principles followed by the
Greeks in their various cities have not as yet in any
degree become conscious of the function which they
exist to fulfil.    In so far as a nation imagines that it
can formulate its purpose it is almost certain to become
the victim of disastrous illusion.    It may become
enormously effective but nearly always in the pursuit
of some object by achieving which it will win disappointment for itself and in all probability secure the
hatred of mankind.    We have instances of this in
recent history : France under Napoleon was immensely
self-conscious ; she believed herself to be carrying the
gospel of the Revolution through Europe by armed
force ; so no doubt in a sense she was, but this was
nothing like what the real contribution of France to
civilisation was meant to be, and the glory won in
the great campaigns brought very fleeting satisfaction
to the French and ranged all Europe among their
enemies.    Similarly at the present time the German

Empire is self-conscious to an almost unique degree. This is not in itself surprising. There have always been two causes which have made the sense of nationality strong ; one is the excitement caused by national unity when recently won, and the other is the sense that this unity, and the national life which it makes possible, are in danger. German unity was only won in 1870, and that by means of a war which secured the permanent hostility of France. Consequently in the case of Germany the two causes which make the members of a nation strongly conscious of their nationality have been operating together. It is not surprising that Germany is self-conscious to a degree without parallel in the history of European nations ; but while it is not surprising it is none the less disastrous both to them and to the rest of the world. This intense self-consciousness leads to the concentration of all attention on such objects as a national consciousness can set before itself. The easiest and most obvious is power and even world domination. To this the German nation has given itself ; we, watching from the outside, know perfectly well that even by achieving this Germany would win no satisfaction for herself, but would merely withhold the means of full national life from other peoples. She would be starving, and indeed has been starving, the vast depths of the German soul for the sake of glutting a very superficial appetite. Here then once more, while a nation which has no conscious purpose is likely to achieve very little and to live a poor kind of life, it is still true that to allow what falls within consciousness to be the whole determinant of action is the way to sure disaster. As with the individual so with the nation, the wise course is to become conscious so far as may be of the capacities and aspirations of the soul, while at the same time remembering that there are vast depths still unplumbed.

In England we tend, if anything, to be excessively

unreflective.   Certainly we should find ourselves unable even to begin formulating the purpose which unites us as Englishmen.   But its negative side is plain enough ; it is a long while now since Englishmen, for instance, first felt a distinction between themselves and foreigners, discovering a common purpose at least as against the latter.   In early stages war is the great consolidator of nations ; and it is so, because it brings into clear consciousness the unity of purpose in a nation's citizens by placing it in practical contrast with a hostile purpose.   The unity is still only germinal, but it is enough to be one term in a distinction—a negative judgment.   In all cases the existence of ideas in our minds is liable to become apparent through their figuring as the subjects of negative judgments. Long before we are able to form positive judgments we are able to exclude various suggestions.   Negation as the form of distinction is no doubt equally fundamental with assertion ; but the negative judgment as conscious act of thought always represents partial ignorance ;   we only say " That is not the way to London " when some one suggests by word or act that it is (in which case the ignorance is in his mind)—or because we ourselves know that there is a road to London but not which road it is, and therefore wish to exclude as many opportunities of error as we can so as to narrow the field of enquiry.[1]   Thus early morality consists of negatives ; it is not known what the ideal life is, but it is known that it cannot include murder or theft.   Just so we may not know what our national purpose positively is, but we know enough about it to sing with real conviction that " Britons never shall be slaves."   This, however, can only be because the term " Briton " is felt to be incompatible with the term " slave " ; whatever ideal it represents is one contrary to slavery.   But to resist, it must have some character of its own.   What is this character ?

[1] Chap. V. pp. 60, 61.

It is the product of a mass of tradition and sentiment which permeates all individual citizens. We were born into a people reading the Bible, Shakespeare, Milton, Bunyan, and so on ; into a people who had finally broken with the feudalism once common to all European nations by the precise expedient of beheading a king in a moment of Puritan fervour ; and so with the rest of the story. We brought some new element ourselves into being when we were born, but even this was moulded by a history embodied in institutions and prejudices and principles ; and even those who are keenest in criticism of British methods are Britons themselves as soon as they have to choose between their own country and another ; and often their criticism is a kind of patriotism, perhaps even the best kind. The national purpose in civilised countries is still only germinal ; it has no clear conscious aim or accepted methods ; but it is there. It does not as yet directly influence more than a tithe of our lives ; for the rest our activities go chaotically on their own way, just as the impulses and instincts do in a child, before any conscious purpose is formed by which some are checked, and others guided, and method is gradually introduced into life.

Just as the child is guided into freedom by external influence and control, so the nation must guide itself and be guided into full freedom and self-government. For alike in the individual and in the society freedom and self-government can mean only one thing—the control of the parts by the whole which they constitute. If a man is to be free, he must have self-direction as against compulsion by other people ; but also his self-direction must be direction by his whole self, and not by passing desires which impel him to act against his real interest. And if a nation is to be free, it must have self-government in the sense that it is bound by no laws except those it makes for itself ; but also its self-government must be government by its whole self in the light of its whole interest and not the mere supremacy of the most numerous class or of passing fancies of the mob.

It may well be thought that this line of reflection would lead to a direct personification of the State. And indeed the conjunction of this language with the previous suggestion of a Common Purpose as the uniting bond of society may seem to lead up to such a theory as that of Cardinal Newman, who sometimes entertained the idea that a spirit or demon presided over every nation, on the ground that only so could one account for the difference between people's individual and collective action.   What is the seat of this Common Purpose ?   Where does it exist ?   There is no evidence whatever for the existence of a social consciousness in society other than the consciousness of the individuals that they are members of the social body, and the modification of their consciousness consequent upon their being so.

The common purpose therefore appears as a purpose set upon a single object, but formed by many individuals. If by will we mean a direction for action—then there is one social will ; if we mean the seat of actual volition—then there are as many social wills as there are citizens.   Perhaps it will be in closest conformity with the ordinary use of language if we adopt the formula—Many Wills, but One Purpose.   Of course it does not follow that society is any less real than the citizens, or that they are primary while it is secondary.   All we have said is that, in the fact which we call society, the citizens, the members, are the organs of consciousness.   But we shall find later on that this involves serious results.

Let us now see where we stand.   We have found that Value is an irreducible mode of being, to be apprehended by intuition alone ; that there is no reason to suppose that all men ought to realise the same values, and great reason to the contrary ; that a man's ideal

character, and with it those values which he ought to
realise, is fixed by his place in the social economy of
the spiritual world. So that in dealing with Value as a
general term we already had to introduce the principle
of Society. Passing on to Moral Value, we found that
the words particularly belonging to the Moral Category
—Duty, Obligation, Ought—all express a relation of
the individual to his fellow-members in Society; that
Society itself is a union of individuals whose several
wills are at one in a common purpose; and that the
aim of society, as of the individual, is freedom and self-
government.

In the light of these considerations we may pass on
to the further question of the relation of Ethics and
Politics, which appear sometimes to lead to conflicting
estimates of duty. It is often held that Aristotle
did an inestimable service to human thought when he
deliberately distinguished Ethics from Politics, and we
are sometimes told that the advance upon Plato which
he made is mainly to be found precisely in this distinction. And of course there can be no doubt that the
distinction contributed very greatly to the advance of
the two sciences, for the field which Plato tries to
cover in one comprehensive survey, in the *Republic*,
is so vast that it is practically impossible to examine it
minutely without first dividing it into sections. Yet
the distinction should be provisional and transitional
and not regarded as affecting the real subject-matter
under consideration; and I believe that even in
Aristotle's hands it damaged his view of both Politics
and Ethics, and has been disastrous to both sciences
ever since. Human life is, in fact, too closely knit to
be broken up into sections which can be treated in
isolation. We all know what happened when Political
Economy tried to be an independent science. That is,
no doubt, an extreme case; but the same difficulties
beset the effort to distinguish Ethics and Politics.
Each of them is given a province whose boundaries

represent no real distinction in the facts. There is in reality only one science of human good, as Aristotle, of course, was perfectly aware. It is easy enough to find examples of the disaster in question. We may hear a preacher say, " What is morally wrong cannot be politically right " ; or a politician may say, " Such an act was no doubt morally wrong, but the political circumstances were such as to justify it." In both these sayings the distinction is implied ; in the former ethics-was taken to impose limits upon politics, and in the latter not ; but both assume the distinction. Yet it is quite clear that at any time, when all the considerations called ethical and political have been taken into account, there is one right thing to be done (or else a choice between two equivalents, in which case the choice is morally indifferent). This right thing may be not easily discoverable ; but if there is one right thing, it is simply misleading to call it a wrong thing. We may hear people talk about the " medicinal lie " as morally wrong, but defensible. What they probably mean is that lying is nearly always wrong, though in the special circumstances it was right. But the way in which this was expressed was bad, in as much as it suggested that what is morally wrong may be defensible on the whole ; and this suggestion tends to weaken the authority of moral rules. The habit, which is engendered by the separation of Ethics and Politics, of laying down abstract moral rules, which do not enjoin the actually best course of action for the special occasions, on which alone any rule is required, inevitably suggests to practical people the irrelevance of moral notions to the real course of life.

The same thing is manifestly true in the case of religion and the science of it, theology. Here too I should maintain that we are dealing with the same subject-matter and that Plato was right, at least in aim, when he set out to deal with Ethics and Politics and Theology in a single treatise. All of them are endeavouring to elaborate and articulate the conception of the Good. So far as they forget that this is their primary object, they wander aimlessly and suggest false ideals, false methods, and false hopes. The conception of Good may be treated from many points of view, individual, social, or cosmic. But all the time it is this same concept which is being articulated ; to exhibit the Idea of Good as the governing principle of the individual, the state and the universe is the only aim of these three sciences ; and as Plato's Justice expands under investigation from an ethical to a political and at last (as the Idea of Good) to a cosmic principle, we see in outline the accomplishment of the aim of all human thought. It would be easy to give instances of the vagaries of theology and theological ethics when disjoined from this guiding principle. But this lies beyond our present subject, and we may leave the matter with a remembrance of the words, "The Sabbath was made for man, and not man for the Sabbath."

Theology can, however, be more easily distinguished from Ethics and Politics than these from one another. It is impossible that there should be two right relations for a man to hold towards his fellows—one morally right and the other politically right ; if ethics and politics thus conflict, there must be some further science which will tell us which is to be adopted ; and then, of course, this alone is right. To assert that such a conflict is possible, adding that morality should prevail, is to adopt a position which is either quite arbitrary or else must rest on some deeper ground—a metaphysic which would assign their provinces to each.

Aristotle regarded Ethics as a branch of Politics. And one result of this was that he had no real test of the value of a constitution except its capacity for permanence. Though he never lays it down, I think it is fair to say that that is his main test. Ethics being for him a relatively independent branch, it is possible for the terms, "good man" and "good citizen," to fall apart ; and though here too he lays down nothing explicitly, I think it is fair to say that on those occasions he prefers the good citizen to the good man. By Ethics he means the science of the good of the individual —which appears to consist primarily in philosophic contemplation and secondarily in "action according to virtue" ; and this latter turns out to be action determined by the rule by which a reasonable man would determine it. But who is this reasonable man ? He is to be appreciated at sight, but we are given no certain means of detecting him. And the result is that we fall back in the main on pure Intuitionism. Respectability holds that some acts are right and some wrong—and that about them, at least, there is no more to be said. And Aristotle's Ethics is a summary of the moral judgments of Respectability, illuminated by profound psychological analysis.

Before discussing whether this is all to which Ethics can legitimately aspire, it may be worth while to contrast Plato's method with Aristotle's. In the points that now concern us the contrast is complete. In the first place, as we have seen, Plato combines Ethics, Politics, and Theology in a single survey. He sets out to investigate Justice in the individual ; it expands into the guiding principle of the Ideal State ; and it expands again to become the supreme principle of the Universe under the title, "Idea of Good." It is, moreover, quite intelligible, for it is εἰς ἓν κατὰ φύσιν—co-operation according to capacity. But, whereas with Aristotle Ethics is a branch of Politics, with Plato Politics is practically a branch of Ethics ; the test of a constitution with Plato is not its capacity for permanence, nor even in the first instance its power to make the citizens happy ; but the test lies in the question, "What type of individual soul does it represent and tend to reproduce?" That is the meaning of the analogy between the State and the Individual, and of the long series of parallel States and Men, in Books VIII. and IX., on which Plato lavished all the treasures of his literary store. If a State is aggressive and jingoistic, that can only be so because of the predominance of the aggressive element in the souls of the citizens. Jingoism is bad because it is the product and symptom of a bad state of soul. If a society is plutocratic, that must be due to the predominance of avarice in the souls of the citizens; and it is to be condemned on that ground. The constitution expresses by an inevitable law the value-judgments of the citizens; it embodies them in its institutions, and it impresses them again on the minds of the young citizens. Hence constitutions must submit to an ethical test, as symptoms and as causes of moral character.

This Platonic treatment has at least one important point in its favour—namely that it supplies as the End in Politics something certainly good in itself. The one thing of supreme value to Plato is the Justice of the individual soul; the expansion of this in the state is only εἴδωλόν τι τῆς δικαιοσύνης (iv. 443 c). And when the Ideal of individual excellence conflicts with the Ideal of citizenship (as in this very miserable world it is bound to do), Plato is emphatic that the former is to be chosen, and the man will cower under a wall as out of a storm and will be happy if he can escape unspotted to the other world (vi. 496 E).[1]

This introduces the one great flaw in Plato's supreme achievement: he has no doctrine of development. We cannot complain that he who anticipated so much failed to anticipate that also. But the lack of this conception leads to the two great blots on the book—the failure to appreciate sacrifice (as where he apologises to the Guardians for bringing them back into the cave to govern); and the practical sacrifice of the individual (specially in the lower orders) to the State in Book V. Having no doctrine of progress, he had to look to revolution alone for the establishment of his state

---

[1] On the whole question, see my *Plato and Christianity*, Lecture II.

(the philosopher-king, having obtained power, is to banish every one over the age of ten and train the rest in sound citizenship) ; but also he had to make his ideal such as to fit the assumed permanence of the political incapacity of the majority. Without a very radical doctrine of progress democracy is lunatic—and such it appeared to Plato. The rigidity of his system is of course due to the same cause.

But if progress is either a fact or a real possibility, the dilemma, "Good man" or "Good citizen," no longer arises in the old acute form. The old alternatives were, "Work a rotten system at a moral loss to yourself" and "Leave the world and save your soul." But now there is a third, always recognised in practice but not always in theory—"Go and make the world a better place, even if you do have to dirty your hands in the process." And if all moral obligation springs from our membership in society, it is clear that this is not only permissible but obligatory, and that a "cloistered virtue" may be exquisite but cannot be moral, except in so far as it is attempted in order that its influence may benefit society as a whole.

It is the principle of Society which determines what values each individual ought to realise ; and therefore such obligations as are essential to the maintenance of Society itself take precedence of all others. The imagination of the artist, for example, may exalt and purify what was, before he handled it, merely gross ; but whether or not his work should be made public must depend on the extent to which its true nature will, at any given time, be appreciated. Here, as in most cases, a balance of good and evil has to be struck ; and at present we can lay down no general rule, except that whatever is vital to the existence of society itself must take precedence of all else, because if society perish, there is no longer any means by which the individual may realise his own good or even discover what it is.

The art or science of social life is called Ethics when

O

it considers how an individual should act, and Politics when it considers how a community should act ; but it is a single science ; and as the great name of Politics has been so debased by modern usage, it is inevitable to use the name Ethics for this whole science when its political and its strictly ethical departments are considered together.

# CHAPTER XV

## THE MORAL CRITERION AND THE SOCIAL ORDER

"We are plainly constituted such sort of creatures as to reflect upon our own nature."—BUTLER.

Οὐ γὰρ δεῖ οἴεσθαι δουλείαν εἶναι τὸ ζῆν πρὸς τὴν πολιτείαν, ἀλλὰ σωτηρίαν.—ARISTOTLE.

WE have found that moral good is a particular form of Good, which is itself an ultimate term; and the particular form is differentiated precisely as that of members in a society, or organised life dominated by a common purpose. Duty, then, is the obligation to serve that common purpose and the society which it sustains and through which alone it can be realised. But if so, it may be asked whether bees and wolves are the subjects of duties; and the answer is that they are not so, if we are right in denying to them self-consciousness and the capacity to reflect upon their own nature. Man certainly has this capacity; he can observe his own tendencies and impulses; he can sit in judgment on them and pronounce whether they conduce to the maintenance of society and the realisation of its common purpose or not; those which tend to this he calls right, those which tend otherwise he calls wrong.

But it is very seldom that men thus actually reason out the question of right and wrong; and it is not at all often that they are capable of doing it wisely. The issues involved are nearly always exceedingly subtle and intricate. To tabulate them is practically impossible.

But this does not mean that we have to choose between blind instinct and crude reasoning. So far as the greater part of our conduct is concerned, the reasoning has been carried on by successive generations of those who share our civilisation. Gradually under the pressure of experience certain conventions have grown up ; probably no one is or ever has been able to state the whole case for any one of these. Yet they are a rational, and indeed a strictly scientific, product. Just as a work of art embodies an infinitely delicate logic, which the critical intellect can only clumsily draw out, so the great conventions by which members of civilised societies regulate their actions represent an immense inductive process too vast to be adequately traced out. Reason has been at work in this process, but it is not the reason of an individual ; it is the collective reason of innumerable individuals, who all agree (though it may be unconsciously) in the major premise that it is desirable to maintain social life.

Human nature is so constituted that we are all exceedingly susceptible to influence ; consequently as we grow up in a society which has long ago learned to regard some actions with favour and others with disfavour, we catch by a kind of infection the same principles of judgment. There are certain acts which we instinctively admire and others which we instinctively condemn because of the effect which this pervading influence of society has had upon us. Most of our moral judgments are, as a matter of fact, to ourselves intuitive. We cannot give the reason for them, though we say that we perceive more goodness in one course of action and more evil in another. So far our whole attitude to moral questions is very like our attitude to æsthetic questions ; just as in the latter case our sensibility can be trained by following the advice of those whose artistic experience is richer than our own, and by deliberately contemplating those works of art which we are assured are good, though we at first may not

care about them, so, too, the moral judgment develops
if the man is ready to let himself be guided by those
whose insight into the principles of moral life is deepest.
But in either case the judgment itself may be pro-
nounced independently of reasons which the individual
can offer for it.

Because of this many have regarded the moral faculty
as more analogous to sense than to reason.   But, as we
have said, these intuitive judgments, while unreasoned
in the mind of the individual, are in themselves to the
last degree rational.   They have an immense basis in
experience, though that experience belongs to the race
rather than to the individual.   There is no doubt
some danger in trying to pass behind the intuition
to the reason which underlies it.   Men are liable to
weaken the authority of conscience if they look for
rational grounds for its precepts and fail to find any
that are very cogent.   But there is also great danger in
acquiescing in the simple moral sense ; for this puts us
in a very high degree at the mercy of our imagination.
The result is seen when people estimate the moral evil
of any action, as they very commonly do, by its power
to disgust them.   Some acts make us feel literally and
physically sick, and we are very liable to suppose these to
be the worst acts ; while pride or a cold and calculating
selfishness have no effect at all upon the nervous system,
and consequently are liable to meet with far less severe
condemnation.   It is only in obedience to some great
authority, such as that of the New Testament, or else
through reasoning out the relative harm to society in
its deepest interests, that we are able to correct the
balance which our feelings tend to disturb.   The only
wise course here seems to be that we should remember
in the first place the immense authority which the
ordinary moral conventions have, simply because they
embody the experience of so many generations, and
then, remembering this, we should seek for the underlying ground of the conventions and criticise them in

its light. We are never at liberty to break an accepted moral rule because we do not see any reason for that rule ; but we are not only at liberty, we are even bound, to break an accepted moral rule when we actually realise that it is defeating its own end, for then we only repudiate the convention in order more perfectly to serve the end which it exists to serve.

Yet here, too, plainly a word of warning is needed. It is very hard, and perhaps impossible, to think out all the results which will follow from the adoption of a new moral habit, and the process of thought must therefore be exceedingly thorough before the authority of the generations is set aside. The classical instance of slavery illustrates all these points. There was a great deal to be said for it in reason ; it had been accepted by the Church for generations ; but Wilberforce and his friends criticised it in the light of the fundamental principles by which it was regarded as being justified. He convinced men that as a matter of fact those principles condemned it ; and thus he swept it away. But it is open to very serious question whether the suddenness of the abolition did not introduce a number of evils which might at least have been modified by a more gradual process. Probably it was impossible, human nature being as it is, to effect any result at all by the gradual process ; the enthusiasm necessary for the work would have had little patience with such methods ; and yet it is true that while the abolitionists were plainly right on the main issue, they did incident-ally a certain amount of harm, because they had not thought out the whole problem in all its details. To say this is not to blame them ; very likely it was impossible to think the matter out ; but the warning stands and is of value.

The activity or faculty which is usually designated by the name of conscience is the reaction of character trained on certain principles to any act or suggestion. The difference between right and wrong is indeed ultimate ; but the judgment with regard to the question—What acts are right and what acts are wrong ?—is determined for the most part by the tradition of that civilisation, by which the individual forming the judgment has been moulded.  It is the failure to distinguish between these two points that has led to so great a confusion in the discussion of moral questions.  Sometimes men, who have only late in life realised that other nations have different standards from their own, come to the conclusion that all morality—including the fundamental principles of right and wrong—is a matter of convention only.  More commonly people who are convinced that right and wrong are in principle absolutely distinct proceed to attribute the same absolute character to the moral conventions which they themselves accept. The relative isolation of England, due to its insular position, has made us particularly liable to this latter error.  But man is by nature a social being, and the moment society exists, the difference between right and wrong comes into being with it.  For all the terms that go with right, such as "duty," "ought," "obligation," and so forth, have reference to a social context ; there can be no moral law with regard to an entirely isolated being, for the moral law regulates the relations between persons ; and so we may say, without fear of contradiction, that the distinction between right and wrong is itself absolute and ultimate.

It is clear that if the moral sense of the citizens is itself so largely a product of environment and its influence, the form of social order becomes invested with immense importance.  As Plato perceived, it is here that the real importance of constitutional questions lies ; for the broad outlines of the constitution will inevitably reproduce the standards of value accepted by the citizens.  Wealth, for example, will only be prominent in the State if the citizens set a high value on it. But for this very reason the form of the constitution tends to reproduce in the souls of the citizens the

standards of value from which it springs. There is
here a circle, either virtuous or vicious, and it is impossible to separate questions of personal ethics from
the more fundamental of the questions of politics. At
root the two are the same, for their root is the standard
of moral values.

Now, if there is one best way of living for all people,
then there must also be one best code of moral rules ;
if not, the morality of different nations will differ in
detail though not in principle. There are certain
moral requirements without which society can hardly
exist ; one of the most obvious of these is honesty ;
and it may therefore be laid down, at least in
general terms, that honesty is always an absolute
duty. But it is to be noticed that honesty is a quality
of a person, and that when we have said it is a man's
duty to be honest we have still not said what in many
cases he ought to do ; and it is in fact always impossible
to lay down universal moral rules with regard to acts.
The history of the Sixth Commandment is an illustration of this point. Its original form was—"Thou
shalt not kill" ; at the date when that command was
given there was not the slightest possibility of any one
supposing that it forbade the killing of enemies in
battle ; a very meagre knowledge of the Old Testament
would be enough to make that point clear. But as
time went on it became necessary to distinguish one
sort of killing from another, and the modern form of
the Commandment is—"Thou shall do no murder."
Murder is always wrong, because murder is killing when
killing is wrong, and it is a familiar fact that juries are
often called upon to determine whether a given case of
killing, where the act itself is not disputed, is or is not
a case of murder. As long, then, as we keep to actions,
we can reach no universal rules ; we can only live by
general rules which admit of exceptions.

Kant holds that it is possible to lay down universal moral rules of conduct, maintaining, for example,

that it can never be right to tell a lie, on the ground that the principle involved in lying is self-destructive, for if lying becomes universal it also becomes ineffectual, since no one will believe the lie ; but plainly this is a very abstract treatment of the topic. A man seldom thinks with regard to his own conduct— "I lied" ; what he thinks is—"Under circumstances uniquely provocative I said what was perhaps not a quite exact representation of the facts as I knew them." No doubt as a general guide we may lay down the rule that in judging himself a man should always attend to the general principle at stake, and in judging other people should attend to the particular circumstances constituting the temptation or possible justification. But it is perfectly plain that there are circumstances in which a man ought to lie. For example, a doctor or nurse who is concealing bad news from a patient dangerously ill is by common consent acting rightly. This instance perhaps gives the clue to determine when general rules of this nature should be broken. It is of the utmost importance to society that a man's word in general should be trusted, and therefore before any one deliberately tells a lie, he must be quite sure that the advantage of his act to society, not of course to himself, outweighs the damage which may be done by a general weakening of credit. In the case of the medicinal lie there is no such weakening of credit at all. Every one understands the exceptional nature of the circumstances, and no one is the more disposed to disbelieve a doctor in the ordinary affairs of life because he has told such a lie in the course of treating a patient dangerously ill. He has done some good and no harm, and has therefore plainly acted rightly.

Now the instinctive consciences of simple people admit these points quite readily ; the healthy and unsophisticated man is quite clear that there are certain instances in which the generally accepted rules should be set aside, and he regards the attempt to regulate all details of life by unbending moral principles as the very essence of priggishness.   There is no damage that can be done to public morals generally so great as what is involved in the attempt to impose rigid principles at all cost ; for this attempt suggests to the ordinary practical man that moral ideals will not work, and that therefore he may ignore them altogether.   In morals, as in knowledge, " the professor is the enemy of his own subject."

Many of these points are most clearly illustrated when we watch the working of a conscience that is developing according to the traditions that have moulded our own, but is at present immature.   For example, every boy at school knows quite well that to cheat in order to gain marks is morally much worse than to cheat to escape punishment.   Schoolmasters very often ignore this distinction ; the result is that the boy supposes the schoolmaster to have a scheme of morals wholly different from his own and with which he need not much concern himself ; but as a matter of fact the boy's conscience is quite right.   Similarly, a boy knows quite well that a lie told in order to save another fellow is much less culpable than a lie told in order to save himself ; and again that a lie which does not incriminate any one else, whatever its motive, is much less culpable than a lie which does bring another into suspicion.   Here again the schoolmaster is very liable to put all of these on a level and vaguely say the boy is a liar, thereby doing great damage to the boy's conscience.   It would seem, as we may remark in passing, that the proper principle for the schoolmaster is to recognise the sound distinctions which the boy instinctively draws, but to apply them on a higher plane ; that is, he will regard as really blameworthy a good number of acts which the boy is disposed to treat as perfectly innocent, but will recognise the scale of degrees.   Moreover, we may say that of the two the recognition of this scale of degrees is far more important than the effort to make the conscience sensitive at those points where it is at the moment insensitive. For the scale of degrees depends upon what is fundamental ; right and wrong are concerned with our relation to our fellow-members in society, and therefore to obscure the sense of degrees in guilt is to undermine the fundamental principle of all morals.

The foregoing discussion has made it plain that there are cases in which conscience may be genuinely perplexed, and some method of ascertaining the right course of action is required. A rough and ready division is sometimes drawn between egoism and altruism, or in the older language, between self-love and benevolence ; and it is then suggested that the right course is always to pursue the good whose fruition belongs to another, rather than the good whose fruition is one's own. As a general practical rule this is indeed very wise. The tendency of human nature, if left to itself, is that each individual should on the whole pursue his own good ; and plainly this needs to be corrected. Aristotle, when he had laid down that the virtuous action is always a mean between two extremes which are both vicious, as courage is the mean between recklessness and cowardice, proceeded to recommend that we should direct ourselves towards that extreme to which by nature we are least prone ; so we should in fact strike the mean. But this still does not determine the right course ; it only safeguards us against our own wrong tendencies. It is no doubt clear that when the greater good is that of another I ought to pursue it in preference to my own lesser good ; but what is to be said when the greater good is my own and the lesser good is the other's ? How, for example, will rational ethics determine the moral problem with which Shakespeare confronts Isabella in *Measure for Measure* ?[1] She is given by Angelo the opportunity of saving her brother's life if she will sacrifice her own chastity. Shakespeare,

---

[1] Cf. A. E. Taylor, *The Problem of Conduct*, pp. 43, 44.

as a matter of fact, simplifies the problem by making the brother a loathsome creature, who asks his sister to pay this price, and from that moment we are perfectly sure that Isabella ought to do nothing of the sort. But supposing the brother had been a hero, many of us would have found our sympathies a good deal torn. It seems clear that the real question at issue is not whether Isabella is to seek her own good or her brother's good, but which of two goods is the greater good, irrespective of the person in whom either is realised. This again may be very hard to determine, but at least it delivers us from the mere personalities of that method which baldly contrasts self-love and benevolence, and there leaves the matter.

If we adopt this more objective method, our question with regard to Isabella will take the following form. Is the preservation of chastity something for which it is worth while to sacrifice life ? It is of course only because Angelo is a tyrant that the question ever arose, and it seems right to answer that, if Isabella truly loves her brother—as she does—so that as between equal goods she would certainly choose his rather than her own, and if she yet prefers to preserve chastity rather than to preserve life, she is then setting this high value not upon her good or his good, or any other person's good, but upon chastity. As this is one of the virtues most necessary to the welfare of society, her choice serves that welfare and is therefore right.

Before leaving this part of the discussion it is worth while to point out that inasmuch as human nature is social, self-love and benevolence are not really antagonistic terms. For my own welfare is bound up with that of society to a great degree, and an enlightened self-love may lead me to devote myself very completely to the service of the community. But in fact it will nevertheless make all the difference in the world—both to myself and to the service which I render—whether I am thinking of myself all the while or whether I have forgotten myself in care for the community. For there is this nemesis pursuing all self-love however enlightened ; it lacks insight into the needs of others. I may persuade myself by reasoning that simply and solely for my own advantage I must give my energies to the public service ; but as a matter of fact that public service will be vitiated and my selfish aim frustrated by the blindness which the selfish aim inevitably brings with it.

While there is no antagonism between true self-love and benevolence, it must be insisted that the attempt to reduce benevolence to enlightened selfishness is bound to fail. It is sometimes said that if a man who could live in cultured ease spends his life working in the slums of a great city, he does it because he likes it, and therefore his act is really as selfish as any one else's. This is the kind of arrant nonsense that is only talked by rather sophisticated people ; for it is as clear as daylight that what really distinguishes the selfish from the unselfish man is precisely what either likes to do. The selfish man finds his pleasure in activities which hardly concern other people, or are even injurious to them. The completely unselfish man finds pleasure only in what gives pleasure, or in some other way does service, to other people. The man who, much against his inclination, forces himself to make some sacrifice is very likely acting nobly, but still there is more selfishness in his disposition than in that of a man who is capable of happiness only in so far as he is conferring it ; for in this latter case even the inclinations have become moralised. As long as duty is distasteful our nature is still only imperfectly moral.

The upshot seems to be that there is no possibility of establishing universal rules, and that in particular cases of difficulty, while we need wisdom to think out the real consequences of the possible lines of action so that we may not do injury while trying to confer benefit, the primary requisite is simply to love one's neighbour as oneself. For only this enables a man to understand his neighbour and appreciate his true interest. To "understand" when used of other human beings always means to "sympathise." When we say "I cannot understand doing a thing like that," we do not mean that we cannot provide the psychological analysis of the state of mind in which such an act is done, but that we do not ourselves feel the motives which might lead to such action. Moreover, it is only to loving eyes that any human being will reveal the deepest that is in his character. The cynic always finds that his experience confirms his cynicism, because to him no one will display the better side of his nature ; and the loving man always finds in his experience confirmation of his love and trust, because love and trust create what they believe in. There is only one ultimate and invariable duty, and its formula is "Thou shalt love thy neighbour as thyself." How to do this is another question, but this is the whole of moral duty.

Normally we show love of our neighbour by genuinely thorough performance of the duties belonging to our position in life. But Mr. Bradley's phrase, "My Station and its Duties," does not cover the whole field. In the first place, it does not help a man who has the opportunity of choosing his profession to determine what "station" he shall occupy. But also it leaves a great deal of conduct unaccounted for, unless the term "station" is extended to include all human relationships ; and then the formula is so vague as to be useless. No formula except the Golden Rule expresses the whole of moral duty.

It appears then that while distinction of right and wrong is ultimate, being indeed the distinction between love and selfishness, the judgment what *acts* are right and what *acts* are wrong varies in different times and places, according to the form of society in which the individual lives. If there is some ideal form of society for man as man, then we might say that the acts appropriate to such a society are in themselves absolutely right, and those destructive of such a society are in themselves absolutely wrong. But such a society is precisely the great object of desire as yet unachieved, and all that we can say without qualification is that such acts as are destructive to all possible society are always wrong ; while those which are required for the existence of any possible society are always obligatory. Duty is service of society. This will only mean the conservation of existing society as it is, if existing society is incapable of further improvement ; often he who tries to improve society is serving it more genuinely than any one else, though it must be expected that those who cannot appreciate the value of what he advocates will regard him as an enemy of society, and therefore a man whose actions are definitely wicked, even if he himself is only thought misguided. If all this is true it follows that Plato was right to a degree not commonly allowed, when in order to illustrate the moral problem of the individual he discussed the whole structure of society.

The problem of the origin of society has exercised thinkers in every age. Plato as usual combines the leading ideas of all subsequent speculations on the subject, but for a long while in modern thought his profoundest intuitions were ignored. In *Republic*, Book II., he shows that he is aware of the line of argument which endeavours to evolve society out of a pure individualism. Glauco suggests that society originated as follows : men are by nature selfish, but as each pursued his selfish aims he found himself at every point opposed by all the rest. Selfishness therefore was unable to secure any of its objects unless it would forgo some of them. The various members of society therefore contract with each other to abstain from inflicting certain injuries upon one another, so that they might also be exempt from such injuries. It is plain that this is the argument of Hobbes, and hardly less plain that it is the conception of Mill, at any rate when he composed his discussion of Liberty. Hobbes

represents the mental condition resulting from the break-
down of the medieval theory. That theory, whether
in its papal or its imperial form, seemed to give a
coherence to civilisation. The practical failure of
the Empire, and the repudiation, both practical and
theoretical, of the Papacy, left civilisation without any
coherent scheme at all. Hobbes attempts, like Glauco,
to build up such a scheme from the foundation. He
assumes individualism. Men are by nature isolated
individuals, striving with each other, and in this state of
nature the life of man is "solitary, poor, nasty, brutish
and short." So the citizens combine to set up a
society. But whereas Glauco made no provision for
the enforcement of the contract which originates society,
Hobbes regards this contract as at the same moment
establishing government. In his theory the citizens
contract with one another to hand over almost all their
rights to a sovereign. The sovereign himself, not
being a party to the contract, cannot break it ; he is
himself above the law, and the scheme therefore provides for just such an absolutism as the Empire and
Papacy had aimed at providing. The doctrine of
Hobbes was unpopular with the court of Charles II.,
because they perceived that it gave this absolute
authority to any sovereign who in fact held power
rather than to a king ruling by hereditary or Divine
right ; and in fact the picture of the Leviathan, that
forms the frontispiece of the treatise of that name,
seems at first to have had the features of Oliver
Cromwell. Revolution, according to Hobbes' scheme,
is no doubt wicked, but only until it succeeds. The
moment it has succeeded, the authority against which
it rebelled becomes in fact the rebel ; and so of course
Cromwell must have regarded the adherents of Charles
Stuart. In the hands of Locke the theory of the social
contract has advanced a stage, though the thought is
far less clear. Here the origin of society and the establishment of government are not regarded as identical.

On the contrary, the government is established in order to maintain a society which it presupposes, and there is a contract between the sovereign and his subjects. Consequently the sovereign can break the contract, and by breaking it forfeit his right to rule. This is precisely what James II. had done according to the Whigs. It is interesting to remember that when James had already fled to France, and William of Orange was indisputably in possession, the House of Lords debated for three days whether they should ask William to occupy the throne which James had vacated by flight, or whether they should ask him to occupy a throne which James had forfeited by breaking the original contract. The former was of course the Tory doctrine ; the latter was that of the Whigs.

It is not until we come to Rousseau that the other and deeper element of Plato's thought again becomes prominent in philosophy. For Rousseau society is the embodiment of the general will, and government derives its authority from the general will. Usually the general will expresses itself best through democratic forms, but these are not necessary to it. The dictator who should carry out the actual will of the people would be governing in accordance with the general will, and therefore with absolute right. This general will is not to be identified with the will of all ; it may be something lying deeper than the purpose which has become conscious in the mind of the separate citizens. We may perhaps illustrate this doctrine by the history of the two great English parties in the nineteenth century. If we were to judge from their conduct at elections we should expect to find the progress of the nation taking a zigzag course as one party went out and the other came in ; but in fact it is not so at all. The two parties no doubt represented different aspects in the whole purpose of the general will, but each of them is its servant. The development of the nineteenth century is upon the whole quite continuous. If we take the

P

three great Reform Bills we shall find the point sufficiently illustrated. That of 1832 was passed by the Whigs and Radicals ; that of 1868 by the Tories and Conservatives ; and that of 1884 by the Liberals. Again it was the Liberal Government which in 1870 made education universally compulsory ; but it was Lord Salisbury who in 1891 made it free. One instance after another could be given of the way in which each party takes up the work of the other and carries it on. Certainly at the present moment the general outlook of Mr. Asquith is far more like that of Mr. Balfour than the outlook of either is like that of the Duke of Wellington. The differences between two parties in the perspective of history become almost unintelligible ; there is a purpose in the nation carrying forward the work of progress by means of both.

But all of this is most simply stated in the Platonic form. It may be true that society would begin even if men were altogether selfish ; it is also true that society would rise quite apart from selfishness altogether, because in the depth of their being men are social and have need of one another. In fact, the individual is always a particular variety of the social institution to which he belongs. I am not first myself and then an Englishman ; I could not be anything but English any more than I could be the child of other parents than my own. My membership in the society called English is as fundamental as anything else about me ; I am, so to speak, " the Englishman " expressed and interpreted in a particular way. Consequently to England I owe all that I value and every ounce of my energy. I shall find the fulfilment of my own will precisely in the service of the country to which I belong, and I can find it no-where else. This indeed would not be true if I were a member of a subject nationality. The Pole cannot feel like this for the alien nations which have mutilated and oppressed his own nation ; his primary loyalty is to Poland which does not any longer (or as yet) exist.[1]

[1] Written in 1916.

Perhaps this more than anything else shows the supreme
wickedness of subjecting one race to another ; for it
interferes with that proper relation of the individual to
his society which makes it possible for him to find
perfect freedom in its service.   But even where the
individual is a member of his own natural society he
will only find this perfect freedom in its service if that
society is such as to correspond with his spiritual nature.
For this it must be so constituted as fully to recognise
his personality.   The struggles for freedom of which
history is full derive all their meaning from this.   They
are an effort to find a society which shall fully recognise
the true personality of the citizens.   But true personality is realised in fellowship and service.   Hence there
is an absolute reciprocity between freedom and obligation.   The State must put first the rights of the
citizens ; each citizen must put first his duty to the
State, that is, to the whole body of the citizens.   " The
quickening principle of a state is a sense of devotion,
an adequate recognition in the minds of its subjects
that their own interests are subordinate to those of the
State.   The bond which unites them and constitutes
them collectively as a state is, to use the words of
Lincoln, in the nature of *dedication*.   Its validity, like
that of the marriage tie, is at root not contractual but
sacramental.   Its foundation is not self-interest, but
rather some sense of obligation, however conceived,
which is strong enough to over-master self-interest." [1]

It appears then that man's duty results from his
membership in society.   What constitutes his duty is
determined by the good of society.   Whatever is
necessary to the maintenance of any society whatsoever
is an absolute and unconditional duty of all human
beings.   In points affected by the diversities in societies,
it is a general principle that whatever serves the society
of which the individual is a member is a moral duty.

---

[1] Curtis, *The Commonwealth of Nations*, p. 8.  Cf. also p. 319 : " Material interests
may bring men together, but nothing can be trusted to keep them together but the
devotion which enables them to forget their interests and themselves."

But society consists of its members, and its good is not separable from theirs. If any institution of a given society in fact militates against the good of the members, loyalty shows itself in attacking that institution even, in extreme cases, to the point of rebellion. The social and political constitution must submit to criticism at the hands of the conscience which it has helped to fashion and train.

This whole effort of man as represented in political history, and in the various theories of politics, is an effort after human fellowship. The nation, with its organ the State, is a means of securing some measure of that fellowship; but the fact that the State relies, and must always rely, upon penal measures proves that of itself it can never lead men to the goal which by its means they are seeking; for fellowship is the life of free persons bound together in mutual love. The State by its penalties enforces, up to a certain point, such action as fellowship demands; but it is clear that penalty is only called for when the spirit of fellowship fails, nor can the penalty of itself ever create that spirit. Consequently it would seem that the goal towards which men are striving in all their political efforts will only be found in a society based on perfect freedom, but endowed with a spirit of fellowship which shall take possession of its members and bind them together in a mutual love, so that all need to enforce the conduct appropriate to fellowship is at once removed.

# CHAPTER XVI

## LIBERTY : INDIVIDUAL AND POLITICAL

> Within a cavern of man's trackless spirit
> Is throned an Image, so intensely fair
> That the adventurous thoughts that wander near it
> Worship, and as they kneel tremble and wear
> The splendour of its presence, and the light
> Penetrates their dreamlike frame
> Till they become charged with the strength of flame.
> SHELLEY.

THE people of Great Britain are as a rule ready enough
to agree that the ideal State will rest upon freedom.
A vast amount of popular sentiment is always available
in support of that cry, but it appears after a very slight
investigation that there are two quite distinct senses in
which people use the word "freedom," and that while
no doubt these are connected at their root, they lead
to the advocacy of very different forms of social order.
The first and most elementary sense of freedom is
simply the absence of external control. Without this
there can indeed be no freedom at all. So long as a
man's conduct, or the conduct of a State, is literally
imposed by an alien authority freedom does not exist.
In the case of an individual the abrogation of freedom
may be complete. If, for example, I am standing on
the edge of a cliff and somebody pushes me over, my
fall is in no sense my own act. In the case of a State,
on the other hand, freedom can never be entirely given
up or suppressed so long as the State exists at all. No
doubt it may sometimes be said that an action is forced

upon the State, when what is meant is that the
alternative was something which no set of persons
could be expected to endure ; none the less there is
here still some element of choice and therefore of
freedom. It is not possible actually to coerce a State
as one can, by superior physical force, coerce an individual—literally seizing and carrying him off. But
it is plain that the presence of such choice goes a very
little way towards giving that freedom which men
value. It is an indispensable condition of the kind of
freedom that is precious ; but in itself it may be no
more than a choice between two evils, each so great
that the selection of either is utterly contrary to the
will which chooses. And this remains true, even where
there is no external pressure. The man who is free to
do what he likes, but has no control of the impulses
which constitute his own nature, has not won effective
freedom. The State which is subject to no alien rule,
but which is driven into certain lines of action by the
rebellion of an ungovernable minority is not in the
complete sense free.

Liberty or freedom has no doubt often been regarded
as consisting in this mere absence of control. Legislation is then regarded as a partial restriction of liberty
for the sake of an increase of liberty on the whole. So,
for example, Mill regards the matter. My effective
liberty to go about my duties and pleasures is secured
to me by the repression of the homicidal and predatory
impulses in others ; and their liberty is secured by the
repression of similar impulses in me. This repression,
being enforced by an external power, is a curtailment
of liberty, but by means of it the greatest amount of
liberty actually obtainable is afforded. This is very
like the Social Contract theory as Glauco and Hobbes
express it. The individual is the unit, and it is for his
selfish interest that any order is constituted at all. The
result of this doctrine in practice is the policy of
*laissez faire*, and liberty so understood is simply

anarchism tempered by so much of government as may make it tolerable. Legislation therefore appears as a necessary evil, and should be reduced to a minimum. It seems probable that this position derives its attractiveness for some moral philosophers from the fact that they belong to the respectable and leisured classes. In their natural desire for simple illustrations they turn to elementary laws, such as the prohibition of murder and theft ; being conscious of no temptation in themselves to commit these crimes, they easily regard the law as directed primarily against other people. This view derives further plausibility, and indeed much ground in fact, from a system under which a small section of the community controls legislation ; for this section will tend to legislate against tendencies in the other rather than against its own. The old laws, and indeed even our existing laws, with regard to poaching, illustrate this point.

But it is to be observed that this kind of liberty may be complete in principle and yet negligible in result. There may, for example, be perfect freedom of contract in an industrial system ; and yet the men have no real choice but to accept long hours, low wages, and bad conditions because the only alternative is starvation ; the employers, on the other hand, may feel unable to improve the terms from fear of being driven from the market by others less scrupulous. Something like this was the actual state of affairs in the early part of the nineteenth century in industrial England. There was perfect freedom of contract but no effective choice, because of the available alternatives one was intolerable. For the law to step in and regulate these matters looks like a curtailment of liberty ; the Factory Laws were opposed by John Bright and many others on precisely this ground. But we know now that the Factory Laws actually increased effective liberty by widening the area of real choice.

Moreover, quite apart from political and social

problems, mere absence of external control will not confer true freedom upon the individual in his own personal life. A licentious man might be free in this sense of freedom; of him it would be true to say, as Plato says of the tyrant, that he never satisfies his real will precisely because he can at every moment do what his fancy suggests, and so he gratifies one isolated impulse after another but never attains to peace and joy for his soul. This can only be won in a life which is dedicated to some purpose, wide enough to afford scope to every faculty in his nature, and lofty enough to claim the dedication of them all. The man who aims at being a great scholar or a great artist, having faculties that fit him to become one or the other, but who is unable to control appetites and impulses which blunt these faculties, has no freedom in any sense in which freedom is valuable. The freedom that is precious is to be found, not merely when a man can say of his act, "I did it and no one compelled me," but when he can say, "I did it, and I am glad I did it, and if the opportunity comes I will do it again." The act then not only springs from, but definitely expresses the man's personality; it is the externalisation of his own self; but to secure such freedom a man must first submit to discipline.[1]

A child when he comes into the world consists of a whole mass of unrelated impulses and interests, and the purpose of the earliest education is to teach the faculty of attention, that is to say, of concentrating the mind upon some one object, however attractive may be other elements in the surrounding world. The child who is learning to read, or who is playing with sand upon a tray, is learning the elements of that power by which a man pursues a great goal ignoring all seductions and overcoming all obstacles, by which the hero dies for his country or a martyr for his faith. This is the real freedom which is worth having, and it is

[1] Cf. Chap. XIII. pp. 169, 170.

the direct product of discipline. At first indeed the discipline must be externally imposed. The chaos of impulses which constitutes our original nature cannot possibly organise itself; but gradually that faculty of purpose which we call the will is built up, and in proportion as this takes place, self-discipline becomes possible. Through this, advance is made to true self-control and to that perfect harmony of the soul where all capacities are used and all instincts satisfied in the pursuit of a life's purpose. That ideal may never be actually reached, but where it is reached it clearly constitutes a real mastery over the successiveness of Time, such as was described as the culmination of the development of Will.

In legislation we see the same process at work in the community. At first, for the sake of that degree of public order which is essential to an even moderate prosperity and happiness, a nation submits to a strong central government which is more or less autocratic. At this stage the control is mainly external. As the fundamental principles of social life become more widely accepted, authority is transferred to a body more and more representative of the whole community. Legislation then becomes a form of corporate self-discipline.

The essence of legislation, at least in a democratic community, is that the citizens condemn in advance any one of themselves who shall at any future time be guilty of certain acts. The only reason for doing this is that they know that these acts would be contrary to their real purpose and yet that they may be tempted to perform them. The motive for making the law is not only that it will be bad for each if some one else does the act, but that it will be bad for the man himself who does it. Legislation with its penal sanction is like a resolution which an individual takes, except that it is more effective because the penalty enacted is more likely to be inflicted; and it is simply true in the ultimate sense that the criminal against whom the law is put in motion suffers by the act of his own real will (though it may be of course contrary to all his conscious desires), unless he has gone so far in criminality that he does not desire the maintenance of society at all. Legislation therefore need not preserve freedom in one by restricting it in another, but may directly increase real freedom all round by strengthening the deliberate purpose of our lives against the impulses as yet undisciplined, which would cut across and interfere with that purpose. For example, it is my deliberate purpose to be honest in all my dealings ; but in a host of small ways I am perpetually tempted to dishonesty, and there can be little doubt that I am often saved from yielding to that temptation by the law, which, if I yielded, would involve me in varieties of inconvenience and inflict upon me the stigma of public censure. The true individual freedom then is found when the character is fashioned into so true a unity that in all its acts it expresses itself completely. Similarly liberty in the State is found when the citizens combine together in a common purpose which they are agreed in maintaining against any impulse, not only in others but also in themselves, which would thwart that purpose. In both individual and society *liberty is control of the parts by the whole which they constitute.*

It is perfectly plain that this formula can only stand for freedom if the whole is a spiritual unity in which the parts fully realise their membership. Otherwise a great deal of substantial tyranny may be carried out in its name. It is for this reason that the government of one race by another is always an evil, and may be an intolerable evil. The Polish subject either of the Kaiser or of the Czar does not at all feel that in submitting to the laws which the political government imposes upon him, he is realising himself by incorporation into a larger fellowship.[1] The State for him is an alien force which so far as it secures good order provides

[1] Written in 1916. This and the two following pages deal with a political situation now ended, but the argument holds good.

a certain material benefit, but has no moral claim upon him.  An Englishman lately said, in the presence of a number of such Poles, that his country had a claim upon all that he possessed and all that he was, because in each case everything was given to him by the country; he was not merely an individual, but essentially and fundamentally an Englishman.  To be English was part of his essential self.  One of the Poles replied that he did not understand this position at all; a man paid in taxes and the like for everything he received from the State, and he did not see how the State had any further moral claim.  This complete divorce between governmental administration and moral loyalty is plainly an evil to which hardly any in the world is equal.  For it strikes at the root of all real corporate life and tends to make the individual regard himself as an isolated atom whose rational course is to pursue his own interest, except so far as he may forcibly be checked, and whose self-sacrifice for the community, if his instincts lead that way, is from his own point of view sheer loss and no gain at all.  Probably the inhabitants of Ireland in very large numbers feel much. the same with regard to the United Kingdom.  The fact that of recent years English government has at any rate attempted to be benevolent, may mitigate the bitterness of the feeling, but will not alter it.  It is not the harshness, but the alien character, of the government which constitutes the fundamental evil.  In certain departments of life organised Labour has the same feeling towards the existing English State.  The State is in fact so much controlled by men of a certain class and station that Labour perpetually feels itself to be in the position of a subject race. We see the result in the difficulties which the English Government had in introducing a measure of compulsory military service, and in their decision altogether to exempt Ireland from the operation of that principle.

In order that there may be real freedom the government must be the organ of a genuine moral unit, and for this reason frontiers should so far as possible coincide with national divisions.[1]    Here as elsewhere, when once sin has been committed, the right condition cannot be restored without atoning sacrifice.    In Hungary and the Balkan States, for example, the claims of nationality were for centuries persistently ignored.    There are now many Roumanians under Hungarian rule, but it may not be possible simply to transfer them to Roumanian rule because there are patches of Hungarian population scattered about in that territory which is predominantly Roumanian in race, and these will then be subject to Roumanian domination as the Roumanians are now to Hungarian.    That would perhaps be better than the present situation, because the number of those subjected to an alien government would be far smaller ; but to these Hungarians it will be a real injury none the less.    There is also the permanent difficulty which besets a government that has ever been guilty of oppression ; it has stored up against itself a bitterness of feeling which is very likely to retaliate when it is given liberty, and the oppression which began from sheer love of power may be maintained from fear of that retaliation.    There seems to be no way out of this danger, except that the oppressed should be willing to wipe out the past, and voluntarily accept its sufferings without demanding recompense.    In one way and another the only means by which sin can be obliterated is through the suffering of the innocent, and this may take the form of a voluntary acceptance of past suffering for the sake of future peace and fellowship.    That government and people which has been guilty of oppression ought to do everything possible to alleviate the sufferings, and take their share, but if they are simply forced to accept a certain amount of retaliation from those whom they have injured, the evil process seems likely to be continued *ad infinitum*.    No doubt the parties can to some extent meet each other half

[1] But see Chapter XVIII.

way. For example it is sometimes said that one difficulty about Home Rule for Ireland is that Ireland could not manage its own affairs without financial help from England ; if that were all, as of course it is not, then let England give the financial help without demanding any supervision of its expenditure. That will be an act that may go far to mitigate the feelings of resentment still alive in Ireland which result from the bad old times. This illustration is of course given simply to suggest a principle ; whether it is politically possible or not is a question that must be determined by those who have detailed knowledge of the facts. Anyhow two points stand out clearly : the right relation of government to governed is not a matter of administrative expediency, but of fundamental and spiritual principle, and when once that principle has been violated there is something present which can only be removed by the voluntary suffering of innocent persons.

But if this is all that can be said, we shall be left with the picture of a human race divided into a number of moral units, each free in itself but each attempting to be self-sufficient. This is the ideal of Nationalism. This attempt is, in the modern world, doomed to failure if only from economic causes. Every people upon the face of the earth is in fact economically dependent upon many others if not upon all others, and this is only the outward symbol of the spiritual unity which in fact binds all men together. Indeed just as the individual finds his freedom by personally realising his own membership in a community, so that community will only find its own self-fulfilment in realising its membership in humanity.

The principle of freedom seems urgently to require extension in two directions where hitherto it has been given little scope. So far as ordered freedom goes, which is very much the same as saying so far as civilisa-tion goes, the national State has been almost its only expression. But, as we have seen, the national State cannot exist in isolated independence ; and even within itself it is to be remembered that the national State does not by means of its regulations come into perpetual relations with the mass of individual citizens. These do, however, find their lives actually controlled by the regulations of the industry in which they work. These regulations invade their very homes and tell them when they may get up and when they may go to bed. Yet they often have no means of affecting these regulations except by the threat of a strike. Before we can be said to have a free society it will be essential that the control of industry shall pass largely into the hands of those immediately concerned. Here as everywhere else the extension of liberty is dangerous to material prosperity, though, if the experiment succeeds, it results in the increase of material prosperity, inasmuch as the enthusiasm of the workers is enlisted. But for the achievement of the spiritual ideal the extension of liberty is indispensable. The various great movements of recent times since the French Revolution, or the less spectacular but equally important industrial revolution in England at the end of the eighteenth century, have all had their real source more in the spiritual aspiration which is the distinguishing mark of man than in desire for more material goods. Very often the former has expressed itself in terms of the latter, because it was economic bondage that fettered the life of the spirit ; but the inner history of the movements shows plainly that the real energy came from spiritual discontent rather than from material greed. This has been most emphatically true of the Socialist and Syndicalist movements. Working men are not as a rule prone to self-analysis nor highly skilled in it. They may find great difficulty in stating where the seat of the trouble lies. But a sympathetic observer very quickly detects that what really galls is not so much the small proportion of the results of industry allotted as the reward of labour, but rather the sense that the employees are treated as "hands" and not as "persons," so far as the industry is concerned. Their personality apparently is for their leisure time ; only their productive utility counts in industry itself. But this is to say that for the greater part of their waking life they are treated as living chattels, which is Aristotle's definition of a slave. The economic maxim that labour is a commodity to be bought as cheap as possible by those who need it and to be sold as dear as possible by those who offer it, ignores the fact that a man's labour is inseparable from himself. I may sell my coat and another man may buy it without in any way affecting my personality ; but I cannot thus sell my labour for my labour is simply myself labouring. The existing social organism is therefore felt to be unjust at its root, because it does not recognise the real and spiritual nature of man. Charity is no remedy. If all that labour asked were a fairer proportion of this world's goods, charity would be a remedy so far as it went ; but as the demand is for recognition of the workers as rational and responsible beings, charity, far from being a remedy, is felt rather as an insult. As between equals it is only a foolish, and in fact weak, spirit that can be insulted by charity. A man ought not to shrink from receiving money or any other assistance from a friend, for he ought to believe that the friend is genuinely glad to give it. But when the relation of friendship is not there, and the charity is a working off of superfluity to satisfy the impulse of compassion, or is even the giving away of comforts in answer to a general and abstract sense of duty, there is involved the denial of true freedom to the person whose necessities can only be met in such a way. In political life sovereignty has had to be shared ; the Crown which once governed has devolved its authority, no doubt under pressure, upon the representatives of the people. In the evolution of industrial freedom the private Capitalist and the Company must pass through the same process. If we are to have real freedom it must be an extension of our general principle to this sphere ; the parts must be controlled by the whole which they constitute, and to that end must truly constitute the whole by which they are controlled.

It is clear, of course, that the association of Labour in the control of industry must be accompanied by a great extension of education ; but that subject, as also the extension of the principle of freedom beyond the bounds of the National State, will occupy us in subsequent chapters. Before passing on, however, it may be well to remark that Liberty as we have defined it is bound up with Obedience. The principle requires both that the authority, governing the parts of the soul or the several citizens in the State, should be vested in the whole soul or the whole body of citizens, and also that the directions issued by this authority should be accepted and obeyed.

The State must also remember that it exists by no other right or title than that of all associations of men ; it is bound therefore to recognise " Personality " equal in essence to its own in all associations or corporate bodies within itself, whether they be religious, educational, economic, or of any other type. It must aim at their "freedom" as it aims at the freedom of individuals, only claiming, in this case as in that, to be the supreme source of order in virtue of its including all other associations within itself.[1]

What then is the place for the individual conscience? Is there no duty, or even right, of rebellion against corporate wickedness ? Unless we can guarantee the moral perfection of the community—and of course that cannot be guaranteed—we must let the individual judge and act upon his judgment. But he must be sure that his objection is truly conscientious, or in other words that it is based on moral principle, which is the same

[1] On this point, which is of capital importance in practice, see Maïtland *Introduction* in his translation of Gierke and Figgis' *Churches in the Modern State*.

as saying based on consideration for the highest attainable welfare of society as a whole. Nor must he raise any objection if the State puts its penalties in force against him. The State will do wisely to deal tenderly with the consciences of its citizens ; moreover, if the position which we shall advance in Book II. is accepted, the State must remember that its citizens are also children of God, owing an allegiance to Him which transcends all earthly loyalties, and having rights as free citizens in a Commonwealth of greater dignity than any nation or state. But the law-breaker has no right to expect exemption from penalty merely because he can plead conscientious objection to the law. He must be ready to follow his conscience to the point of martyrdom. Moreover, both he and the State must first of all remember that freedom rests upon law ; frequent law-breaking and the contempt for law resulting from it is the way to chaos and the condition wherein the life of man would be " solitary, poor, nasty, brutish, and short." Frequent breaches of the law, however conscientious, are therefore disastrous to society, and if the " objector " is to be truly conscientious he must have estimated as far as he can the harm which he does by weakening the authority of law. The true aim alike of State and individual is that condition which may be called either free order or ordered freedom ; for this is the counterpart of that true fellowship which we defined as the life of free persons bound together by mutual love.

# CHAPTER XVII

## EDUCATION

Μέγιστον δὲ πάντων τῶν εἰρημένων πρὸς τὸ διαμένειν τὰς πολιτείας, οὗ νῦν ὀλιγωροῦσι πάντες, τὸ παιδεύεσθαι πρὸς τὰς πολιτείας.—ARISTOTLE.

IT has already been said that with a view to the only available means of establishing true freedom in an industrial community a great extension in Education is absolutely essential. But it is not only in that connexion that Education is seen to be of primary importance. If the aim of man in his social life is at all that which we have described, it becomes clear at once that Education is the most important department of the State. There is no doubt a sense in which others may, in different stages of development, be more indispensable; for example, a civilised community exposed to barbarian invasion might well consider that the maintenance of its defences was even more indispensable than Education to the maintenance of its standard of life. But that is due to relatively accidental circumstances. The barbarians may become civilised and lose their desire to attack. In such a case the maintenance of defences would cease to be important; but without Education of some kind there can be no life worth defending, and without Education of a very definite kind there can be no attainment of that goal to which all human endeavour, personal and national, is striving.

No doubt merely to live in a civilised community

is itself the most important part of Education. From the general mental and spiritual atmosphere the growing citizen will imbibe the principles of social life, quite apart from any definite instruction or deliberately chosen influences. But in the world as we have it, where society is still in process of passing from barbarism to true civilisation, there is nothing so vitally important as to secure that the influences tending towards the formation of a truly social character predominate over those which tend to develop egoism and self-seeking in the training of the young. We have already said that a man's real freedom is only found when his acts are dictated by some purpose to which his whole life is voluntarily given, and indeed only when this purpose is so large and rich as to afford scope for the activities of all his different faculties. But it is at once perfectly plain that such a result will not be achieved for human nature as it is without a very great amount of discipline ; and the child cannot discipline itself, for it has and can have no purpose in the light of which to control and organise its various interests and impulses.

The first function of the educator is to train the capacity of attention, insisting that the child shall attend to the duty of the moment, whatever that may be, in spite of all sights and sounds which may tend to divert the attention. This faculty of concentration upon the work of the moment is the first and the last business of Education. The teacher who is training the child to read, or it may be only to play with sand on a tray, is engaged, as we saw in the last chapter, in fashioning that faculty by which, when it is fully developed, the hero dies for his country, or the martyr for his faith. For here you still have in principle only what is already present in the most elementary form of teaching—concentration upon a purpose in spite of all obstacles and all seductions.

If by the word " will " we mean the faculty to form

and pursue a purpose, and not merely a determination to have our own way whatever that may happen to be, then it must be said that the primary business of Education is to fashion a will. But it is impossible that there should be merely a will in general ; it must always be a will to something ; and therefore this process of fashioning the will must also—at least after the very elementary stage—be a process of directing the will. This cannot be done merely by argument or reasoning, for the child has little faculty in this direction of which the educator may make use. It must be done by setting the child in such environment that it comes spontaneously to love what is lovely and hate what is hateful. Indeed the former is the one thing necessary, for, as Plato profoundly says, the soul should know evil only by its opposition to what it already loves as good. To know evil by direct and inward experience is to vitiate the soul itself ; to experiment in moral matters is always impossible because the experiment itself vitiates the instrument by which the result is to be estimated. For this reason we cannot leave the child to test the values of various ways of acting or thinking and then choose between them ; but we must so contrive the child's environment that what is good may be attractive, and what is evil either altogether absent (as is best), or at any rate repellent. So the true judgment is formed before the emergence of reason, and when reason comes the child greets it as a friend with whom its education has made it long familiar.[1]

The first requirements for this result are that the home should nurture the soul with love, and then that as soon as the child is becoming definitely conscious of individuality it should be a member of some society of such a kind that it can realise the nature and responsibilities of membership. Of course this does not mean that the child is to be able to formulate its measure of responsibility, but that its outlook should in fact be so

[1] *Republic*, 409 A-D ; 401B-402A.

directed that it naturally and spontaneously considers the welfare of a whole society, and not merely its own point of view. This cannot take place in the family, for there the child must always be a dependent. Of course nothing can be a substitute for the influence of a good family. Especially in early childhood, when there is no critical capacity, and the soul is therefore in the highest degree sensitive to influences, the formative power of the family is incalculable. Here the two requisites are simply goodness of character and love. A child is very imitative. But quite unconsciously it imitates the spirit rather than the outward act. A child surrounded by love will tend to become loving ; a child surrounded by selfishness will tend to become selfish. The selfish parent may be either " kind " or " cruel " or both (for both are rather pleasant things to be) ; but whichever form the selfishness takes, it is the selfishness that will be imparted. The loving parent may be gentle or stern, or more probably both, for both are at different times in place ; but through either the gentleness or the sternness the love will tell, and it is the love that will be imparted. No rules for conduct can be given ; kindness will not " spoil " nor sternness save ; but love will save and selfishness will spoil.

But the stage comes when the life of home must be supplemented by another life in which the child shall be more responsible because at once more independent and more fully a member of his society. In the home the child must always be a dependent. It would be unreasonable for the parents to withhold their guidance if the child were falling into some serious mistake, merely on the ground the child must somehow or other learn to live ; and on realising the mistake the child would in such a case feel some just resentment against the parents' neglect. And yet it is true that we can only learn to live by living ; we cannot first learn to swim and then get into the water, nor can we first learn to live and then start living. But we can learn to swim in calm water and in the presence of friends, who will give us help if necessary, instead of making our first attempt alone in a rough sea ; and so we can begin to live in circumstances carefully devised and controlled, but in which none the less we have to make our own attempts and rely upon our own efforts. For this we need a society which consists mainly of other children of more or less the same stage of development, because if there are many grown-up members in the society the control will inevitably fall to them.

It is upon this principle that the English traditional education is based. The Public School is a society of boys just such as is described. The whole life of the School is really made by the boys themselves within the limits which the School regulations make possible. There are grown-up people—the masters —who both share, and afford guidance in, the general affairs of the life of this society ; but that life is essentially a life of boys, and the masters can at the most be only on the fringe of it. It is here that the great value of the system lies, for there can be no doubt that a boy at school would far rather that some success or honour were obtained by his House or by the School than by himself. No doubt if he can be the one who wins, or helps to win, the honour for the community, so much the better ; for that is the way to win honour for himself ; but the only dignity recognised is a dignity of service. The form of service in a society of boys is bound to be rather trivial ; almost always the service must be rendered in games, such as House matches and the like. Still, it is only by helping to realise a purpose which belongs to the whole community that a boy can obtain any position of dignity at all. It is mainly for this reason that athletes are more admired than scholars ; for it is felt with regard to work in school that the boy makes efforts for his own advancement or improvement, while an athlete, however much he may enjoy the admiration he wins, is by his success helping his whole community. So far the boys are quite right in their moral judgment when it sets the athlete above the scholar. It needs only to be added that this judgment, which is perfectly healthy during a phase of development, may easily become stereotyped and persist into a stage of life where it is positively vicious because it fastens attention permanently upon interests which ought not to be absorbing to the full-grown man.

There can be no doubt that our schools have done harm in just this way. For example, one noticeable fact about games is that they are the natural sphere for unlimited competition ; in fact, games that are played with teams provide an illustration of the immense complexity with which competition and co-operation may be woven into each other. The object of the game is enjoyment of all the players, so both teams co-operate for the main purpose. But this enjoyment depends upon the keenness of the contest ; any sportsman would rather be beaten in a good match than win in a walk-over ; and so the enjoyment for which the teams co-operate is obtained by their competition with one another. Again each team can only be successful in so far as its own members co-operate in their competition against the other team ; the selfish player is a bad player. But the members of the team may compete with one another to be the best co-operator, so that a good player is he who best co-operates with his colleagues in competing against another team for the sake of a pleasure which the two teams, by competing, co-operate to obtain. But the whole essence of a game is that nothing beyond it is at stake ; it is an elaborate form of make-believe. As soon as the question is asked, why one should want to kick a ball between three poles, the game is spoiled. One does not want to do it for the sake of anything except for the fun of the game. One great danger of an education which proceeds largely by means of games, or rather by means of a social life of which games are the inevitable expression, is that it gives an impression that the rules of the game may be treated as rules for life. In England we speak of ."a good sportsman" and "playing the game" as if these phrases embodied all morality ; but in fact they are most misleading. To regard the competition of the business or industrial world as at all parallel to the competition of a game of football is sheer illusion. In one case there is, or should be, nothing at stake except the winning and the losing of the game ; in the other there may be at stake the right to live with honesty and to support wife and children. The two cannot be judged by the same standards, and to encourage the tendency to think of life in terms of games, while it may save us from priggishness and ultra-seriousness, is none the less disastrous.

This is a real danger ; and yet the method is the only sound method. Probably the evil results which have sometimes followed have been due in fact to the exclusiveness of the Public Schools, and to the narrow circle from which their pupils are drawn. The boys have mostly had little perception of the struggle to maintain life ; their notions are healthy, but their outlook and their sympathies limited. It is not likely that the application of the principles of games to serious affairs would still be common, if, in the schools, there were a large number of those who had more experience of the real seriousness of the struggle of life. There is, however, great difficulty, as will shortly be explained, in securing this by any other than an indirect and lengthy process.

It is a noticeable feature of the Elementary Schools in recent years that they have been rapidly developing more of this corporate spirit. Old Members Associations are growing up in many places, and some real pride in membership of a school is showing itself. But all of this takes place under the greatest possible hindrances and limitations. A symptom of the view taken by the legal authorities is to be found in the fact that a child may leave school on its fourteenth birthday even in the middle of a term, instead of at the end of the term in which that birthday occurs.[1] The suggestion plainly is that the school exists entirely for the child and not the child for the school ; the stages of the child's life are alone considered, not those of the school's life. But the school will only give its best service to the child if the child regards itself as a member of the school and as owing it real loyalty and allegiance. Again, the buildings are as a rule not such as easily gather associations, and have little individuality ; the opportunity for organised games in which the corporate spirit of the school must find its chief expression is very little. To provide such educational facilities as are really called for will cost a vast amount of money, but it will prove a good investment, for it will undoubtedly lead to very large reductions in expenditure upon Poor Law, prisons, and the like, and to an immense increase of educational efficiency. When, however, the gain in happiness and in the enrichment of life is taken into account, the advantage secured by such expenditure can no longer be called into question. At the present moment there can be no doubt that much of our expenditure on Education is wasted simply because it is not enough ; it stops short too soon and the size of the classes prevents even the time allowed from being used to the best advantage. Our system has been devised partly under the conviction that what is required for all citizens is a bare minimum. This conviction reveals itself in the lunatic regulation that if a child is clever enough to profit by prolonged education, he or she may leave school before the appointed time ; while the child who is slow and stupid, and therefore likely to profit little by schooling, is kept at school till the full legal time has elapsed.[1] In any case the present leaving age, interpreted as meaning the emancipation of the child from all educational supervision, is disastrously early. The period from fourteen to eighteen is probably that of greatest mental and moral expansion. The early years before self-consciousness is

---

[1] Written in 1916 : the Act of 1918 corrected this.

fully established may be more important in giving to the whole life a certain tendency or bias, but the period of adolescence is that when most is at stake so far as the direction of conscious volition is concerned. That a boy of fourteen should feel himself to be independent, and assume the airs of a grown-up man, is as unwholesome as anything can be. Quite apart from such questions as this, and from " blind-alley " occupations, which leave the boy when he really reaches manhood stranded in the world with no skill in any direction, there is the serious loss resulting from absence of discipline and restraint at the time when the chaos of conflicting impulses within the soul is more complete than at any other after infancy. New interests, tastes, and passions are developing, but the child has no established standards by which to judge them, and very likely no strength of purpose by which to enforce his judgment upon them. Here it may be well, parenthetically, to insist upon the educational necessity of proper physical development. To try to extract moral harmony from a system which is fretful and irritable through lack of proper nourishment or of proper all-round development is like trying to draw music from a violin whose strings are out of tune ; but this would not be the appropriate place to pursue that topic.

It has already been stated that the institutions of the social order exercise a pervading influence upon the characters of citizens by perpetual suggestion. It is undoubtedly true of the educational system as a whole. It is no doubt the case that while all should be under discipline until eighteen years at least, there are many who would not benefit by continued " schooling " up to that time, or at any rate by such schooling as we have yet devised, and which uses books as the chief instruments for training. It is sometimes said that we have already provided scholarships and exhibitions in such abundance that all those who are able to profit by a prolonged school education are able to obtain it. This statement is in itself at the very least problematical, and even if it is true it does not justify the present system.   The boy who has won a scholarship or exhibition inevitably tends to think that he has by his own ability and labours won a prize which he may legitimately use for his own advantage.   The fact that this prize is offered him by the community is not likely to be very present to his mind.   We need instead a complete system of education which shall eject at various stages those who do not seem likely to profit by carrying school education further.   That is to say, the community should train all its citizens to the full extent of their powers for its own service, and cease to train its citizens precisely in so far as further training would be of no benefit to itself. Such a system will perpetually give the suggestion that the faculties developed by the community must be used in the service of the community, and will tend to counteract the whole atmosphere of self-seeking which has pervaded much of our educational progress.

There is a real danger that so thorough a State-system of education may tend to make service of the actual political constitution its main aim rather than the disinterested pursuit of Goodness, Truth, and Beauty. This we have lately learnt to call Prussianism.   We have been saved from it by having no real national system at all.   But the State, while organising the system, should foster that independent life in the schools, whose value we have referred to, by leaving each great freedom to work out its own methods.   Most inspections, whether by the Board or the County Councils, should be abolished, together with nearly all Codes. The school should be as free as possible to devise its own curriculum and time-table, submitting to inspection not as regards methods but only as regards results.

So far as possible, children of all classes should be trained together so that they may have more opportunity of getting to understand each other, instead of growing up in separate departments knowing nothing of each other. But it is doubtful whether the mixing of classes can profitably begin in Secondary Schools. The stage of adolescence is that of the greatest self-assertiveness, and therefore liable to manifestations of envy or contempt beyond what may be expected in children or in grown-up men and women. If the children have mixed in the Elementary or Preparatory School they may go on together through the Secondary School, but to mix children of different classes then for the first time, as is liable to happen through the regulation allotting 25 per cent free places in all schools that receive aid from the Government, is a false policy. On the other hand, at the University the intermingling can take place with great advantage and little or no loss. The society is freer, and if there are any who do not desire the company of some other, they simply keep apart. The great danger at present of bringing working men to the University is simply that they develop tastes and interests of a kind which they can hardly gratify if they go back into the ranks of labour. Quite apart from all social ambition, they inevitably tend to desire a kind of life in which they may have more leisure and more means of satisfying these new tastes than is possible to most working people in the present social conditions. In practice this difficulty can probably be overcome if as a preliminary to membership of a University they are for a time members of a University Tutorial Class[1] in their own neighbourhood, and then go up to the University with their membership of that class behind them. Such men will be rather older than most undergraduates, and therefore less liable to lose their moorings. They are more likely to bring to the University the contribution which labour has to give than boys from Secondary Schools who come from working-class homes ; and the danger of carrying off from the Labour Movement its own ablest members, and planting them out in some other section of society,

---

[1] See *University Tutorial Classes*, by Albert Mansbridge (Longmans & Co.).

is likely to be diminished to such a point as to be negligible.

We have said nothing so far about intellectual training, which most people tend to regard as the essence of education ; but indeed the training in social membership is so much more important that this department should always occupy a secondary place. It is definitely undesirable to develop the intellectual powers of a man who has not learned how to be a member of society. If a man is going to be a villain, in heaven's name let him remain a fool. But if the social purpose is to be formed in him, then he needs intellectual training to make that purpose effective. As a matter of fact, we suffer far more from stupidity than from deliberate wickedness, and tend to forget that alertness of mind is a necessary part of moral goodness. It is not, of course, requisite that everybody should be clever, but it is requisite that everybody should be sensible and mentally honest. It is here that we have especially failed in England. We have, as a nation, practically no regard for Truth. When an Englishman speaks of telling the truth, he usually means the utterance of those ideas which happen to be in his mind ; but if these ideas are false, the utterance of them is falsehood. Telling the truth must mean, not only to speak of things as we think they are, but to speak of them as they really are. To accept a prejudice, or repeat a commonplace of our social class without seriously examining it, is mentally dishonest, just as the incurring of financial obligations which we cannot meet is financially dishonest ; and of the two, mental dishonesty does the more harm. The amount of prejudice which the different sections of society entertain with regard to one another, and which could be removed by the expenditure of very little trouble in the way of investigation of facts, is one of our chief national perils. The ignorance of the shareholding class concerning the aims and purposes of Trades Unions has done an infinity of damage; so has the ignorance of the Labour world concerning the mental outlook and moral qualities of the more well-to-do. Ruskin wisely observes that many of our troubles arise from the fact that the wise of one class habitually contemplate the foolish of the other. That this should be so is not unfortunate ; it is wicked. Intellectually, education must aim chiefly at imparting a desire for the truth, or, in other words, a desire to understand. It is not knowledge in the sense of masses of information that education aims at imparting, but rather the knowledge which interprets what it knows. For instance in History, I may know all the dates of all the events that ever happened and still have no real historical knowledge. For what matters is not when a thing happened, but why it happened when it did. For example, the exact date of the first English Poor Law is unimportant, but the fact that it was enacted towards the end of Queen Elizabeth's reign when the influx of silver from South America had had time seriously to affect prices so that prices had risen while wages remained stationary, is a piece of knowledge of real value because it suggests important enquiries concerning other periods of distress, including our own just before the war.

The most important kind of fact for a man to understand is all that may be gathered up in the phrase "human nature." Whatever we are going to do in the world we shall have to with other men. There is need for a great development of scientific education, but this need must not be allowed to affect the primacy of what are called "the humanities." In a school or University where these obtain the chief place of honour, those, whose special studies are in the field of natural science, will gain from their intercourse with the students of the humanities very much of the education that comes from those studies themselves, while students of "the humanities" gain equally by learning from intercourse with students of natural science how these interpret the world.

We may state the question perhaps in this way.[1]
In order that a man may live his life and discharge his
responsibilities as a citizen he needs knowledge.  What
is the most important sort of knowledge to have?
None can be put on a level with the knowledge of
human nature.  Whatever a man is going to do he
will have to deal with his fellow-men and find his own
place among them.  This knowledge cannot be adequately obtained from books alone, and, as I have said
already, training through membership in a social life is
the best means to it.  But it may be also fostered in
a very high degree by what are called the humane
studies :  the study of the best that men have thought
in philosophy, the study of their highest aspirations
and deepest woes in literature, the study of their
attempts and their achievements in history.  This is
the most serviceable of all scientific studies that a man
can undertake.  But it is no doubt true that we have
allowed two evil things to happen.  In the first place,
we have not sufficiently recognised the value of natural
science in education, and, still more disastrous, we have
tended to identify the study of the humanities with the
study of the classical languages.

The upholders of the classics, taken as a group, have
no one but themselves to blame if the studies in which
they believe are an object of very general attack, for
they have been defiant in manner and retrograde in
practice.  And yet the attack upon the classics is
unintelligent.  It is very noticeable that the most
elaborate study which has ever been compiled of the
British Empire, and of the problems which it must face
in the near future, should find it necessary to begin its
survey with an account of the civilisation of ancient
Greece and Rome.  I am referring, of course, to *The
Commonwealth of Nations*, by Mr. Lionel Curtis.
European history and civilisation are indeed only

---

[1] This and the next three paragraphs are taken from my Presidential Address to
the Educational Science Section of the British Association, delivered at Newcastle in
September 1916.

intelligible in the whole sense of the word by means of some knowledge of those two ancient nations. And there is this great advantage in the study of Greece and Rome, that we can trace there the complete rise and fall of a particular system of civilisation. The modern system is not complete, perhaps it never will be. For that very reason it is impossible to see the events in a perspective determined by an apprehension of the whole. But the history of ancient Greece is a complete thing, so is the history of ancient Rome, and it is possible to study their thought and achievements with a perspective and proportion due to the fact that the whole is known to us. I am not saying that this is always done, for much time is too often spent on studying events which led to no appreciable result at all ; but at least the thing is possible. The study of ancient Greece has this further advantage, that the ancient Greeks asked all the elementary questions of philosophy in the simplest form. All subsequent European thought is to some extent sophisticated, precisely because it takes up its problems where the Greek philosophers left them. It is un-doubtedly best for the student to begin at the beginning ; and the beginning of European thought is to be found in the pages of Æschylus, Sophocles, and Euripides, of Plato and Aristotle, of Herodotus and Thucydides. But the study of these great literatures with their attendant history is largely ruined by two facts. One is that far more boys are driven into this study than will ever seriously profit by it, and for this Universities are on the whole to blame, though it is to be remembered that nearly all professional examinations make a fetish of elementary Latin, requiring not enough of it to be any kind of use, but quite enough to waste a great deal of the student's time. And the other ruinous fact is that we have continued a system appropriate to a time when there were few subjects to supply the place of mental gymnastics, and therefore use the history of two great peoples, and two noble literatures, for this menial office.

But, after all, important as are the subjects of study and the machinery for pursuing them, all of this is subordinate to the spirit which should direct and inspire the whole. I say the less about this because it has been so admirably dealt with by Mr. Clutton-Brock in his recent little book, *The Ultimate Belief*. Broadly, however, my contention, like his, would be that the aim of education is primarily spiritual, and that there are three, and only three, primary aims of the spiritual life. These are Goodness, Truth, and Beauty. It must always be insisted that these are ends in themselves. School discipline must be so conducted as to suggest constantly that goodness of character is not to be sought as a means to happiness or any form of success, but as an end in itself. So much is commonly admitted though seldom acted on, but the same principle must be impressed with regard to Truth and Beauty. With regard to Truth, probably most educators already believe it, but they are shy of appealing to it, and industry is recommended not as a means to the fulfilment of the spirit's destiny but as a means to success in life, or at best as a means to effective moral goodness. In the case of Beauty our education hardly recognises at all that it is an end, with the result that those whose spiritual activity most naturally takes this form find themselves in rebellion against the upholders of Truth, and still more against the upholders of Goodness.

There is danger at the present time that we are about to be plunged into great efforts for educational development resting on purely utilitarian motives. Such efforts may succeed for a time, but in the long run they are doomed to failure because they take their stand upon a lie. Beauty, Truth, and Goodness cannot in the end of the day be sought for the sake of anything beyond themselves, though it is true that innumerable benefits follow even the partial attainment of them. But the search is doomed from the outset if it is not

R

concentrated upon them as themselves being the prize
of the soul.

Understanding, in the case of all human questions,
always means sympathy, and the aim of education may
be summed up by saying that it is the development of
everything about a man which distinguishes him from an
animal or a machine—the discipline of intelligence, the
quickening of imagination, and the widening of sympathy. But if that is true, it is not necessary to argue
further that for liberty, moral or political, Education in
its threefold form of discipline, initiation into social life,
and instruction, is the primary requisite. By means of
it the individual is put in the way of fashioning the
unity of his own soul's internal harmony, and becomes
fit to take his place in the community as one element
in that larger harmony. In the degree in which his
faculties are at once developed and harmonised he
approaches the state of perfect moral freedom wherein a
man's whole life is freely given to the pursuit of a
purpose lofty enough to claim the service of all his
powers and rich enough to give them scope.

But no man can in fact evolve such a purpose out
of himself, nor can any human society supply such a
goal for his energy and service.

# CHAPTER XVIII

## INTERNATIONALISM

For I dipt into the future, far as human eye could see,
Saw the Vision of the world, and all the wonder that would, be.

. . .

Till the war-drum throbb'd no longer, and the battle flags were furled
In the Parliament of man, the Federation of the world.

TENNYSON.

ONE of our earlier conclusions was that so long as the nations of the earth regarded themselves as the sole end of their own action, and each considered only its own interest, so long would each fail to realise its true destiny. It has always been true that the different nations have needed the peculiar gifts of other nations for the fulness of their own life. In the early period the horizon of each nation was indeed comparatively narrow. It would be fantastic to say that for the fulfilment of its place in the world Ancient Greece needed the influence of China ; but Athens needed the qualities of Sparta, and Sparta those of Athens. As the means of communication have developed, the area of mutual influence and need has similarly increased. In the modern world every civilised nation needs the products of the rest. We do not indeed need a breaking down of national distinctions which would result in a diminution of the spiritual variety of men, but rather that each nation should develop its own gifts to the utmost extent in order that all nations may enjoy the finished product. So we see at once that in no country but Russia could Tolstoy and Dostoievsky be produced ; in no country but Germany could the philosophies of Kant and Hegel have emerged ; in no country but England could Shakespeare and Browning have written as they did.  But when once the works are produced, all nations may enjoy them ; we need the gifts of Russia and Germany, and of all the other nations, just as each of them needs ours.  This has lately become more plain than ever through the economic inter-dependence of all nations of the earth.  While under stress of exceptional circumstances a modern civilised nation can for a time be almost self-supporting, this is only by cutting off supplies which minister to the normal fulness of its life.  We are in fact members one of another ; and we shall have no proper politics until our principles of action conform to this given fact.

So much seems to be clear ; but great difficulty arises as soon as we begin to consider the basis of common action.  It has been said very frequently, and with perfect truth so far as the statement goes, that there is more hope of a final settlement as a result of the great European War of the early twentieth century, than there was at the close of the Napoleonic War. This is not because men are now more idealistic, but because many at least are agreed that the settlement should not be dictated by consideration of what any party can claim by right or wrest from the others by force, but rather by consideration of what will conduce to contentment and peace in the future.  In other words, the new factor is the recognition of Nationality. But then what is Nationality ?  There has been a great tendency of late to speak of it as if it were almost identical with race.  Englishmen should be the last to fall into that snare ; to what race shall we say that we belong ?  The Germans before the war, or at any rate as soon as it broke out, claimed that we were Teutons, and that in fighting against them we were entering upon a fratricidal strife.  It would appear, however, that we have never, for many centuries, felt any especial kinship with the Teutonic races ; our Anglo-Saxon forefathers probably provided us with a large number of Teutonic tendencies which we have retained as prejudices, but all our deliberate imitation has been of the Latin races of France and Italy. The argument used by some in Germany who complain of our conduct seems to ignore the Norman Conquest and all that has resulted from it ; but we are not only Saxon and Norman, there is a large infusion of Danish and of original British.

Certainly we cannot begin to base an idea of nationality upon race, if race be biologically or historically estimated. We are a family of people living in an island, and thereby driven to the establishment of social relationships with one another, until, owing to outside pressure and to the mutual influence perpetually in process, we have evolved something like a common purpose in which we feel at one with each other. If Great Britain is a real nation it is so in virtue of its common purpose. A nation is in fact a sovereign society. For a society is held together by a common purpose and exists because of that ; a nation is such a society not included in any other society and able to maintain itself on an equal footing with other sovereign societies. The State is, in the case of any true nation, the organ of that nation for purposes of collective action, whether in control of the nation's own constituent members, or in dealing with other States as representing other nations.

It is well to consider the problem in relation to a country like our own where circumstances have made the chief factors particularly obvious. Both the mixture of races, the influence of geographical and other circumstances in fusing them, and the fact that in the end one nation exists, represented by its own State, are here so plain that argument on the subject is not called for. But we have had our own problems of unassimilated groups, and the war has reminded us of them very sharply. Ireland is a constituent part of the political State called the United Kingdom ; but there is much dispute whether we should say that Ireland is a nation separate and independent from England, and again whether, if there is any such independent nation in the neighbouring island, there are not two nations. Upon these questions the whole of the Home Rule controversy turns. This is enough to remind us that, while ideally a nation is a sovereign society bound together by one purpose and acting through its own State, in actual fact it is often very difficult to determine when distinctions of nationality really exist ; at any given moment the *de facto* State has to act as if it were the instrument of one nation, when as a matter of fact it may hold together under its sway many nations, or many groups only partly fused into a nation. In Central Europe there is a mixture of races so distinct in tradition that the fusing of them into a single nation must be a matter of very great time, even though good-will should prevail upon all sides. To determine that every little society which felt conscious of a purpose of its own, but not conscious of any community with surrounding societies, must therefore form a separate State and have its own government is both practically impossible (for the resources of these communities would be too limited to support upon the material side alone such a system as modern civilisation teaches men to need) and theoretically undesirable because it would stereotype the present outlook and prevent it from merging in something wider and larger. It is inevitable in such countries that one State should contain different communities not as yet fused into one nation. Lord Acton in 1862 wrote words which need to be earnestly considered in this connexion. "By making the State and the nation commensurate with each other in theory, this principle reduces practically to a subject condition all other nationalities that may be within the State's boundary. It cannot admit them to an equality with the ruling

nation which constitutes the State, because the State
would then cease to be national, which would be a contradiction of the principle of its existence.    According,
therefore, to the degree of humanity and civilization in
that dominant body which claims all the rights of the
community, the inferior races are exterminated, or
reduced to servitude or outlawed, or put in a condition
of dependence. . . . The theory of Nationality is
more absurd and more criminal than the theory of
Socialism.    Its course will be marked with material as
well as moral ruin, in order that a new invention may
prevail over the works of God and the interests of mankind.    There is no principle of change, no phase of
political speculation conceivable, more comprehensive,
more subversive, or more arbitrary than this.    It is a
confutation of democracy, because it sets limits to the
exercise of the popular will, and substitutes for it a
higher principle. . . . Thus, after surrendering the
individual to the collective will, the revolutionary
system makes the collective will subject to convictions
which are independent of it, only to be controlled by
an accident." [1]

No doubt it is desirable that as far as possible
frontiers should be drawn between different States as
the mass of the inhabitants of the area concerned would
choose, but in the condition of the world as we have it
there will perpetually be a minority feeling at the
moment alien in tradition and sentiment.    If the State
is based upon the idea of Nationality, then, as Lord
Acton says, these people are put below the level of
full citizenship ; an injury is done to them and conditions are created which must almost inevitably end in
disaster.    The problem of statesmanship must always
be to give the utmost freedom that is at all compatible
with the maintenance of such order as is necessary to
the conduct of civilised life.    Gradually, as people have

[1] Lord Acton, in the essay "Nationality" in *History of Freedom and other Essays*,
pp. 297-299.    I owe the quotation to Mr. A. E. Zimmern.

dealings with one another, the mutual understanding will grow and a true nation emerge as a basis of the State.

The desire that has lately become prominent for some form of international control of questions such as Colonial expansion and the like, can only be satisfied if account is taken of the relation between State and Nation which we have discussed. Actual proposals must always be for inter-state control and the State may in any given case be an artificial and even an unjust construction. Such inter-state control was attempted at the end of the Napoleonic wars by the Holy Alliance. Governments united together in the desire to secure permanent justice and thereby peace ; but the chief practical result of the Holy Alliance was that the Russian armies marched across the Carpathians to suppress Hungarian aspirations towards liberty. The Alliance was in fact an Alliance of Governments, and that too of Governments which were not in any complete or spiritual sense the organs of a national will. It is only in so far as Nationality itself has come into existence that internationalism in this sense is altogether desirable. A central body before which disputes are brought, even if it is called a Council of Conciliation rather than a Court of Arbitration, will always tend to settle any dispute by consideration of precedents and of existing legal rights, and will therefore always tend to be a conservative force, liable to retard legitimate popular aspirations. Only if the conception of the State, as ultimately justified by its capacity to express the general will, is loyally adopted, can anything like a world State or Federation of States be wisely or permanently set up. Probably the change in general opinion during the century that has elapsed since the Battle of Waterloo makes possible the erection of a Central Council for the direction of certain specified activities, so far as the civilised nations of the earth are concerned. But all the dangers must be squarely faced and the experimental nature of the undertaking fully realised.

But there is in the world a political institution which, just because it is a natural growth and not an artificial construction, seems to supply the clue to one part of the problem. The so-called British Empire was never planned by any persons or group of persons; it is the spontaneous product of the energy of the British people left, as it has been, comparatively unfettered by exigencies of European war. Our island position, while not cutting us off from the civilisation of Europe, which was to some extent brought to us by the Roman Conquest and more richly by the Norman, has at the same time secured us against the perpetual waste of strength in frontier bickerings, or in such wars as those of Louis XIV. and Napoleon. It was only our army and navy that fought Napoleon; the Nation as a whole was not engaged; and above all the country itself was not harried.

The different parts of what we call the British Empire were added to it for a great diversity of reasons, but latterly, at any rate, the extension of Imperial control has been due to a desire to protect the natives of different parts of the earth against the aggression of British or European traders. So, for example, in New Zealand it was necessary that there should be some Government which the white man would respect, if the Maoris were to be saved from the most abominable exploitation. That Government was bound to be a European Government; and the British Crown took control in order to restrain its own subjects. Here already we see in the Imperial Government the germ of a World Government deriving its authority from a moral need. This Empire does not stand in the line of succession with Assyria, Babylon, Macedon and Rome; it is a new kind of fact. Until lately no one, even among ourselves, seems fully to have appreciated it. In the summer of 1914 the

Germans had observed that we held the Empire with
very light grasp ; some among them thought that if
they could, so to speak, shake our hand it would fall
out and they might pick it up. But then they discovered, but also, which is much more important, we
discovered, that we were not holding it at all ; it was
holding on to us. So far at least as concerns the
Dominions inhabited by white peoples it is true to say
that the Empire exists for no other reason than that
its constituent parts desire it to exist. If Australia
preferred to " cut the painter " we could hardly prevent
her, and certainly should not try. If Canada preferred
to join the United States we should not talk about
fitting out an expedition for the reconquest of Canada.
But most remarkable of all is South Africa. Canada,
Australia and New Zealand are united to us by ties of
race and sentiment ; but alike in race and sentiment
South Africa is predominantly Dutch. That a rebellion
should have been attempted and failed is more remarkable than if none had been attempted at all.
That the Dutch leader, who so lately commanded the
troops of his people in war against the Empire, should
have now, with their support, been winning victories
on its behalf is as remarkable and as promising a fact
as any in secular history, for it proves beyond all
dispute the possibility of that free family of nations,
whose establishment at last shall be the guarantee of
the world's peace. However far off the establishment
of such a society throughout the civilised world may
be, what has happened in South Africa definitely proves
its possibility.

In this fact of the British Empire, then, we have
" the noblest project of freedom that the world has
seen." [1] It has grown, but in its growth has been true
upon the whole to the principle of freedom, and in
that principle has found its bond of unity. That is the
new fact ; other empires were united by a force imposed

[1] Curtis, *The Commonwealth of Nations*, p. 705.

upon them from above ; the Commonwealth of the British Empire is united by the free loyalty of its constituent parts. No doubt, the United States offer an illustration also of a Federation of Free States, but there the whole extent of the territory is continuous, and the life of the separate States can never feel itself so independent as in a Nation such as Australia, separated by leagues of sea from the seat of Imperial Government.

But the British Empire also illustrates the difficulties that need to be faced. Every one is familiar with the problem of India. It is our professed aim to guide India forwards into national self-government, but no thoughtful person desires merely that the alien rule should be withdrawn at six months' notice. Here we have a State which has not yet secured its national basis ; but the national feeling is there, and the possibility of training it by education and a steadily increasing share in administration towards real self-government is admitted. If the task is carried out with complete good-will and the consummate wisdom for which it calls, it is not at all unlikely that free India would choose to remain a constituent part of the commonwealth called the British Empire.

Now the Federation of the World cannot proceed merely by the bringing in of different States freely under one national government ; but the British Empire itself is not likely to last for very long if it maintains its present constitution, which puts one member in control of all the rest so far as foreign relationships are concerned. The principle of freedom, the control of the parts by the whole which they constitute, has not yet found political expression in the British Empire taken as a whole. We must arrive at a real Federation of the Empire if we are to be true to its own root principle ; but so soon as that is done there seems no reason why other nations should not seek incorporation in this Commonwealth, thereby of course gaining the right to a voice in its control, so that on the basis of freedom and equality all nations might be linked to one another. In that case of course the title "British Empire" would have to go, for it would no longer be specifically British. The final stage in such incorporation would be a definite Act of Union, but this would only be attempted when, by the gradual building up of treaties and the establishment of machinery for the determination of international disputes, a result had been reached which would in fact be the same thing. The other sovereign States would not have sought admission to the British Commonwealth, but the British Commonwealth and they would have coalesced in the new union, so that gradually, by extending through the world the principle of freedom according to the formula that we have given—control of the parts by the whole which they constitute—we should reach the time when the spiritual varieties of the various nations would no longer be a source of antagonism and strife, but all would be bound together in a unity which, far from denying its differences, would rest upon the recognition of those differences and upon the realised need of each for all and of all for each.

But what guarantee can we have, even then, that the civilised nations will not combine to exploit the more backward, or even that they will all permanently realise their community with each other with sufficient clearness to be free from all temptation to break the pact for the sake of some great individual gain? The British Empire itself has often sinned against its own root principle of freedom. The nations themselves need some society that may include themselves, whose basis shall be a common purpose, not springing from merely individual interest and a preference for fellow-ship, as against the horrors of war (which were to rest our international fellowship on the principles of Hobbes), but arising out of loyalty to an all-inclusive Kingdom and a common Master, and expressing itself in common action in service of that Master and Kingdom.

# BOOK I—*continued*

## PART IV
### RELIGION

# CHAPTER XIX

## RELIGION, THE CULMINATION OF SCIENCE, ART, AND MORALITY

"The eye is not satisfied with seeing, nor the ear filled with hearing."— ECCLESIASTES.

" Canst thou by searching find out God ?   Canst thou find out the Almighty unto perfection ? "—JOB.

WE have considered three of the chief activities of Mind in its attempt to reach an experience in which it may find satisfaction.  In each we have seen it trying to order multiplicity in unity ; confronted with a chaos it seeks a cosmos.  In Science it does this on the basis of the huge assumption that the chaos actually is a cosmos, and that by seeking out the principles which govern our apparently haphazard experience it will find an order expressive of rational coherence.  As Science develops it gives perpetually increasing justification to this assumption.  In one department after another it finds the order that it seeks, and thus the confidence is increased that it was right in its initial belief that the universe is indeed an orderly whole.  But the only kind of order that Science reaches is one which satisfies the intellect and it alone.  The conquest of transitoriness which it achieves is reached only by the discovering of laws which, remaining constant, govern that which passes away.  When we passed to Art, we found Mind achieving a deeper satisfaction and a completer conquest of Time, but only because it selected its material and

255

concentrated attention upon objects which were created with a view to affording such satisfaction. We passed on to the Ethical aspirations and endeavours of men, and found the same process carried still a stage further in the life-purpose of a man who is genuinely moralised; we found a conquest of the transitory greater than that of Art, for it included the element of indeterminism or real choice, and consequently of variability, within the perfect unity achieved. And in the principle of Morality by which such a life is governed we found the unity that binds together different persons and societies in one corporate life or fellowship.

We notice that each of these efforts delivers man from his own isolation and from the sense that all passes away, and that as we advance along the stages of Mind's effort the deliverance becomes constantly more complete. Science is not only the means of reducing the chaos of experience to order, but is also in fact, though not in aim, a link between men otherwise far separated from one another. But just as it reaches its relative eternity through abstracting from the process of Time, so it binds men together by abstracting from everything which separates. It ignores passions and desires, except the desire for truth, and therefore its unity is easily broken when passions are uppermost, so that men who had been fellow-seekers after truth in England and in Germany before the summer of 1914 were found, immediately after the declaration of war, hurling manifestos at each other across their frontiers. Art is in both respects less abstract than Science. In some respects, indeed, it may seem to ignore precisely those elements on which Science fastens itself; but this is rather by taking them for granted than by leaving them out, for, as we have already seen, a work of art is a strictly logical structure, though its logic is so subtle and its detail so minute that it cannot be reproduced in the rough-and-ready machinery by which the logic-books teach us to test either coherence or cogency.

Inasmuch, however, as Art is concerned with the value of fact rather than the actuality of fact, it is clear that its main sphere is in the realm of appreciation, which requires both thought and feeling ; its subject-matter is therefore less abstract than that of Science, and the unity between men which results from fellowship in pursuit of it is also richer and fuller.    But those who are so united remain rather a small group of men, liable, in proportion to the intensity of their concern with Art, to be unsympathetic towards those who have little artistic capacity ;    and the very concentration upon personal value-judgments which the activity of Art involves leads to a peculiar vigour of divergence when divergence is found to exist.

In Morality, Science and Art both find their place. The man who is pursuing a purpose must think out the means to his end, and it is essential to the realising of a moral life that he should think them out correctly ; otherwise his purpose remains a mere good intention. But his purpose itself is determined by appreciation of values, and the good life is an artistic masterpiece. This is the half-truth which lies behind the whole conception of Nietzsche's Superman ; for the beginning and end of Nietzsche is this, that he treats all morality as if it were a form of Art.    From this point of view we may rightly say, " What matter how many canvasses are spoiled, provided the masterpiece is there at last ? " So Nietzsche cares not how many men are crushed, provided the superman, who is the expression of all that humanity can be, is at last evolved.    But the very principle of the moral life is fellowship with others, so that this masterpiece can never be produced by crushing another.    The spoiling of a canvass is of no consequence ;   the spoiling of another human life is the very infringement of the principle which the masterpiece is to set forth.    We find, then, that, just as we have here a greater conquest of the transitory than in either Art or Science, so, too, we have here the principle which

S

binds together men, even the most diverse, in a unity or fellowship, membership in which is the indispensable condition of individual achievement.

But the goal of Science is not reached ; Science only exists in departmental fragments : physics, chemistry, biology and the rest. The goal of Art is not reached ; there is no experience obtainable through the æsthetic faculties in which the soul can find satisfaction for ever. The goal of Ethics is not reached ; it would be realised in the pursuit of a purpose, lofty enough to claim the allegiance of all our faculties and rich enough to exercise them all, conducted in a fellowship bound together by ties of mutual love ; but man cannot evolve out of himself that purpose, nor can he of himself create that fellowship.

All of these efforts of Mind in its search for satisfaction demand the actuality of an ideal to which they point but which they never reach. Ethics suggests a Will which is perfectly self-determined, and yet is active altogether in love ; such a Will, if it be made manifest, will satisfy the aspiration of Art, for its manifestation will claim and deserve eternal contemplation ; such a Will, if it control the Universe, is the very principle of unity which Science seeks, for Will, while remaining constant in its Purpose, chooses now this, now that, as means to its end, and is the only principle which, self-explanatory in itself, explains what it orders or informs. Is there such a Will ? Only if there is, can the Universe be deemed rational ; Man's creative mind can find satisfaction only if there be a Divine creative Mind with which it may have communion.

That such a will exists may be said to be the basal conviction of every developed religion. It is indeed true that for some religions, notably for Hindooism, the ultimate principle is not definitely conceived as volitional. Yet inasmuch as for Hindoo philosophy everything is dependent upon the Absolute Spirit, the difference for our purpose becomes negligible. For reasons which the whole course of this book has made plain, we should maintain that only when interpreted in terms of will can the Supreme Spirit be so conceived as to supply the ground of rational unity in the universe.

Religion has very many roots, and unites within itself the principles alike of Science, Art and Morality. Its natural history, so to speak, traces it back, as everything else in life may be traced back, to very humble origins ; but all the great religions of the world reach out towards, though they do not all affirm, the belief in a single ruling power, and, moreover, rest upon some experience which is interpreted as communion with that power. This experience in itself may carry absolute conviction to the mind of the individual or group to whom it comes. When, moreover, it is found that the Being with whom men believe themselves to have communion is such as would supply completion to the fabric of philosophy, the whole weight of reason seems to be on the side of affirming the reality of that Being. Science, Art and Morals seem to require for their own completion, and for their unity with one another, the existence of God ; and there are men in almost every part of the world and almost every period of history who believe themselves to have had direct experience of communion with God. Religious experience, therefore, confirms and is confirmed by the whole tendency of philosophy.

Philosophy by itself only shows that God must exist if the world is to be perfectly reasonable ; it can never refute ultimate scepticism ; it can only say that the being of God is the ground of the possibility of all certainty. The sceptic, who is content to deny the possibility of certainty, remains irrefutable so long as he does not argue, though, no doubt, if once he argues he is assuming the validity of his argument, and through that the rationality of the world and the being of God which is essential thereto. Similarly, religious experience by itself proves nothing ; it may be the mere projection from the soul of that for which the soul

so intensely longs ; self-hypnotism may be conceived
to account for its whole range, more especially inasmuch as it is in groups that men are most susceptible
to this experience, and it is then, too, that self-hypnotism
most easily takes place.    But when the two are found
supporting one another the ground for belief would
seem to become almost complete.

But still not quite complete ; and the failure is of a
kind to threaten the whole structure with utter ruin.
For both the philosophical argument and the religious
experience affirm the goodness of God.    If He is merely
omnipotent Will without goodness, He may indeed be
supposed to account for the mere existence of the
world, but He does not satisfy the demands of mind as
expressed in morals, and the universe is left unreasonable just at that point where unreasonableness is most
intolerable.    And yet, in view of the world's history,
how can it be affirmed that the ruling power is good ?
The problem of evil, the great religious problem, the
only problem which prevents men on any large scale
from rising to faith if their nature otherwise desires
to do so, threatens the whole fabric which the mind of
man builds up.    For Religion, like Science, Art and
Morals, is fundamentally an attitude of the human
mind or soul, and Religion, unless it has some other
basis than even the combined witness of philosophy and
its own experience, may be turned to sheer scepticism
by the fact of the world's evil.    This does not mean
only the fact of human sin, for there was evil in the
world before moral choice emerged, and what we call
sin, whether it be more than this or not, is at least in
part the evil that is in the universe as it passes into the
moral sphere.    No doubt, in becoming conscious of
good and evil, man also made the evil in his nature
worse, because from that time on it was something
realised and deliberate.    But it is not only in man that
it is found ; nature, too, is full of evil : " The whole
creation groaneth and travaileth in pain together."

# CHAPTER XX

## THE PROBLEM OF EVIL

"The religious mind . . . views the world as ruled by Divine Providence, and therefore correspondent with what it ought to be. But the harmony between the 'is' and the 'ought to be' is not torpid and rigidly stationary. Good, the final end of the world, has being only while it constantly produces itself."—HEGEL.

In Tragedy, as we saw, the main elements of the problem of evil are brought before us—the positive force of evil itself, the apparently irremediable deficiencies of certain forms of good, the hideous loss through which alone the purging out of evil is accomplished; and combined with this we have the sense, which the poet conveys in the secret manner of art and without any express statement, that the conflict is abundantly worth while; for Man is revealed in it as great and Goodness as triumphant.

But, as was said, the solution of the problem is felt, and not understood. The intellect is still perplexed. The tragedian gives us faith that the problem is soluble; he does not solve it. This faith is no doubt given by the very act of isolating the problem and revealing the facts from which it springs in their uttermost truth; but we have still the task of understanding scientifically what we artistically appreciate.

What, then, is the nature of the problem? When people ask dismally about the problem of evil, what is it that perplexes them? Plainly no mere history of the emergence of evil would satisfy them, even if such a thing could be given. The problem lies in the realm of final, not of efficient, causes, as indeed is the case with every perplexity if our account of human knowledge is correct. The problem, therefore, is the hopelessly paradoxical nature of the question which we are bound to ask—What is the good of evil? We have agreed that in the end the explanation of everything is to be found, if anywhere, in the good Purpose of an Eternal Will; why does a good God either create or permit evil in His world?

One obvious solution is to be found in the denial of the Divine Omnipotence. It is urged that we may retain all that is of real value in that belief while still allowing that God made the world imperfect because He could not make it perfect. Dr. Rashdall, in his work, *The Theory of Good and Evil*, maintains the position that "whatsoever evil exists in the world must be supposed to exist because it is a necessary means to the greatest good that the nature of things makes possible," a view which I cordially adopt. But his further development of the theme does not altogether satisfy; he proceeds as follows:

But it will be said, in thus talking about the best possible, in justifying the world's existence because it is good on the whole, in speaking of evil as the condition of good, are we not limiting God? I answer: 'If Omnipotence is to be understood as ability to do anything that we choose to fancy, I do not assert God's Omnipotence.' I am content to say with sober divines like Bishop Butler that there may be some things which, with adequate knowledge, we should see to be as impossible as that God should change the past.[1] And if it be urged that the existence of conditions limiting the possibilities of the divine Will is inconsistent with the idea of a God who is infinite, I answer that neither Religion nor Morality nor, again, reasonable Philosophy have any interest in maintaining the infiniteness of God in the sense in which a certain tradition of the schools is accustomed to assert it. The limitation must not be conceived of as a limitation imposed by the existence of some other "being"—some other spirit or a "matter" with definite properties and an intractable nature of its own. The suggestion

---

[1] In what sense is this impossible? Cf. Chap. XIII.

that a limit necessarily springs from without is due to that ever-present source of metaphysical error, the abuse of spatial metaphor. The limitations must be conceived as part of the ultimate nature of things. All that really exists must have some limits to its existence; space and time are unlimited or infinite just because they are not real existences. And the ultimate nature of things means, for the Idealist, the nature of God. All that we are concerned with from the ethical point of view is that God should be regarded as willing a Universe that is the best that seems possible to a Mind to whom all the possibilities of things are known, and who wills the existence of all that is actual because he knows it to be best.[1]

Thus it is urged that ethics is in no need of a strictly Almighty God to make its injunctions rational, but of a God who is good and is the supreme power of the actual world; His power is regarded as limited—not by anything external to Himself but simply because there is so much of it and no more. And we may agree that, if we are driven to choose between the Infinite Power and the Infinite Goodness of the Eternal and Omniscient Spirit, it is no prejudice that leads us to choose the latter; the wish may be father to the thought, but the thought can quite well maintain itself independently on logical grounds. As Dr. Rashdall argues later on—

"It may be impossible to prove—even in the sense in which any metaphysical truth is capable of proof—that that ultimate reason " (sc. why greater good should not be attainable) " is not to be sought in a defect of goodness in the Being from whom all reality is derived. But the dilemma forces itself upon us that the explanation must be sought either in such a moral limitation or in some other kind of limitation—a limitation which, in the doubtless inadequate and analogical language which we are always compelled to use in speaking of ultimate Reality, may be described as a limitation of Power. To adopt the former alternative would involve the strange idea that the Being from whom all our ideas are derived, and who cannot reasonably be thought of as subject to the limitations which are connected with the life of the bodily organism, deliberately acts in a way contrary to the dictates of His own thought, to

---

[1] *The Theory of Good and Evil*, vol. ii. pp. 237, 238.

judgments which present themselves to him as necessary truths : the latter view has nothing against it but a groundless assumption." [1]

Whatever objection may be raised on theoretical grounds to this position, it is at any rate immeasurably superior, alike on theoretical and practical grounds, to the doctrine that evil can be dismissed as an illusion or reduced to unimportance by the application of negative terms. The position of Dr. Rashdall recognises the reality of evil ; the importance, even from an ultimate point of view, of our action in regard to it ; and the certainty that victory will in the end crown the efforts of Good. Many theories that claim to be more optimistic are in effect a disguised pessimism ; I do not see how Mr. Bradley's treatment of the subject can escape from this charge. " Heaven's design, if we may speak so, can realise itself as effectively in ' Catiline or Borgia ' as in the scrupulous or innocent. For the higher end is super-moral. . . . The discord as such disappears if the harmony is made wide enough." [2] Or again " since in ultimate Reality all existence, and all thought and feeling, become one, we may even say that every feature in the universe is thus absolutely good." [3] It is essential to optimism of this type that the final harmony is only realised at a level " higher " than that of the finite self, so that the very doctrine which proclaims the illusoriness of evil from the Absolute's point of view proclaims in the same act the irredeemableness of evil for every finite self. The good which is thus characteristic of the Real, is none the less itself eternally unrealised by man, who is condemned for ever not only to incompleteness but to error, pain, and, apparently, sin, that the Absolute experience may " enriched." How even this can be the result is a question which gives rise to some perplexity if, as Mr. Bradley has lately maintained, "The Universe is nowhere but in the lives of the individuals, and . . . the

---

[1] *Op. cit.* pp. 287, 288.  [2] *Appearance and Reality*, p. 202.  [3] *Op. cit.* p. 412.

Universe realises itself not at all except in their differences." [1]    At any rate it seems quite clear that on this theory human experience is necessarily and permanently afflicted with evil, and the problem is solved, even for the Absolute, not by the overcoming of evil with good but by the transcendence of the distinction between good and evil.    The verdicts not only of the Moral Consciousness, but of all our value judgments are quashed in that higher court.    But if so, the whole scheme becomes not only pessimistic but irrational. We have seen that for us value is the highest of all categories ; [2] only in terms of value can a satisfactory explanation of any fact be given, for the Good is our only self-explanatory notion ; [3] and moreover knowledge itself can only be acquired by serious effort which must be " vitalised by a general will to know " [4] —so that it is only as being good that knowledge is either sought or brought into being.    The good is, logically, [5] the presupposition of knowledge and of fact ; it is above being and beyond knowledge, as Plato maintained, since it is the common source of both.    Consequently to allow it to be " merged " or " transcended " is to arrive at a conclusion that contradicts its own premise.    This type of Absolutism not only deadens moral effort ; this might not be important as an objection to the theory, for we are told that the theory itself condemns the application of ultimate truth to practical questions ; but the doctrine is found to be internally defective, for it pronounces irrational the impulse that gave it (or any other doctrine) birth, and it explains away the only principle by which anything is explicable. [6]

[1] *Mind*, N.S. No. 62, p. 176, cf. p. 179 :  "I do not believe in any reality outside, and apart from the totality of finite mind."

[2] Mr. Bradley also seems to hold this (*Mind*, N.S. No. 60, p. 472), but it is hard to reconcile with his treatment of value-terms elsewhere.

[3] See Book I. Chap. IX. pp. 88, 89, cf. p. 177.

[4] Bosanquet, *Knowledge and Reality*, p. 35.

[5] Or, if we may coin a word on the analogy of Metageometry, "metalogically."

[6] In the closing chapter of this book I hope to indicate what I conceive to be the truth underlying this type of Absolutism.

Yet if we refuse to adopt a theory of the "transcendence" of good and evil in the Absolute, are we not driven back upon the denial of Divine Omnipotence in its strict sense? For whatever objections are valid against a "transcendence" theory are still more fatal to any view of the ultimate unreality of evil. It plainly does not make matters any better to call evil negative names; it may or may not be true to say "Evil is a negative, not a positive term. It denotes the absence rather than the presence of something. It is the perceived privation of good; the shadow where the light ought to be. 'The devil is a Vacuum.' . . . Good is being and evil is not being. . . . It is not a thing in itself; it is only the perceived privation of what you know to be good."[1] This leaves us where we were; for our whole problem is, Why is there a shadow where the light ought to be? If evil is a "perceived privation," there is no reason to call it "*only* a perceived privation"; for the perceived privation is just as bad as the "thing in itself," being indeed another name, whether more accurate or not, for the same experience.

It may be worth while to point out at this stage that evil cannot be regarded as a necessary consequence of the very existence of finite spirits. Of course it is true that inasmuch as I am finite I am not infinite; that, being a part, I am not the whole. But if all the parts fitted harmoniously together, there would be no evil; each would be imperfect as against the whole, but perfect in its own relations. Our problem is not that the parts are only parts, but that they refuse to regard themselves as parts (or at any rate as the parts which they are) and enter into mutual hostility. Evil cannot be accounted for on the mere ground of finitude any more than it can be dismissed as a mere negation.

We seem, then, driven to a denial of Divine Omnipotence. And yet it may be that this is due to the

---

[1] Rev. R. J. Campbell, *The New Theology*, pp. 43, 45. But this book no longer represents its author's views.

abstract way in which we have been treating the subject. We have been speaking of Good and Evil as if they were terms with meanings quite intelligible apart from our actual experience of the world. Moreover, it is questionable whether any precise meaning can be attached to the notion of the finitude of the Universe ; its infinity may not be any more intelligible (though I believe that it is), but in that case we must refrain from making deductions from our ignorance. We are told that " the suggestion that a limit necessarily springs from without is due to that ever-present source of metaphysical error—the abuse of spatial metaphor." But the question arises whether the category of Quantity can reasonably be applied to the Whole or to the Principle of the Whole. What is really meant by saying that the Power of the Creator is so much and no more, if, in fact, it originates and controls all that exists? The All or the governing principle of the All may be improperly described as infinite ; but it does not on that account become " finite." It must be the self-explanatory ground of all finite beings ; and only the Good is self-explanatory. To speak of it as " limited " without showing grounds in its very Goodness for the limitations is to destroy its self-explanatory character, at least so far as these limitations are concerned ; indeed, if Goodness is the only ground of existence, the distinction of Goodness and Power in God is only " provisionally " justifiable.

But if we take this view, it will be incumbent upon us to show that Evil is a necessary means to the greatest good that the nature—not of things, but—of Good itself makes possible.

Here we must remind ourselves of the dual nature of the problem. We have to deal with positive evil, symbolised by Iago, and with the ineradicable faults of certain specific forms of goodness, symbolised by Hamlet, Othello, or Cordelia. The former, though difficult enough, is the simpler of the two.

As soon as we consider the term Good in its concrete forms it is apparent that many of them owe part of their excellence to the difficulty of attaining them. We do, as a fact, value more highly what costs us trouble. I see no reason to regard this as a negligible freak ; it is an element in the value of things as we experience it. And further, one of the most conspicuous forms of good is Victory. A world in which there was no victory would be, so far, an inferior world. But if there is to be victory, there must be opposition. To demand the good of victory without the existence of an antagonist is to demand something with no meaning. It is no limitation of the divine power to say that it could not give us the good of Victory without any antagonist, for this good is not a real or possible entity ; the words are strictly meaningless. For Victory is not a result of overcoming, it is the overcoming ; and its good is not a result of it, but it is itself a form of good. We are not speaking of any subsequent enjoyment, but of the essential excellence of Victory itself, and particularly of moral Victory. If, then, this form of good is to exist, the nature, not of "things," but of good in this form requires the antagonist.

But it may still be urged that the evil over which the victory is won is also real, and thus, when the whole process is considered, the nett result is at best neutral. Certainly the evil is real ; but I maintain that there are cases where, the evil being overcome, the good of the victory preponderates, and the world is better on the whole than if there had been no evil. I can see no way of avoiding dogmatism at this point. Our value judgments, when they are concerned with intrinsic good or evil, and not with utility, proceed from our character and not from argument. A change of character will alter the objects which one pronounces excellent ; but short of that, each man's value-judgments are for him final. Without further argument, therefore, I submit the view that evil overcome by good is often justified.

It will be seen that according to this theory the ultimate solution of the problem of evil in its details is to be found not in thought but in action. We have found a principle which may supply the formal justification of the existence of Evil in general ; but the evil as it exists is only justified when every given case of it has been forced to yield up the good that is obtainable through its destruction. Evil does not appear good from a higher point of view, while yet remaining evil (whether in appearance or reality) for us ; but precisely for those who feel its badness it is found, at least occasionally, to be a necessary means to a good that they wring out of it by overcoming and destroying it. At the end of the tragedy evil has served to enhance the excellence of good and is itself utterly purged out; the sacrifice involved is a problem which will engage our attention later. But we have already seen that the value of a past event may be entirely reversed by its future context.[1]

It is, of course, manifest that Victory is only good when Goodness wins the Victory. It is not suggested that there is no absolute Goodness ; rather the existence of such Goodness is required by our whole argument. What is contended is that such Goodness when it is attained by a struggle, and still more, when it maintains and reproduces itself through struggle, wins thereby an added excellence. And, in particular, it will be suggested that Love is in itself the best form of Good, and is never so true to its own character, never so much itself, as when it breaks down apathy and hostility by its own self-devotion and wins responding Love. There may be some forms of Good which involve no struggle, and these may even be among the highest forms. All that is required for the argument is that there is a

---

[1] Cf. Chapter XIII. pp. 172-174 ; especially the words : " The point is that they (the past evil states) do not cease to be evil, but their very evil becomes an element in good."

particular type of Good—the Victory of what is itself
independently Good—whose existence depends on the
existence of an antagonist.

The question at once arises—what is to happen
when the process of conquering evil is complete ? To
which the answer is that there is no reason in the nature
of things why it should ever be complete. We have seen
that the Good, as the only self-explanatory principle
we have, must be taken as the ground of all existence ;
and our problem is to find some way of understanding
this without flying in the face either of plain facts or of
the moral consciousness. Now if Reality be taken as
timeless this is clearly impossible ; without real progress
we must either say that our moral judgments concern
mere appearance and are irrelevant to ultimate Reality,
or else that ultimate Reality is, to put it mildly, imperfect. But if Reality be taken as temporal, it must
either have a beginning and end or not ; and as the
former is meaningless, seeing that it involves the
impossible notion of empty time, we seem committed
to the infinite series. To such a series there are
two main objections : (1) that it involves complete Indeterminism ; (2) that it makes the idea of progress
unmeaning. Let us take these two objections separately.

(1) The first objection refers to the apparent need
of a beginning for the series. It is urged that if the
series is infinite, then, though every part may be linked
to every other part, the whole at any rate is indeterminate. But this argument can be satisfied only by
the positing of a First Cause, which is after all itself
undetermined. But if the whole be regarded as the
gradual realisation of a Purpose, it becomes not undetermined but self-determined, which is, by the nature
of the case, the only sort of determination that can
possibly affect it. Now if Good is our supreme principle, the world must be the realisation of Purpose ;
and if Victory is to be included in that Good (and
otherwise it is a defective good), the realisation must

be gradual.    Still we are inclined to insist that it must
have had a beginning ; but there is no necessity.    If,
as the doctrine of evolution suggests, the world has
developed hitherto by the perpetual generation of new
qualities and capacities, I see nothing self-contradictory
in the notion of an infinite regress.    The musician may
introduce a new theme when the development of those
already introduced approaches completion, and the new
combination thus affected supplies the material for new
developments.    So the world apparently generates perpetually new qualities and thus gives rise to new
problems.    Or we may look at the matter from the
side of analysis instead of construction.    No limit can
be set to the course of analysis.    Wherever we stop in
the analysis we find related individuals, and each of
those individuals admits of further analysis, which will
in turn result in the discovery of other related individuals.    It is, of course, quite impossible to *imagine*
an infinite regress, but it is, I think, not impossible to
*conceive* it, though it is true that a concept for which
no adequate percept or image is forthcoming can never
be fully appropriated by the mind, and carries with it
a sense of strain and a suggestion of unreality.    The
theological image for what I am trying to express is
the Eternal Generation of the Son or Divine Word ;
some will find that image too remote from our habit
of thought to be of any real use, but its meaning is
what we need to express.    In any case, our failure fully
to grasp the principle which requires the whole universe
for its full manifestation need not distress us ; the
utmost that we can do is to synthesise the elements
that constitute our own experience (taking care to make
that experience as wide as possible), knowing that this
synthesis, however inadequate to the whole of Reality,
may be true so far as it goes.    If, then, there is no
intrinsic self-contradiction in a self-determined process
with no beginning, we are not at liberty to reject it
*a priori* merely because we can find no image for it ;

and as the evidence points in this direction, we are bound to accept the conclusion which it suggests.

(2) The other objection to the infinite series concerns not its beginning but its end. It is maintained that all progress is judged by some goal and must come to an end when the goal is reached, so that to attribute a temporal character to Reality as a whole is to defeat one's own object, for the time of the whole must be infinite, and thus progress becomes impossible. Eternal progress is another name for unlimited failure. One is tempted to reply that so far the alternative is at least as bad, for a world statically perfect would be far less interesting and even less noble than the process towards it ; but that is no answer to the objection. The answer consists in the denial of the objector's major premise, which is that all progress is the approach to some goal. Need it be so ? Much progress is of that nature, but not all. And in the particular case of ethical development, progress seems to consist in the continually wider application of a principle that sets no limits to its own application. There is nothing self-contradictory in such a notion. The world may quite consistently be conceived as an entity consisting of elements which it is for ever harmonising and systematising, new elements being continually produced as the process reaches the completion of any one stage. Certainly, if we believe in immortality without pre-existence, we must regard at least the spiritual world in precisely this way ; for no element is lost, yet new ones perpetually come into being. And the doctrine of evolution suggests that such a growth has taken place in the past, new qualities and capacities perpetually emerging and introducing new problems both theoretical and practical. The harmony of the whole thus becomes perpetually richer in content, and there is no limit beyond which its wealth cannot increase. Thus we may conceive Evil as perishing in one form after another and yielding up that good which consists in the

Victory of Good which destroys it.  At every stage Good has an antagonist, and at every stage a new antagonist.  Each antagonist must perish, and in every epoch the struggle is at a higher level than before. Virtue at one time lay in utter devotion to the clan or tribe against all others ;[1] now such a "patriotism" may be positively vicious.  We cannot tell what problems will arise from the solution of those of our own day ; but they will be such as to recognise our achievement and at the same time give the basis for new triumphs.  Evil, in the general sense of opposition to Good, may never perish ; but every special form of evil perishes and the Progress is not illusory but real.[2] In the progress of the individual this principle has familiar illustration in the relation of the Pharisee to the Publican, or again in the deadly sin of spiritual pride to which men only become liable as they rise above the ordinary temptations of humanity.

Of course this does not prevent the struggle within any individual soul from reaching its completion.  But the spirits of just men made perfect may be engaged in the warfare against that spiritual wickedness from which they themselves are for ever become free.

It is incumbent upon any one who adopts such a view as this to justify it with reference to the main types of evil ; for though the precise good that is made possible by any given case of evil can only be known in detail by the actual conquest and destruction. of that evil, it must be true, if Good is the supreme principle, that every essential form of evil has its peculiar utility.  Of such forms there are, I think, three —Intellectual Evil or Error, Emotional Evil or Suffering, Moral Evil or Sin.

Error appears always to consist in unwarrantable

---

[1] Cf. The Song of Deborah.

[2] I am fain to hope that such an infinite progression fulfils the conception of the "true infinite," which "consists in being at home with itself in its other, or, if enunciated as a process, in coming to itself in its other" (Hegel, *Logic*, § 94, Wallace).

T

synthesis ; it is a thinking what is not, or what is other than, the supposed and intended object of thought.[1] It is a disregard of the negative element in things, of their difference from one another. It is a mis-taking one thing for another. So long as we only analyse the content of our experience we cannot err ; error is only possible in synthesis, in the assertion of the identity of different objects. The people who thought the sun was a living god were (in all probability) wrong ; the man who said it was a red-hot stone was perhaps in a sense nearer the truth ; a man who contents himself with saying it is a source of heat is quite right as far as he goes, though there may be truths about the sun— æsthetic or perhaps religious truths—which he ignores. He contents himself with analysis, and is in no danger of his judgments becoming either erroneous or interesting. Even in cases where the error immediately arises from a wrong insistence on difference, it may be shown that this itself rests on a presupposed but unwarrantable synthesis. Thus, for example, the objector to Plato's scheme for giving men and women the same occupations pleads that the difference of their sex will require that they have different occupations ; and the answer is that the difference of sex is not relevant, that is to say, that the distinction was pressed only in virtue of the unwarrantable generalisation—" All differences in the agent are relevant to his appropriate action." Thus the root of the error was not analytic or due to emphasis of distinctions, but was a failure to distinguish between relevant and irrelevant differences.

This is, after all, only a cumbrous way of stating the old rule : when involved in contradiction, make a distinction. But if error creeps in through the synthetic activity of our minds, and only so, then it is part and parcel of the experimental character of our lives. And this feature seems to me wholly good. A great deal

---

[1] Plato, *Sophist*, 254-258. Hegel, *Logic*, § 80 (Wallace) : " Knowledge begins by apprehending existing objects in their specific difference."

of the interest in life is due to the fact that we never know " whether shall prosper, either this or that, or whether they both shall be alike good." There is an element of adventure in all our generalisations, and the life of the intellect derives much of its stimulus from that fact. If all our intellectual experiments at once succeeded, this interest would vanish. Hence it is good that some of them should fail. Error is an element in the very goodness of the search for truth.

But error involves another difficulty, which is stated with great clearness by Mr. Joachim.[1] If our philosophy leads us to believe in an Omniscient Spirit, we seem to be involved at once in a contradiction. For while this Spirit may know the errors of finite minds as facts, He cannot Himself experience error at all ; for it is of the essence of error that it claims to be true. Doubt is not in itself error ; nor is partial knowledge error unless the man who has it supposes that his knowledge is complete. Hence we seem to be involved in the paradox that an Omniscient Being, just because He is omniscient, is incapable of knowing fully one of the real facts in the world.

To deal with this difficulty adequately, it would be necessary to discuss the whole series of arguments on which belief in an Omniscient Being rests. But if we adopt the position on which the whole of this argument is based we shall be led, I think, to quite definite conclusions. That assumption is that in Purpose, or the Good, we have a self-explanatory principle ; that there is no other such principle in our experience ; and that we are therefore called upon to employ that principle as our clue to the explanation of the world.

Now Good, as we know it, is nowhere so manifest as in personal affection and love. Love is only possible if there are more persons than one ; hence we see the necessity of a plurality of spirits. But the Good must be willed, if it is to be realised, and must be good for

---

[1] *Nature of Truth*, ch. iv.

somebody in order to be good at all. And the Good
of the whole is not and cannot be the object of a finite
will, or (if you like) of the will of a person whose
intelligence is finite. Unless, then, our plurality of
spirits is to involve chaos, we need to believe in one
Will from which all things are derived. The method
of the world's creation and history—the Divine Word
—is just the method of the realisation of the Purpose
of that one Will. But again, in order that there may
be Love, this Will cannot be the sole and immediate
power which effects all that happens. The finite wills
which proceed from it must not be absorbed into it.
Yet if they remain independent, how can all be due
to the one creative Will ? We seem driven to choose
between an Absolutism which destroys personality, and
a pluralism which implies intellectual chaos.

But the alternative is not exhaustive, and is only
suggested by the ease with which our thinking slips
into the mechanical category. When we consider the
normal action of one will upon another, we find that
the latter is in no way paralysed or annihilated. In
cases of hypnotism this may take place, but not where
one person responds to the greatness or goodness of
another and takes that other's purpose as his own.
When St. Paul says " Not I, but Christ liveth in me,"
or again, " The love of Christ constraineth us," he does
not mean that, much against his will, he is forced to
certain actions ; he acts freely, but his choice is wholly
determined by the will of Christ because his own will
has freely accepted Christ's purpose as his own.

Thus we are led to regard the spiritual world as a
society of individuals, each with his own capacities and
opportunities, and each responding at any one time in
his own degree (or not at all) to the influence of the
creative Spirit. Beyond this Society is a Volitional
Intelligence or Intelligent Will, to whom as Intelligence
the whole system of the Society and its components is
present, and from whom as Will it all proceeds. In

one sense, therefore, there is an irreducible plurality—
for as a centre of consciousness each is himself and no
one else ; but in another sense there is a perfect unity,
for all is the operation of a single Purpose, originating
in a single Will, however many may be the wills
through which it is effected.

Two of the many difficulties in this view must be
met. Is the relation of God to the individual just that
of two individuals to each other? In one sense—yes.
There is the otherness involved in the fact that there
are two centres of consciousness and not one. But in
another sense—no. For I do not derive my whole
existence from other individuals, as I do from God.
In one sense a father is a member of the family ; but
the relation between my brother and myself is not the
same as that between each of us and our father. But
our entire being is not wholly dependent on our parents,
whereas it is wholly dependent upon God, who thus
alone realises the ideal conception of Fatherhood, and
of whom it may therefore be said that "of Him all
Fatherhood in heaven and earth is named." [1]

The contradiction, therefore, in which the fact of
error threatened to involve us is not inevitable. The
unity of the world, as rooted in the Divine Will, does
not repudiate but rather demands the plurality of
spirits ; and the Divine Omniscience, not being regarded
as an all-inclusive experience, need not be conceived as
suffering itself the error which it yet knows to be the
condition of finite minds. These difficulties arose from
the tendency of our thought to revert from the category
of subject to that of substance ; [2] they can be avoided
by a consideration of the relation of subject to subject,
of Person to Person, as that is revealed in our actual
experience.

Error, then, may be regarded as the symptom of the
adventurous character of the intellectual life ; if it were

---

[1] Eph. iii. 15.
[2] Mr. Joachim's typical Monist is Spinoza.

impossible, that character would be gone ; if it were never actual, that character would be unperceived and therefore valueless. The justification of each particular error must be sought in the circumstances of its origin and the joy of its removal. But in general terms we may say that part of the real excellence of the life of reason depends, not accidentally but essentially, upon the existence of error.

When we pass to evil in the form of suffering the difficulty of the question is considerably increased ; not that the argument is complicated, but because there can be no hope of agreement until we arrive at far greater unanimity in our value-judgments on such subjects. I can only assert my own judgment that there are cases of suffering which, by drawing out real sympathy,[1] such as is effective in overcoming the suffering, are justified ; the existence of the suffering and the sympathy together is better than the absence of both. The sympathy takes the pain into itself and makes it an element in its own good. It is true that the average tolerably selfish man can only be roused to real sympathy by the sight of real pain ;[2] but that is not the point I wish to empha- sise, for it seems that so far the dependence of the sympathy on the suffering is accidental. But there is a peculiar quality about sympathy of this kind which *consists* in the nature of its object, and it is a quality of supreme excellence. Pain, coupled with fortitude in its endurance, especially when this is inspired by love, and meeting the full sympathy which at first lightens it and at last destroys it by removal of its grounds, is some- times the condition of what is best in human life. It is of no use to argue the point ; we think so or we do not ; what may be of use is to present the true fact as far as possible in such a way as to show its real value instead of stating it in the colourless language of prose, which, because it stimulates no emotions, leaves us at

---

[1] I mean, of course, what Mr. McDougall calls " Sympathy in the fullest sense of the word " (*Social Psychology*, p. 173).
[2] Cf. Browning, " Ferishtah's Fancies : Mihrab Shah."

the mercy of the hedonism which besets every man
when his imagination is vacant or slack.

When God formed in the hollow of His hand
This ball of Earth among His other balls,
And set it in the shining firmament
Between the greater and the lesser lights,
He chose it for the Star of Suffering.

I think, when God looks down the ranks of Heaven,
And sees them, not as we see, points of fire,
But as the animate spirits of the spheres,
He doth behold the Angel of the Earth,
Stretched like Prometheus on the promontory
(Upon the outermost verge of rocky seas
That sweep to shadow as they turn in Heaven,
Swept with the earth, but trembling towards the moon),
Bound to a perpetuity of pain,
Willing and strong, and finding in his pain
God, and his one unbroken note of praise
In the full rush of cosmic harmony.

    ·    ·    ·    ·    ·

For God has other words for other worlds,
But for this world the Word of God is Christ ;

    ·    ·    ·    ·

So that for ever since, in minds of men,
By some true instinct this life has survived
In a religious immemorial light,
Pre-eminent in one thing most of all :
The Man of Sorrows ;—and the Cross of Christ
Is more to us than all His miracles.

    ·    ·    ·    ·    ·

What better wouldst thou have when all is done ?
If any now were bidden rise and come
To either, would he pause to choose between
The rose-warm kisses of a waiting bride
In a shut silken chamber—or the thrill
Of the bared limbs, bound fast for martyrdom ? [1]

For all the anguish of the world there are three
consolations. The Epicurean says, "It is but for a
time; ere long we fall asleep in the unending
slumber"; which is comfort of a sort. The Stoic
says, "Rise above it all; to the wise these things are

---

[1] Mrs. Hamilton King, *The Disciples.*

nugatory"; which is no comfort at all if we are not wise. Christianity says, "Christ also suffered"; and that, with the Christian interpretation of "Christ," is real consolation, a human answer to our humanity.

If it be thought that I am illegitimately introducing, without warning, a vast amount of controversial matter, let me go back to the presentation of pain or grief as the great artists give it—not the great religious artists who give us the Virgin of Perugino's Crucifixion or the "Qui Tollis" and "Crucifixus" of Bach's great Mass, for here too the further controversial questions enter, —but as it appears in great Tragedy, or in Turner's *Fighting Temeraire*, or in the Adagio of a symphony:

> Grey memories that haunt us yet,
> Sorrow too deep to break in tears,
> When dauntless love has challenged fate
> And learns its doom too late, too late,
> Or time has buried in regret
> A hope that kindled earlier years—
> Sad, tearless eyes, my own were aching,
> Hearts that have broken, mine was breaking.[1]

The last couplet gives the key; the artist can reveal suffering as beautiful because he so reveals it as to make us sympathise. But what of all the sorrow that finds no sympathy; the sense of oppression, or of faculties that cannot be exercised; the agony of love that spends itself on others who receive it with indifference or hatred? Our solution does not touch such cases. All we can claim is that we have found a principle on which, where we can trace its operation, suffering becomes a necessary element in the full goodness of the world; that in some cases this principle can actually be traced; that in others its action must be assumed if we are to maintain the rationality of the world. This immense and most audacious assumption religion makes, discovering in the Love of God the justifying principle, and believing that in other worlds if not here that love is

---

[1] G. F. Bradby, *A Symphony of Beethoven.*

realised by every individual sufferer.   The assumption
is immense and audacious ; yet our choice is between it
and an unintelligible world, and it is not irrational to
make it.

Clearly this justification is only formal.   To justify
the actual sufferings of men we must seek them out
and extend our sympathy, spending ourselves in the
removal of pain and sorrow which are elements in the
good of the world precisely, but only, so far as they
are overcome.[1]   The theoretical and the practical are
not really two functions, but one, and it is not sensible
to give one a priority to the other.   Always our aim is
to systematise or harmonise experience ; sometimes the
mind does this by " thinking," sometimes by " acting " ;
to leave out any of the mind's functions will make it
incapable of the full apprehension of Reality.   The evil
we are considering is not a concept, but is the actual
pains and sorrows of men.   To make a harmony of
these, within the beneficent Purpose of God as so far
understood, involves not the concept of sympathy but
actual sympathising effort.   In the degree in which we
are capable of love we have the right to say to any who
in this world are in tribulation, " I have overcome the
world."

Perplexity seems especially to fasten on the suffering
which befalls the innocent and the noble.   But if once
we have escaped from the foolish notion that the only
justification of pain is when it balances moral evil in a
character possessed of moral evil, the suffering of the
innocent is the least difficult of all forms of suffering to
explain.   Pain as a discipline may be wholesome for the
evil ; sometimes it is the indispensable preliminary to
all reform.   But to a bad character it can never be of
more than negative advantage.   Its full value is only
seen when it is borne by a noble character which becomes
nobler in the bearing of it.   Such pain there is no

---

[1] " There is no general answer to the problem of evil, but a particular answer
whenever it is embraced as suffering and confessed as sin " (A. C. Turner in
Concerning Prayer, p. 382).

difficulty in attributing direct to God ; it is His last best gift, short of the perfect union with Himself, to many a noble soul. Christ in the Garden of the Agony prayed that the cup might pass from Him ; but after His prayer He knew that it was the Father's gift : " The cup that the Father hath given me, shall I not drink it ? " He Himself is chief among those who have been " made perfect through suffering." Pain may brutalise the coarse ; it is only the pure who are further purified by its influence. But, above all, Love is made perfect through suffering. Suffering is naturally a selfish state ; when we suffer we are full of ourselves, and want other people to think of us in pity and kindness. When in extreme suffering a soul still cares for others and gives itself to their service, it is rising to a pitch of love not elsewhere to be found nor otherwise attainable.

It may be urged that I have mentioned only to ignore the most apparent use of suffering, as the occasion of fortitude. But frankly I see little merit in fortitude as such. Merely to endure for endurance' sake is a barren virtue. Endurance as a form of moral discipline may be good as a means ; but no discipline is an end. The courage we really admire is that which endures suffering for a friend or for a cause ; and the " cause " can only be the good of men in some shape or other, so that devotion to a cause is only an indirect form of sympathy ; heroism is a part of love. It is true that in such cases the suffering is a consequence of sympathy, and not *vice versa* ; but it is still the sympathy or love, the devotion to the cause, that makes it good, and the peculiar qualities of this type of suffering must be discussed when we come to moral evil.

Midway between suffering or passive evil and sin or active evil stands what I have called the tragic fact— the conflict of right with right or the inherent defects of certain types of goodness, as represented in Sophocles'

*Antigone* or in the characters of Othello and Cordelia.
This apparent conflict within the nature of Good is
to me the hardest problem of all, for the fact seems
undeniable.    Situations do arise where the fulfilment
of one obligation involves the violation of another ;
duty to family and duty to the State may oppose each
other ; the follower of Christ must be ready to hate his
own father and mother.[1]    Yet this is merely part of
the mal-adjustment of the world ; if our morality is to
involve both effort and progress this problem must
arise.    For if the adjustment were already perfect and
complete there could be no progress ; and if it were in
process of realisation unopposed there would be no
effort.    But if we remove progress and effort we have
spoiled life.    The manifestation of the Divine Glory
in Christ's utter self-surrender is only possible if the
proclamation of the Gospel brings Him into conflict
with those who trust in what has hitherto been the
divine dispensation—and this is true not only of a
single epoch but of History as a whole.[2]

And in the same way with the great virtues ; they
carry with them an element of moral risk.    In almost
all circumstances the immense devotion of Othello is
good, but in the circumstances he had to meet it would
have been better, at first glance, to have it tempered
with sanity.    Yet only at first glance ; if we begin to
tamper with Othello on this side we shall spoil him.
But still we ask, why should Othello and Iago be
brought together ?    Why should the one demand be
made which the man's very virtue makes him powerless
to meet ?    There seems to be some malice implied in
the ruling Power of the world.    Here I confess to an
apparently insoluble perplexity ; but I suggest that
this combination of characters, being the most effective

---

[1] "Yea—and his own life also," which leaves the demand harsh, but rids it of
all excuse for cynicism.

[2] If Christ is the Logos, whatever is true of the essentials of His earthly life is
true of history as a whole ; but this, equally with the words above, anticipates an
argument not yet developed.

for the construction of great tragedy, is such as to elicit sympathy of peculiar value. Drama is not real life but a portrayal of it, and the aim of a drama is that it may be performed before an audience, and its merit must lie in the effect produced on them ; it appears that in the arousing of the great sympathetic emotions of pity and tragic fear this type of evil is especially potent. But we also saw that where tragedy reaches its greatest heights it becomes permissible and desirable to introduce a hint of a further reconciliation beyond what the play reveals—as in *Hamlet* and *King Lear*. That there is a great value in the sympathy called out by the tragic fact is undeniable ; that it counterbalances the evil which tragedy isolates and presents I could not assert ; we must leave it to find ultimate justification, if at all, in " the undiscovered country."

Hitherto we have not come into contact with positive moral evil. The forms of evil which we have considered affect our personal and individual feelings, and the discussion may on that account have seemed hedonistic, even in the justification of pain. The evil lay in the feeling, and in feeling, therefore, the justifying principle had to be sought ; and the pursuit of good feelings is hedonist. But now we pass on to the region where hedonism is out of the question ; for the acutest form of our problem still remains.

Throughout this discussion we have been constructing our conception of God in the image of Man, as all religion, and pre-eminently Christianity, requires us to do. But this is only justifiable if Man is created in the image of God ; and how can this be asserted in the face of human sin ? The wonderful myth with which the Bible opens, profound as it is in many ways, gives no help here ; it simply puts the creation of man in the Divine likeness and the rebellion of man against God side by side ; man by disobedience obtained knowledge of good and evil ; he discovered the moral law by running

against it and suffering its reaction.   So by falling into
sin he rose from mere innocence to the possibility of
virtue.   This is illuminating indeed.   But it still leaves
us unillumined as to the justification of sin either from
the Divine standpoint or from the human.   If man
became self-conscious, the evil in him must become
deliberate until he had been purged of it.   But why
was it there at all ?

What is the essence of sin ?   All the actions which
make up its particular manifestations are the satisfaction
of impulses which have a true place in the economy of
life and can be morally exercised.   But as all morality
consists in the recognition of the claims of other spirits
whether Divine or human, so does all sin consist in
the ignoring or repudiation of those claims.   There
are, as Plato saw, three relations in which we may stand
to other men, and only three : we may ignore them ;
we may set ourselves against them ; we may recognise
them as forming with us one corporate whole.[1]   Indifference, hostility, and fellowship are the only primary
relations that are possible between one man and another ;
and the former two, except as regulated by the last, are
immoral.   The essence of sin is self-will.   By Pride
Satan fell in the myth, and the myth is right.   Of the
forms of self-will, complete indifference to other people
is the worst.   Hatred at least recognises the other
person as being of importance, and in essence, as well
as by our psychological tendencies, is nearer to the
moral relation with its culmination in love than is
indifference.

But if sin is essentially Self-will in one or other of
these forms, why is there Self-will ?   And I answer
quite confidently : because Love is never so completely
itself as when it enters on complete self-surrender to
conquer the indifferent or the hostile and succeeds.
This is not due to any accident.   Love is not only a
motive to self-surrender, but rather, as Nettleship said,

[1] $\epsilon\pi\iota\theta\upsilon\mu\iota\alpha$ : $\theta\upsilon\mu\delta$ς : τὸ λογιστικόν.

" Love is the consciousness of survival in the act of
self-surrender." [1]    The fact that there is more joy over
one sinner that repenteth than over ninety and nine
just persons who need no repentance is based upon the
further fact that love perfects itself by the conquest
of hostility through self-surrender.    "God commendeth
His love towards us in that while we were yet sinners
Christ died for the ungodly."    So far forth as the
self-surrender of love is made absolute, love becomes
completely itself and supremely excellent.    And so St.
John's Gospel brings the embodiment of the Divine
Character and Method to the threshold of His Passion
with these words upon His lips, " Father, the hour is
come ; glorify thy Son, that thy Son also may glorify
thee. . . . And now, O Father, glorify thou me with
thine own self with the glory which I had with thee
before the world was." [2]    All that prayer refers to the
approaching sacrifice ; the full manifestation of God's
glory is the Cross.    When the self-surrender is complete,
the manifestation of the eternal glory and excellency of
God is complete also.    But the self-surrender cannot
be complete if there is not the utmost opposition that
can be quelled.    Love whose return is achieved by
struggle is better than spontaneous affection, not
accidentally but essentially ; for the specific ardour of
the struggle enters into the fibre of the love itself.    In
fact a sinful world redeemed by the agony of Love's
complete self-sacrifice is a better world, by the only
standards of excellence we have, than a world that
had never sinned.    " O felix culpa, quae tantum et talem
meruit habere redemptorem ! "

This position is not unlike St. Paul's, and is open at
first sight to the same retort.    "Shall we then continue
in sin that grace may abound ? " [3]    St. Paul answers in
effect that if we are in such a state as to cause grace to
abound, we are in a state where the suggested course

---

[1] R. L. Nettleship, *Philosophical Remains*, p. 41 (" The Atonement ").
[2] St. John xvii. 1, 5.                    [3] Rom. vi. 1.

of action is psychologically impossible. "How shall we, that are dead to sin, live any longer therein?" If we really desire grace to abound, we cannot continue in sin. The two states cannot co-exist in the same will. For we are not dealing with actions, but with volitional states. Sin is not the doing of this or that, but is self-will. And the man whose heart is won to return the love that is lavished on him cannot say, "And now, for the fuller victory of that love, I will harden myself against it." We cannot hate a man precisely on the ground of loving him. But so far as our hearts are not yet won, so far we are self-willed and do not need to be made so. Our ordinary morality does not indeed depend upon a love of God ; but it does depend on a relation to other men the nature of which is only clearly manifest in love of men ; and a morality which is finally and universally secure can only be attained through a love of God which answers His love for us. And of course it is only so far as self-will is conquered by love that it is justified as an element in the world's history. But when conquered it is justified. It may become good for me that I have sinned, that I may love God as my Redeemer ;[1] it may prove good for Him that I have sinned, that He may have the joy of my redemption. We postponed the justification of the suffering that is bravely borne because it is inspired by love ; but we have found it here.

It may, however, be objected that, while it is true that if or so far as my love has been won I cannot any longer be self-willed, yet this doctrine may be used by those who still resist as a justification for their resisting

---

[1] Cf. the well-known hymn :

> There's a song for little children
>   Above the bright blue sky,
> A song that will not weary
>   Though sung continually,
> A song which even angels
>   Can never, never sing ;
> They know not Christ as Saviour,
>   But worship Him as King.

the more steadfastly, or may lead those who follow God's will to commit deliberate acts of sin "that grace may abound." I admit a minute danger in the former case. People who want to obfuscate their consciences will seize on any means of doing it ; they will be acting quite logically, and I shall of course admit that they are preparing for a yet more splendid victory of Good than would be possible without their resistance. But those who regard this objection as really serious are involved in the worst form of the intellectualist fallacy. We are not discussing the doing or refraining from certain actions, but the possession or not-possession of love. Nor can the plea that we should deliberately sin to experience redemption be admitted. We are sinful without effort. The doctrine of Original Sin is strengthened, not weakened, by the thought that the "ape and tiger" have a hereditary place in our constitution. The "man" in us needs to be developed by the "humanity" of our environment. So far as we act morally without religious motives it is either for some selfish end—the advantages of being respected and liked—or because we recognise in our own wills the claims of others upon us. This recognition is not imparted by argument, and any one who likes to deny it is free, so far as I can see, from all danger of logical refutation. We recognise the claim of others on ourselves because we find it is expected of us ; the expectation acts as a suggestion, and we do what is suggested. We then find that it is a good thing to do ; but we are not led to it by argument. A man who has a moral sense cannot ignore it ; it is part of his nature as much as his instinctive impulses, and to ignore it or defy it is a sure method of failing to achieve satisfaction. But the moral sense is not deducible from elsewhere.

So it is with our immediate problem. There is no danger that a man will meet the love of God with apathy in order to increase the ultimate triumph of that love. We do not love men because we have been argued into a belief that they are lovable, or refuse to love them on the contrary ground. We love them, if at all, because we and they are we and they. And in the case of the Divine, " We love because He first loved us." To act wickedly because of our love for Him is as impossible as to harden our hearts against Him because of our love for Him. The eternal victory is eternally progressive. It is new triumph, not a perpetual repetition of the old, that brings joy in heaven. The sinner that repents is in a state of progress ; the " just person " is stationary ; a man who deliberately resumed sinful habits would be retrograde. Our theory cannot, as is sometimes suggested, lead men to commit sin because of their love to God. In this case, as in the other, " we that are dead to sin " cannot live any longer therein.

But our love must be drawn out by His love for us. If we do not realise His love we neither do nor can love Him.[1] Love is not a commodity to be manufactured at pleasure. Our fundamental volitional attitude is the thing about us over which we have least control. As St. Paul and St. Augustine bitterly learnt, if we will to move our bodies they move ; but if we will to move our wills they remain unmoved. No doubt Augustine was right in his explanation : the effort of the will to move the will proves a division in the will itself ; when the will is wholly set on something it has no need to move itself. But that does not concern us now. Our wills move us ; but they themselves can only be moved, in the sense of " changed," by something other than themselves. " Who shall deliver me from this body of death ? " To seek the ideal we must first appreciate it. We can only strive to love what we already love in a feeble way or with part of our nature. We cannot will to love God if we

---

[1] Cf. McDougall, *Social Psychology*, p. 132 : "If tender emotion is the emotion of the parental instinct whose impulse is to protect, how can this emotion be evoked by the Divine Power? The answer to this question is : In the same way as the child's tender emotion towards the parent is evoked, namely by sympathy."

U

do not love Him ; and if we do, there is no need to
will, except for a deepening of the love. The issue
lies with Him, not with us. At His own time He will
call out from our hearts the response to His own love
by the full manifestation of it in its irresistible power.
So far as we have felt it, we prepare ourselves for a
fuller response ; so far as we trust those who tell us of
it, we prepare ourselves to respond when the time shall
come. But in the end the work is His. This experience
shows ; and this the doctrine of His omnipotence
requires. Pelagianism is Ethical Atheism. The work
is His ; yet we are not abolished or absorbed. It is
our hearts that love, but it is His love that draws our
hearts to Him. " The love of Christ constraineth us."
" We love, because He first loved us."

Thus all history appears as the method of the Divine
Love. That love requires beings whom it may love,
and requires their varying forms of evil for the perfecting of love. Inasmuch as it is love, it enters by
sympathy into all pain and sorrow, and spends itself
in the redemptive agony. Eternally it operates. From
the infinite past to the infinite future it continues its
course of irresistible victory ; at every stage there is
advance ; every epoch has its own determinate goal to
reach, and in reaching it finds that new problems arise.
The endless growth of the world provides for ever new
material on which love may exercise itself, and we
witness the continually wider application of a principle
to whose application no limit is set either by the
principle itself or by the nature of the subject-matter.
Yet the victory is that not of force but of tenderness,
and the Word of God which goes forth conquering and
to conquer must be first symbolised by the figure of a
Lamb as it had been slain.

So we can believe that the problem of evil finds
solution—for God, if God is Love, and for Man so far
as he is loving. Whether or not we regard such a view

as satisfying will depend on our own moral nature. What seems to us good is determined by our character.[1] If we are selfish, the world is for us the worst of all possible worlds ; but if we love, it is the best. That is why the Man who reveals the Divine Character and Glory as infinite self-sacrifice can be represented as saying, " No man can come to me except the Father which hath sent me draw him. . . . Ye neither know me nor my Father ; if ye had known me ye should have known my Father also. . . . If God were your Father ye would love me : for I proceeded forth and came from God ; neither came I of myself but He sent me. Why do ye not understand my speech ? Even because ye cannot hear my word. . . . He that hath seen me hath seen the Father." [2]

Yet what is the evidence for this immense assumption? We are to assume that all the futile struggles of the eliminated species, all the useless sordid misery, all the baseness and hardness of heart, find their justification in the eternal realm (for manifestly they do not find it here) ; and we are to assume that the character of the Cosmic Power, which can only be known through its work in history, is infinite love, though the world it has made is as selfish as it is loving, and has " progressed " by the savage way of competition and the struggle for existence ; and why? Because otherwise there is in the world an irrational and inexplicable element. Were it not better to accept that element at its face value, at the risk of scepticism, than to indulge in speculation such as this ? Some tell us they have experienced the Divine Love—but there is no limit to the fanaticism of men, and their superstitions are past all counting. Were not ultimate scepticism itself, if that be involved, more rational than a hypothesis which flouts experience in the interest of an *a priori* rationality ?

Yes, it may be so ; unless there is one fact ascertain-

---

[1] Τὸ φαινόμενον ἀγαθόν is determined by ἦθος.
[2] St. John vi. 44 ; viii. 19, 42, 43 ; xiv. 9.

able.    But if there has ever been a manifestation of love
on the scale required, and if the Supreme Power of the
Universe has been plainly co-operant in its redemptive
work, carrying the Spirit that displayed it through the
ultimate self-sacrifice that He might see of the travail
of His soul and be satisfied, then the theory we have
constructed is forced upon us by the facts as well as
by the demand of reason.    If the Gospel is a myth,
agnosticism is at least as scientific as faith ; but if Jesus
lived and died and rose again, then God must be His
Father.

NOTE.—As the position taken in this chapter is of paramount importance to the
subsequent argument, especially in Chapters XXIII. and XXVII., I venture to add
Dr. Bosanquet's eloquent statement of it in *The Principle of Individuality and Value*,
pp. 243-246 :—

"It is not an imperfection in the supreme being, but an essential of his completeness, that his nature, summing up that of Reality, should go out into its other to
seek the completion which in this case alone is absolutely found.    The 'other' in
question can only be finite experience ; and it is in and because of this, and qualified
by it, that the Divine nature maintains its infinity.    And, therefore, it may be said
that the general form of self-sacrifice—the fundamental logical structure of Reality
—is to be found here also, as everywhere.    Not, of course, that the infinite being
can lose and regain its perfection, but that the burden of the finite is inherently
a part or rather an instrument of the self-completion of the infinite.    The view
is familiar.    I can only plead that it loses all point if it is not taken in bitter
earnest. . . .

" The comparison of pleasure and pain in respect of quantity, even if we disregard
the difficulties pointed out in anti-Hedonist polemic, betrays an inorganic point of
view.    The question cannot surely be how many moments of pain you have
experienced, and whether you have had enough moments of pleasure, allowing for
the intensities on each side, to outweigh them, but whether the experience has done
its work, and returned you to yourself a complete or at least a completer being.
So, it would seem, the problem should be stated about the universe.    Not, if we
could reckon up moments of equal pleasure and pain (to simplify the question by
reducing it to a matter of counting) which of the two classes would be found to
outnumber the other, but rather, is there reason for thinking that pain and finiteness
are elements playing a definite part in the whole such that its completeness depends
upon containing them ?    Broadly speaking, I suggest, experience indicates that a
soul which has never known pain, like a nation which has never known war, has
no depth of being, and is not a personality at all.    Of course, this way of looking
at the matter does not by itself dispose of the suggestion that the cost even of
perfecting a soul may be too high ; but the conviction that there essentially must
be a certain cost corresponds to our best insight in the sphere of every day
experience."

# BOOK II

## GOD'S ACT

# CHAPTER XXI

## THE NEW START

The very God! Think, Abib; dost thou think?
So the All-great were the All-loving too.
So through the thunder comes a human voice
Saying, " O heart I made, a heart beats here ;
Face my hands fashioned, see it in Myself.
Thou hast no power nor mayst conceive of mine,
But love I gave thee, with Myself to love,
And thou must love Me who have died for thee."
BROWNING.

AT a particular time in the history of the world and at
a particular place upon its surface there was born a Child
who, though He corresponded to none of the anticipations, was recognised when grown to manhood as the
promised Messiah of Israel, and by men and women
who had shared His life was worshipped as Lord and
God. There is elsewhere no sort of parallel to this.
There were heroes who received Divine honours long
after their deaths, but these honours were not in any
way comparable to the worship offered by the Jew to
his God. To admit Heracles to the Greek Pantheon
was merely to add another to that list of superhuman,
but quite finite beings, to whom the worship of the
less reflective Greeks was directed. The same was
true of the deification of the Cæsars ; moreover the
Cæsars, though recognised as divine in this lower sense
of the word immediately after their deaths, and in
remoter provinces of the Empire during their lifetime,
had won that position by a combination of military and
political power which had literally controlled the world.

It is not so with the story of Jesus of Nazareth. In outward circumstances His life was humble and commonplace until the Ministry began. For thirty years He lived in obscurity ; for three years He moved about making His proclamation and gathering around Him a small band of intimate followers, who, towards the end at least, shared all His movements ; and it was these very men who came to regard Him, not as one among the host of Divine beings, but as the very God of Heaven and Earth.

The historical records both of His life, and of the transformation of His followers from a group of disciples about a Rabbi into the nucleus of the Catholic Church, have been the subject of more investigation than any other records which the world contains. It would be impertinent, therefore, for one who is not a specialist in the matter to give as part of such an argument as we are developing the views which he has formed concerning these records. But in general I would say this, though I know what I say is bound to be superlatively annoying to those who do not agree. The evidence seems to me to be just as good as it is desirable that it should be. If the evidence were complete and cogent, faith would become dependent upon intellectual proof and intellectual apprehension of the proof. It would thus lose a great deal of its spiritual quality and value. To believe that Christ is a revelation of God and wish that He were not, is a condition about as far from discipleship as anything that can well be imagined. Loyalty of heart is more important in the spiritual world than correct opinions, though no doubt it is true that correct opinions may foster loyalty of heart. For those who know their need of just such a revelation as this, the evidence is sufficient, for it shows that reason is on the side of the faith that such a man desires to accept.

What after all is the evidence broadly considered ? First and foremost comes the very existence of the

Church.    Somehow this society, with its perpetual
capacity for renewed life, apparently out of all relation
to the circumstances in which that renewal comes, must
be accounted for.    Something must have started it.
The books collected together in the New Testament
give a record such as is required to account for the
origin of this society.[1]    The evidence, were it not for
the uniqueness and inestimable import of what the
records state, would be amply sufficient to give historical
certainty so far as that is ever obtainable at all.    Man
rightly requires weightier evidence before believing
some otherwise unparalleled event than for accepting
the statement of some quite commonplace fact.
Similarly he demands weightier evidence before he
believes something which must affect his whole life
from beginning to end, than is required for the
acceptance of some proposition which will have no
influence upon his conduct.    It is right, therefore, that
such records as these should be subjected to the most
ruthless criticism ;  but that criticism must be strictly
impartial.    It must not begin with a bias either for or
against the acceptance of events which are unique, but
must simply and cold-bloodedly state what the evidence
actually is.    No historical evidence ever affords absolute
proof of the mathematical type, and our acceptance of
even well-attested facts depends to some extent upon
their harmony or discord with what we already believe ;
though of course in history, as in the other sciences,
a new fact may sometimes force acceptance of itself and
shatter the system of belief which tried to reject it.
In such a case the evidence for the new fact is weighed
against the grounds of the accepted belief ;  if it is
sufficient the accepted belief must go.

So it was, according to the record, with the actual
life of Christ in its effect upon contemporaries.    We
watch its actual effect upon the whole mental outlook

[1] My own view of the historic origin and value of the Gospels is given in *The
Faith and Modern Thought*, Lecture III.

of St. Paul. It did not fit into his previous scheme of things ; it shattered that scheme and forced him to construct a new one around itself. Our position, however, is the exact opposite. Where the whole general outlook seems to demand some fact not hitherto known, the mind will naturally tend to believe as true the record which affirms precisely such a fact. Astronomers were puzzled by the movements of Uranus, and concluded that there must be a planet, though no one had ever seen it, in a certain position. They turned their telescopes on to the point indicated by their conclusions, and there they found Neptune.

If the argument of this book is sound, the main constituent sciences of human philosophy present four converging lines which never meet. Philosophy is able to conceive in general the kind of fact which would constitute the point of their ultimate convergence. It is the historic Incarnation of God in a human life of Perfect Love, issuing in a society bound together by the power of that Love. The record of such a fact the mind must therefore welcome ; it could not have affirmed the necessity that such a fact should exist ; it could only affirm that the sole choice lay between its existence and an ultimate scepticism. But it finds in the New Testament evidence, which in these circumstances is sufficient, for the belief that God has wrought precisely what man needs.

At the time when Christ was born the wheel of history seemed to have come full circle and reached a standstill. The religion of Israel had worked itself out and settled down into the observance of legal minutiæ. Greek philosophy had worked itself out and in the moment of its finest bloom had been carried by Alexander the Great through Asia as far as India, through Syria, including Palestine, to Egypt. Roman politics had worked themselves out and settled down into the stagnation of the Empire. Progress seemed to be at an end. But the development of Israel's religion had made possible the understanding of Christ. Greek philosophy provided a vehicle for its intellectual state-ment, and the handing down of the tradition. The Roman Empire provided a world peace in which the Gospel had opportunity for establishing itself in men's minds without the disturbance of wars, or the question of national claims and allegiance over against those of the Catholic society. From one side previous history constituted a real preparation for Christ, but on another side His advent is a new start. The previous history of the world does not account for Him. Before turning, however, to consider the way in which the life of the Incarnate Word supplies philosophy with its most urgent need, we must look more particularly at two strands in that preparation.

Our method hitherto has been (I hope) philosophic ; from now onwards it will be theological. Hitherto we have moved towards the central unity by attempting to understand the world ; now we begin with the revelation which God has given of Himself, and claim that it supplies the unity which we seek, and thus interprets the world.

# CHAPTER XXII

## ISRAEL AND GREECE

" For ask now of the days which are past, which were before thee, since the day that God created man upon the earth, and from the one end of heaven unto the other, whether there hath been any such thing as this great thing is, or hath been heard like it ?   Did ever people hear the voice of God speaking out of the midst of the fire, as thou hast heard, and live ?   Or hath God assayed to go and take him a nation from the midst of another nation, by temptations, by signs, and by wonders, and by war, and by a mighty hand, and by a stretched-out arm, and by great terrors, according to all that Yahweh your God did for you in Egypt before your eyes ? "—DEUTERONOMY.

> Greece and her foundations are
> Built below the tide of war,
> Based on the crystalline sea
> Of thought and its eternity ;
> Her citizens, imperial spirits,
> Rule the present from the past,
> On all this world of men inherits
>     Their seal is set.
>                     SHELLEY.

OF the three great factors in the Preparation for Christ one need detain us but a moment.   The creation of the Roman Empire provided, as has been said, a wonderful opportunity for the spread of the Gospel, and formed a kind of shell within which the growth of the Church as an organised society might take place.   Very much of the Church's constitution, so far as concerns administration and the like, was taken over from the Roman Empire, and there is a true sense in which the Pope is a successor of the Cæsars.   But vital as the existence of the Empire was, its place and value are so easily perceived that no time need be spent in discussion of them.   It is otherwise with the preparation that takes place in Israel and in Ancient Greece.   In

order to understand what was happening in these
countries, we have to secure a new orientation of
thought.   The modern man is quite sure that if there
is a God at all there is only one, for the thought of
God has become so greatly deepened and extended that
it now excludes plurality ;  there can be only one
Supreme, only one Absolute.   But in the ancient world
the matter was otherwise ;  every one was sure that there
was a realm above the human, but the unity of God
was only reached through growth and struggle.

The Old Testament contains the record of how a
certain nation came to its faith in One Holy God.   For
understanding this record we must first of all remember
that it is written, in its present form at least, by men
who accept that faith, but that the story is to a great
extent concerned with people who did not accept it.
When sayings of the early Israelites are quoted they
often imply the existence of many gods ;  but the
editorial comments, so to speak, are all written under
the inspiration of faith in the One and Holy God.

It is moreover worth while to keep in mind the
religious condition of other peoples in the Mediterranean
basin during the same period, for this will help us to
appreciate the real meaning of the religion of Israel.
It is good to remember that throughout the history
of Rome down to Julius Cæsar there was a religious
official in the Imperial city called the " Flamen Dialis."
" He was forbidden to touch a cat, a dog, raw meat,
beans, ivy, wheat, leavened bread.   He might not walk
under a vine and his hair and nails might not be cut
with an iron knife.   He might not have any knot or
unbroken ring anywhere about him." [1]   The curious
condition of mind among the Romans is illustrated by
the fact that a young aristocrat of dissolute habits,
C. Valerius Flaccus, was in 209 appointed to this priesthood in the hope that its various taboos might be
helpful in the discipline of his character ;  and moreover

---

[1] Warde Fowler, *The Religious Experience of the Roman People*, p. 34.

the effort succeeded ; he became an eminently respectable citizen. Here you have at once so great a contempt for a priesthood that a profligate young man may be put into it, and yet so great a respect for its rules that under them his character is changed. The Latin word " Religio " does not stand for what we call religion, but simply for anxiety in the presence of the supernatural. The object of worship was to maintain the *pax deorum*. Gods and men inhabited the same city and the same house, and the peace between them was preserved as long as men rendered their dues. When things went wholly wrong, there was a great outburst of " Religio." Nearly every section in Livy's account of the war with Hannibal records such an outburst. On these occasions the one idea of the government was to find an outlet by means of which the excitement might work itself off without doing damage, and various devices largely borrowed from other countries were used for this purpose. In fact, Livy says, on one occasion, that there was so great an outburst of religion, and that too so forced in character, that either men or the gods seemed to have changed their nature.[1] One more celebrated instance of the Roman habit of mind may be recalled. When Cæsar as Consul was passing democratic laws, his aristocratic colleague tried to render the procedure void by sending repeated announcements that he was seeing lightning, at which announcement, according to religious rules, the assembly should have been dispersed. But men were outgrowing old superstitions, and Cæsar's refusal to take any notice did not cause the same sort of excitement as Flaminius, the first democratic Consul, when he set out to put himself at the head of an army without taking the auspices, an act of impiety for which his crushing defeat at Lake Trasimene had been regarded as punishment. These are illustrations of one side at least of the religion of Rome in the days

[1] Livy xxv. 1.

of her rise and attainment to greatness. They supply a standard by which we may estimate the extraordinary elevation of Old Testament religion.

In the religious history of Israel there are certain marked points. One is the call of Abraham and the revelation to him in Genesis xvii. 1, 2. Another is the further revelation to Moses recorded in Exodus iii. and vi., and the deliverance from Egypt which follows. Another is the emergence of the great prophets, teaching, as we shall see in a moment, a new doctrine concerning God. Yet another is the exile and return, and another again the development of Apocalypse. We may consider the significance of each of these in its place in the history.

It would appear that Abraham was brought to believe in what we may call natural monotheism ; but this is not made very clear. All we can say is that there was a recognisable identity between the God whom he worshipped and the Most High God of whom Melchisedek was Priest. In this period, however, the question concerning the relation of the God of Abraham to any other deities does not definitely arise. When Israel with his family went into Egypt, they came into contact with a highly developed civilisation and system of worship, and it would seem that there was a decided acceptance of the belief that each nation had its own god. Whether or not Moses believed this he seems to make use of it in his pleading with Pharaoh ; but of course there would be no doubt that the Egyptians would regard the God of Israel as an alien God.

The revelation to Moses marks a definite new stage, and puts the religion of Israel once and for all on a different footing from that of any other nation. Yahweh explicitly spoke to Moses, and joined to Himself the Israelites by a Covenant which He made with them. Yahweh was not a God of Israel alone ; He was apparently the God of Mount Sinai. Jethro, who was

a Midianite, was His priest.   He claims to be the God
of Abraham, Isaac, and Jacob, but explicitly states that
His name, or, as we should now say, His personality,
is revealed to Moses for the first time, at any rate in
the definiteness which the revelation now receives.[1]   To
people of that period Yahweh was of course one god
among others—a god who chose Israel for His people
and delivered them from Egypt ; that the Israelites
took such a view is made plain, for example, by the
story of Jephthah who recognises Chemosh as the
Moabite god in just the same sense as Yahweh is the
Israelites' God.[2]   The God of Israel is the one tribal
God for whom it has ever been claimed that He is
the only God of all the earth, and who has become
recognised, in proportion as his worshippers have truly
known Him, as indeed the One God.   To us looking
back with the subsequent history to help us, with the
prophetic revelation in our minds and everything that
has resulted from Greek thought into the bargain, the
matter must appear otherwise.   We shall rather say
that the One God of Heaven and Earth used the figure
of Yahweh the God of Sinai as the means of revealing Himself to a particular nation.   We may put
it if we like in this way : at first, Yahweh was a
tribal deity like Chemosh, a mere figment of man's
imagination in his search after the divine.   God
used this figure of the contemporary belief as the
medium for His revelation of Himself, and we can
partly understand why He did it.   No doubt the God
of Sinai was an austere deity to be worshipped with an
awful reverence and in complete detachment from all
licentious rites ; this the whole picture in the Book of
Exodus suggests.   It would have been of no use, even
on the intellectual side, to implant the conception of
One God, the Governor of Heaven and Earth, at that
stage, unless the whole course of human history and
the development of man was to be altered fundament-

---

[1] Exodus vi. 2, 3.                    [2] Judges xi. 23, 24.

ally. Only a few could possibly have risen to the
height of the conception, just as the philosophical
beliefs attained by Plato concerning God remained even
among the Greeks the property of a select few.

But there was a reason beyond this. Human life is
fundamentally social, and if the revelation of God is to
have in it redeeming power for human life, it must be
given to and in a divinely ordered society. Such a
society Israel was, or at any rate was capable of
becoming. Consequently the revelation must in the
first instance be to a nation rather than to mankind,
for mankind was not then, and indeed is not now, an
organic society. But there was always this difference
between the relation of Yahweh to Israel and that of
other tribal deities to their tribes : it was based upon
a Covenant. Chemosh belonged to Moab as much as
Moab belonged to Chemosh ; but with Israel this was
not so. There might indeed be complete confidence
that God would not cast off His people, but this was
not because He could not do so, nor because His
honour would thereby suffer irreparably. Faith was
grounded in His character of faithfulness, not in any
need for Israel on His part, otherwise than because
of His love for Israel. In other words the relation of
Israel to its God was from the outset a moral relationship. It is impossible to lay too much emphasis upon
this, for it is this which makes possible the development
which we find in the prophets. Again it is impossible
to lay too much emphasis upon the great historical act
which accompanies this stage in the revelation, namely
the deliverance from Egypt. Very likely much legend
is gathered about this event, as it is natural enough
that it should, but Israel's history as a political or a
religious fact demands for its explanation just such a
story as we have here given to us. They are led out
of Egypt by a power that seemed to them at any rate
to be not their own, nor that of Moses for all his
greatness. And it is upon this fact that the subsequent

x

religion of Israel most firmly stands. To it the prophets perpetually appeal, and to it the mind of simple men went back when the circumstances of their own day were utterly perplexing. It is as though they said, "We cannot see what God has planned for us now, but God brought us out of Egypt and God will guide us still." [1]

We may regard Abraham as a natural monotheist; his God is a God of Nature, but not also a God of a Church. When Israel came into Palestine they were at once Church and Nation; and their God was Yahweh. They did not at present maintain that Yahweh was the God of other nations also. This first appears with Amos and the great prophets. The declaration of these teachers is not that there is one God who appears under the name and person of Yahweh, but that Yahweh Himself is the only God. There is therefore a difference between the monotheism of Amos and Isaiah and that of either Abraham on the one side or Plato on the other; and this difference is seen to be important when we remember that human life is essentially social, and that therefore man's relation to God must be interpreted through a society. Until the Exile the prophets remained in a minority. The greater part of the people, while regarding themselves as worshippers of Yahweh, even though they frequently added the worship of other gods, did not accept the great declaration that Yahweh alone is God. What is the source of that declaration? The prophets plainly did not reach it by any process of philosophic reasoning, nor was it an outcome of any movement of thought in the nations. There is no possible source from which it can have come except the direct revelation of God Himself in their souls and consciences.[2] That there is One God, and that the One God is Holy, Amos, Isaiah, and Jeremiah knew through experience of Himself.

[1] Cf. Psalm lxxvii.
[2] Cf. Hamilton, *The People of God*, vol. i., to which I am greatly indebted in this chapter.

Jeremiah, when confronted with others who claimed to prophesy in the name of the Lord, could only be sure that they had not sat in His counsel by the fact that they did not know His Holiness and Unity.[1]  Here, then, is the next stage in that act of God which we call the History of Israel.    The first was the Call of Abraham ;  the second the Deliverance from Egypt ;  the third is the Revelation in the Prophets.

There remain three more.    The first of these is the Exile.    The prophets interpret the expansion of Assyria and afterwards of Babylonia as an act of God for the purpose of dealing with His people ;  and historically they were right.    It would have much surprised Sargon or Nebuchadnezzar to be told that the reason why he really mattered was to be found in his dealings with these tiny tribes ;  yet so it was ;  the rest of their acts have vanished and left historically no result.    When Judah went into captivity the adherents of the prophetic faith were still in a minority.    At Babylonia those who considered that Yahweh, the God of Israel, was first and foremost the God of Sinai and Palestine, would easily lose so much of their national identity as was safeguarded by religious faith.    Those who returned from the Exile were mostly, if not entirely, those who had held together through loyalty to this faith.    The Exile, therefore, inverts the previous situation ;  the mono-Yahwehists are now supreme.

The Return is the next act in the drama.    After it Israel had little national existence.    Its aspect as a Church now entirely predominates.    So the last act begins with a religious persecution.    The first collision between Hellenism and Judaism on a large scale comes with the attempt of Antiochus Epiphanes to stamp out the worship of Yahweh and to supplant it with that of Zeus.    This was resisted by the loyal in Israel, headed by the Maccabees, and out of the suffering of their affliction comes the Book of Daniel, representing the

---

[1] *E.g.* Jeremiah xxiii. 16-29.

complete establishment of Apocalypse as distinct from Prophecy, and the confident hope in Immortality, at least for the supremely righteous. Alike in the prophetic and apocalyptic writers we find the expectation of the Messiah. In the days when Israel was a nation as well as a Church the Messiah had been thought of chiefly as a King ruling from the throne of David. So Isaiah had pictured Him. But when the life of the Israelitish Church entirely overshadowed national questions the conception of the Messiah was spiritualised, and He came to be regarded as one who should appear in the clouds of Heaven, establishing the Kingdom of God by an act of the divine authority. So He is pictured in the Similitudes of Enoch. There were indeed great diversities of expectation ; Second-Isaiah hails Cyrus as Messiah,[1] and, whether written by the same hand or not, we have in his book the picture of the Servant of the Lord which seems rather to take the place of any Messiah so far as concerns the future, a picture which carries the Old Testament, at least in the fifty-third chapter, nearer to the New Testament than it is elsewhere able to come. Under the Maccabees it was commonly expected that the Messiah would be one of the Tribe of Levi, not of Judah ; and it is possible that Psalm cx. is intended to hail Simon Maccabaeus as himself the Messiah.[2] But at least the supposition that God's Kingdom should be inaugurated by normal human agencies and methods is in this period abandoned ; it must be the work of God Himself or of one whom He shall endow with special powers for the work. It is a supernatural Kingdom and must be supernaturally founded. Neither this nor the prophetic anticipation was literally fulfilled, but the fulfilment of each is included in the Act of Christ.

Meanwhile, another people had, in the persons at least of its loftiest thinkers, been led by a very

---

[1] Isaiah xlv. 1.
[2] Cf. Charles, *Religious Development between the Old and the New Testaments*, p. 81.

different road to a belief in the unity of God. Such a belief is really involved in the Doctrine of the Logos in the hands of its first formulator, Heraclitus.   The Logos in his philosophy is the supreme principle of all existence, its name, of course, intimating that it is a principle of reason.   It operates through all nature and in the mind of man, and that too whether they know it or not.   It is the one fixed point in Heraclitus' philosophy of universal flux ; it is, as it were, the unchanging principle which governs the incessant changes of everything besides itself.   It was through combining this principle of the eternal flux of all matter with Socrates' conviction that real knowledge is attainable in regard to morals that Plato came to formulate his Ideal Theory.[1]   It does not closely concern us here except in so far as it led him to speak of an ideal state which is in the heavens, and upon which he who will may gaze, and fashion the constitution within his own soul after its likeness.   For Plato the meaning of life is to be found in a spiritual world which our experience here enables us in part to apprehend, but only in part.   The immortal soul in which he always believes, though his arguments for immortality vary from time to time, may have the vision of the perfect truth if it is freed from the body.

In its doctrine of God, Greek philosophy, like all other philosophy, was confined to forming conceptions to meet the requirements of argument.   The demand of reason for unity led therefore to Monotheism.   But while Plato conceived a living God who cares for the world, the one supreme God of Aristotle apparently does not even know that the world exists.   This inferential knowledge of the divine unity could never have the spiritual power of the prophet's direct experience of the divine uniqueness.   Greek civilisation, the effort for an ordered freedom and for the application of moral ideas to social life, is something that still has

---

[1] See my lectures, *Plato and Christianity.*

supreme importance and value for us.   But in theology proper the great importance of the Greeks is limited to the perfect confidence of their great philosophers in the unity of the world's ruling principle, which Heraclitus had called the Logos.   This belief, expressed in this name, the Stoics upheld and made universally known.

Just when Greek culture had reached its zenith it was carried through the world by the conquests of Alexander the Great, whose career is, even more plainly than those of Nebuchadnezzar and Cyrus, a providential provision for the furtherance of the divine purpose in history.

Platonism met with Judaism in the new city of Alexandria which Alexander the Great founded largely with Jews taken from Palestine.   In the fusion of the two streams there arises a new interpretation of both, and in particular an identification of the Logos of the Greeks with the expected Messiah of the Jews, so that the former becomes a personal power of righteousness in this world, and the latter becomes, not merely the deliverer of a nation, or the renovator of the earth, but the controller of the Universe.   Everything is ready now for the appearance of the Son of God.

# CHAPTER XXIII

## THE WORD INCARNATE

'Ο λόγος σὰρξ ἐγένετο.—St. John.

" Ich lehre euch den Übermenschen.
" Der Mensch ist Etwas, das überwunden werden soll. Was habt ihr gethan ihn zu überwinden ? Seht, ich lehre euch den Übermenschen."—Nietzsche.

WE have pointed out already that at the time when Christ was born the history of the world seemed to have worked itself out. All the chief forces of civilisation around the Mediterranean basin had done all that it was in them to do. Now must a Deliverer come or the reign of death begin. There had been in the religion of Israel two forms of anticipation of a Divine Deliverer.[1] The earlier of these had represented Him as accomplishing His purpose by the ordinary methods of an earthly monarch. His purpose would indeed be perfect righteousness, but His means would not be different from those which other kings employed. In a certain sense the deification of the Cæsars may be said to represent a similar outlook among other nations. These, indeed, had not anticipated any heaven-sent king ; but the impulse to hail as divine the Cæsars who had established peace throughout the world and had given to mankind the undoubted benefits of Roman law, was akin to the earlier form of the Messianic hope. At a later time among the Jews an anticipation had arisen that the Messiah would do His work by Divine

[1] For a fuller treatment of the subjects dealt with in this and the next chapter, see my volume *Church and Nation*.

authority manifestly displayed. He would give the sign from heaven which would convince the most obstinate ; in other words, He would inaugurate the Kingdom by miracle. This view of the matter holds the field with many variations in the apocalyptic writers of the second and first centuries before Christ. The Jews' demand for a sign comes quite straight from it, and the Greeks' desire for wisdom is not essentially alien from it. For their hope was to receive a proof which would entirely convince the intellect.

Mingled with both of these anticipations there is a certain strain of selfishness, for each of them requires that the claim of the Kingdom shall make itself good through the process of rendering it worth while for men to accept it. And so lying behind both of them there is in reality the suggestion that the Messiah shall bribe men to accept Him. There was, however, a profound truth in both the anticipations. The Messianic work was to be the culmination of all that kings and kingdoms strive to be ; it was also to be a manifestation of the Divine power and wisdom in their fulness ; but in the form which the Jews had given to their hope, it was defective because it failed to operate through the free will of men. The Kingdom of God must be the Kingdom of the Almighty, the All-Ruler ; but the Almighty only rules over all if He controls not only our conduct but also our hearts and wills. These can neither be bought nor coerced. A man's action may be determined by force through his fear of penalty ; his heart and will can only be controlled by the manifestation of love. There is as a mere matter of fact nothing else which is effective to change the motives and inclinations. Consequently the political Messiah and the apocalyptic Messiah were alike inadequate to the task which they were to accomplish.

At the beginning of His Ministry our Lord faced and rejected all these suggestions. The power with which, as Messiah, He was endowed could not be used merely to satisfy His own or other people's creature comforts. In the service of His Kingdom, He would indeed feed the hungry and heal the sick, but this was not to be the basis of His work ; it was the mere automatic action of love possessing power when confronted with human need. Those whom He healed were to say nothing about it ; and when His works of healing created popular excitement, He immediately withdrew and would not continue his proclamation of the coming Kingdom in that atmosphere. So again when He thought of the kingdoms of the earth and the glory of them, He would not claim them as He might upon their own terms, the terms of the Prince of this world. To do that would be merely to repeat the rule of Cæsar Augustus on a higher moral level. Not so should the Kingdom of God come in. Nor will He give to Himself or to others the sign from Heaven which shall establish His authority for ever. What could be further from discipleship than one who was convinced that Christ is the revelation of God, while wishing all the time that He were not ? In rejecting the three temptations He has resolved that He will not cajole, He will not coerce, and He will not demonstrate. He will use none of the means by which men's conduct may be controlled otherwise than through the free devotion of their hearts and wills. But He will live in the spirit of Holy Love and in that spirit die. By the Resurrection, God set His seal upon this life as that of His own Son, and so while the Greeks seek wisdom and the Jews a sign, the disciple of Christ proclaims "a Messiah on a Cross, to Jews a scandal and to Gentiles an absurdity, but to the very people who are called both Jews and Greeks a Messiah who is God's power and God's wisdom." [1]

The Kingdom was to be based upon the free response of the human heart to the love expressed in love's own act of sacrifice. But it was to be a real

[1] 1 Cor. i. 23, 24.

Kingdom, which has laws that are the fulfilment or completion of all other laws. Other legislation aims at maintaining the life of a community or fellowship against the impulses and passions that would lead men to destroy the community or make its life impossible. The laws of this Kingdom are for those who have come to understand what fellowship is and to value it for its own sake. They are the laws which regulate the relations of men who are already in fellowship with one another. This is the whole significance of the Sermon on the Mount ; it is the climax or " fulfilment " of the Mosaic law and all other legislative systems.[1] Its method is different because the objects at which those systems aim are steps to be secured before it is set in operation. In fact its laws merely work out the principles involved in the belief that man's true nature is found in his membership of the Kingdom where Christ is King.

But as the Kingdom is a real one and the anticipation of the earlier prophets is fulfilled, so is the manifestation of Divine power and wisdom also real and the anticipation of the apocalyptists is fulfilled. For when once the love of God is declared there is found in that love the one power which can convince the heart and will, a power stronger than even irresistible force. The Lion of the tribe of Judah is no Lion but " a Lamb standing, as it had been slain " (which is to say, living with the marks of sacrificial death upon Him).[2] This faith can only maintain itself if it is accepted in all its completeness. If we begin by saying that God is Love and then make up our image of love and our own suppositions with regard to its action, we may very easily produce a conception of God which the whole of the universe at every step repudiates, and which is morally enervating to ourselves. Everything depends upon what we really think good for man.

[1] See my lectures on *Church and Nation*, I. and II.
[2] Rev. v. 5, 6.

The parent who supposes that enjoyment is the end
of life will show love for his child by leniency and
indulgence, and when God's government of the universe
seems to be the very opposite of lenience and indulgence
both the man and his children will be likely to say that
God is no loving Father.   But if what is good for man
is to be made like Christ, to be used and used up in
the service of God and men ; and if love aims rather
at the formation of a character which has in itself the
secrets of joy and peace because it is rooted in love,
discipline will at once appear to be as essential an
activity of love as any indulgence can ever be.   Men
have so long spoken of Christ as one who was most
obviously meek and gentle, that other elements in His
nature have been obscured ; but certainly the fierceness
of His anger against hardness and self-complacency are
quite as conspicuous features of the Gospel portrait as
His gentleness towards those whom the world called
sinners.   He is in many respects a terrible figure—an
austere and lonely figure.   Only once did one of His
disciples venture to offer Him advice ; then the answer
was—" Get thee behind me, Satan."   Many men were
afraid of Him ;  even those who came to arrest Him
went backward and fell to the ground when He came
out from the garden enclosure and stood defenceless
before them.   It was only children who were entirely
free from fear or wonder in His presence ; and perhaps
this fact is connected with His requirement that we
should become as little children if we are to enter His
Kingdom.[1]

Those who were still innocent, or who knew themselves to be sinners, found from Him the readiest and
tenderest welcome ; but those who were full of self-
concern, who had a pride to maintain and appearances

---

[1] We are liable to forget how very difficult this saying must have been.  Cf.
*Philochristus*, p. 103.   " But I returned marvelling greatly at his words and pondering them in my mind.   For I could in nowise perceive how we could redeem Israel
and drive out the Tetrarch from Tiberias and the Romans from Jerusalem, and set
up the Kingdom of God, and all this by becoming as little children."

to keep up, did not find in Him unmixed gentleness. On the contrary there are no denunciations so terrible as those which He launched at the self-satisfied good folk. They are all the more terrible because of their complete freedom from personal bitterness. He stood among men ready to save, but for that precise reason always pronouncing judgment; for He offered life, and those who rejected the offer were thereby involved in condemnation. So He spoke of Himself as a stone whom the builders rejected, a stone on which whosoever should fall would be broken: but on whomsoever it should fall it would scatter him as dust. This picture of Him as inevitably pronouncing judgment is one great characteristic of the Fourth Gospel. St. John sees Him standing among men unchanged Himself while they react to His influence in the most diverse ways. Gradually the followers and rejectors are sifted out from one another and stand in two opposing groups. His presence in the world constitutes the world's judgment. It supposes itself to pronounce judgment on Him; but therein it is in fact itself subjected to judgment. "Now is the judgment of this world" are words spoken in close connexion with the sentence of death which He knows that the world is about to pronounce upon Him.[1]

All of this is in the strictest harmony with the Figure set before us by the synoptists, when we have learned to read their story rightly and without the sentimentalism which we have allowed to colour our interpretation. But it also fits peculiarly with the governing thought of St. John's Gospel, which pervades and interprets the whole. The Lord is here set forth not merely as the promised Messiah, but as the manifestation once for all of the eternal principle which governs the universe. The Logos was a familiar enough conception at that time; it stood for that

[1] This suggestion with regard to Judgment and that below with regard to the Holy Spirit are further developed in Chapter XXV.

over-ruling and unifying principle which the mind must inevitably presuppose when it starts upon its work of explaining the world in which we live. With this sense it had been used by heathen philosophers, and by theologians in Alexandria it had been connected with the Word of the Lord in the Old Testament. St. John begins his Gospel with commonplaces; yet these commonplaces are full of the most far-reaching implications; for they involve that it is of the very nature of God that He should reveal Himself. The Logos, thought or speech, is the means by which a mind reveals itself to another. To say then that this eternally exists in relation to God and is itself Divine is to affirm of God that He is in His own nature self-revealing. The whole process of that revelation which has been going on through nature, through history and through prophets, comes to complete fulfilment in the Incarnation.

We are thus given the union of two points of view, which as a matter of fact it is very hard to hold together, but on the combination of which all real understanding of the revelation in Christ depends. Upon the one side this revelation is an altogether new fact; it does not rise out of the previous history of the world, though the previous history of the world had been so guided as to prepare for it. It is an invasion from without. And yet what thus breaks in is itself the power which had always been in control. It was not an alien principle coming into the world but precisely He by whom the world was made and apart from whom, as St. John with emphasis declares, there has not even one thing happened. We cannot therefore think of the world as something which, even for a moment, moves independently of God, and which God intervenes to correct or adjust; but neither on the other hand can we think of the world-process in anything less than its entirety as supplying an exposition of the Divine purpose in Christ. Only in the life of

Christ is this manifestation given. What we see in Him is what we should see in the history of the universe if we could apprehend that history in its completeness.[1] What have been called immanence and transcendence are here perfectly combined, and this without the smallest sacrifice of one to the other. They are not merely held together ; they are fused into each other. Our faith is fixed upon One "Who for us men and for our salvation came down from Heaven," and who yet had been always in the world, the Creator of all things and the Light that lighteneth every man.

This complete fusion of the transcendent with the immanent is made most of all manifest by St. John's habitual use of the term "glory." St. Paul had used language suggesting that our Lord had left the glory of Heaven when He came on earth, returning to it after His Resurrection ; and this language of course expresses one truth about the matter, for the humiliation and the sacrifice were voluntarily undertaken. Yet St. John takes us deeper with his insistence that the humiliation and the sacrifice are themselves the culmination of the glory. "The Word was made flesh and we beheld His glory." The word "glory" is used with increasing frequency as the Passion approaches. The threefold expression—"The hour is come that the Son of Man should be glorified" ; "Now is the Son of Man glorified" ; "The hour is come, glorify thy Son" ;— all have direct reference to the Passion and its fruit. In the High-priestly prayer, in which the Son dedicates

[1] And even then it is to be remembered that we have not the World-History without the Incarnation as one expression of the Divine Will and the Life of the Incarnate as another ; for that Life is a part of History, though it reveals the principle of the whole, and it is through its occurrence in the midst of History that History is fashioned into an exposition of the principle there revealed. We have here a series which is part of another series and is yet perfectly representative of it. (Cf. the Supplementary Essay in Royce's *The World and the Individual*.) But here the series which is contained (the Life, Death, Resurrection of Christ) only becomes representative of the series which contains it (the entire history of the world) in virtue of the influence which by occurring within the latter it is able to exercise upon it. Therefore, though Transcendence and Immanence are fused into one, the Transcendent aspect is always dominant.

Himself to the final sacrifice, His prayer is that He may
now be glorified with the eternal glory which He had
with the Father before the world was.    When the
sacrifice is made perfect, the manifestation of the glory
is made complete.    And what is thus manifested is
something eternal and not momentary.    The Passion
and the Resurrection are two sides of one truth.    It
was necessary that they should be set forth successively.
If we think of a triumph won by sacrifice either the
cost will dim the brightness of the triumph or the
triumph will irradiate the darkness of sacrifice.    He
must pass through the uttermost defeat, and the sense
that even God has deserted Him, if out of the very
depths of defeat He is to bring victory, and light from
the darkest of all possible gloom.    But this is His glory
—the completeness of the sacrifice and the completeness
of the triumph which by that sacrifice He wins.    Therein
His work is in one sense accomplished ; the perfect
revelation has been given, and through it the power of
God in its plenitude is at work among men.

But if the victory is won, its fruit is still to be
gathered.    The realisation, in actual effect and upon the
plane of history, of all that is involved in God's self-
revelation is the work of the Spirit.    God's power and
love had indeed been guiding and controlling human
history before Christ came ; the eternal Word was
operative from the beginning and without Him hath not
one thing happened.    But one department remained in
which this power could never reach its fulness while it
remained to a great extent unknown.    The free spirit
of man, his heart and will, can only fully respond to an
influence which it understands ; and so, though God
was guiding men in all the ages before the Incarnation,
that guidance took a new form from the time of the
Incarnation onwards.    It is this new power of God
(which is after all the old power mediated through its
complete revelation) which St. John calls the " Spirit."
It could not come before the Incarnation simply

because it is the operation of God through the revelation of Himself in intelligible form. "There was not yet Spirit because Jesus was not yet glorified." The Holy Spirit is the Word of God with the new power or influence which the Word acquired by becoming incarnate.[1] So it may truly be said that it was in order to make possible the coming of the Spirit that Christ was born. It is not to the historic figure living at men's side that we are to cling, but to the same Divine Being present within our souls : "It is expedient for you that I go away : for if I go not away, the Comforter will not come unto you ; but if I depart, I will send him unto you."

But while it is true that it was only to make possible the advent of the Spirit that Christ was born, it is equally important that it is only through His Birth and Life and Death and Resurrection that the Spirit could be sent. The new power is precisely that which is won through giving men a real understanding of and insight into the Divine love. To know that love is to be one of the elect who are sanctified by the Holy Spirit. St. John after his manner represents this new power that should come upon those who had received the full revelation, by means of two contrasted episodes in the life of one of the Apostles. Before the Crucifixion the Lord declared that to the place where He was now going His disciples could not yet follow Him, for He was going to that innermost presence of God which is the absolute self-sacrifice of love, and there they could not follow. "Whither I go, thou canst not follow me now ; but thou shalt follow afterwards." When the sacrifice had been completed, and the Lord had given His charge to this same Apostle, He looks forward to St. Peter's death, contrasting his submission then with his earlier impulsiveness : "'When thou wast young, thou girdedst thyself, and walkedst whither thou wouldest : but when thou shalt be old, thou shalt stretch forth thy hands, and another shall gird thee,

[1] This is not all that is to be said, but it is true as far as it goes.

and carry thee whither thou wouldest not. Now this He spake signifying by what manner of death He should glorify God. And when He had spoken this He saith unto him, Follow me." The following to that uttermost sacrifice, in which love is made perfect and which is therefore the presence of God, is now enjoined upon that Apostle for whom it was earlier impossible ; for the revelation has been given and therein the power.

This episode recalls us to the fact already glanced at, that Christ in His earthly life is the greatest of all heroes. In the manner of His own life, and in His appeal to His followers, this is the supreme characteristic. He is one who is ready to face anything, and calls upon His followers to be ready to face anything, for the sake of the cause with which He is entrusted, and for the service of the Kingdom which He came to found.[1] His life is a life of love ; but His love shows itself not so much in giving comfort as in calling others to a love like His own, and, if that be involved, to sufferings like His own. His love is very terrible to all that is soft or self-indulgent or even self-regarding in our nature. He offers us Love, the greatest of all gifts. If we reject it, we reject the very principle of life and commit ourselves to death and destruction. Therefore though the purpose of His coming is our salvation, its result is always judgment. By the judgment which crushes and breaks up the hard crust of self we are made at last if not at first responsive to love's appeal, so that the very pain which our self-will causes becomes, when the judgment is fallen, the means of winning us from self and moulding us in the likeness of the Love which we had despised.

The Cross and Resurrection of Christ are the conquest not only of death, but of sin which brought Him to death. The powers of evil never achieved anything so great as when they secured the condemnation of the

---

[1] Cf. my lectures on *Church and Nation*, I. and VI.

Y

Lord of glory. Never was darkness so deep as that darkness of despair out of which the Divine Sufferer cried, " My God, my God, why hast thou forsaken me ? " This was no failure of right, due to the fact that its supporters were themselves tainted with evil or lacking in wisdom. When our attempts to serve God fail, we naturally suppose that we ourselves must be failing in some way or other to follow His will. But on the day of the Crucifixion the very cause of God, served with undeviating loyalty to the very method of God, was failing. God was rejected, and successfully rejected, in His own world. Evil was triumphant. So for the time at least it seemed to the Lord Himself ; the God who had sent Him was failing Him : " My God, my God, why hast thou forsaken me ? " And this deep anguish, beyond what any of us can ever know, stands before us for evermore as something that has place in the very life and experience of God. For He who cried thus to His Father is He who also said, " He that hath seen me hath seen the Father." The evil that is in the world, and in our own heart, could bring this agony of despair upon the omnipotent and eternal God.

It is out of that uttermost gloom that the light breaks. The light does not merely shine upon the gloom and so dispel it ; it is the gloom itself transformed into light. For that same crucifixion of the Lord which was, and for ever is, the utmost effort of evil, is itself the means by which God conquers evil and unites us to Himself in the redeeming love there manifested. Judas and Caiaphas and Pilate had set themselves in their several ways to oppose and to crush the purpose of Christ, and yet despite themselves they became its ministers. They sent Christ to the Cross ; by the Cross He completed His atoning work ; from the Cross He reigns over mankind. God in Christ has not merely defeated evil, but has made it the occasion of His own supremest glory. Never was conquest so complete ; never was triumph so stupendous. The completeness of the victory is due to the completeness of the evil over which it was won. It is the very darkness which enshrouds the Cross that makes so glorious the light proceeding from it. Had there been no despair, no sense of desolation and defeat, but merely the onward march of irresistible power to the achievement of its end, evil might have been beaten, but not bound in captivity to love for ever. God in Christ endured defeat, and out of the very stuff of defeat He wrought His victory and His achievement. Language must be tortured to make it express what we see here. It is not only the enemy that was conquered ; defeat itself was defeated, captivity was led captive, and its shame converted into the splendour of triumph.

Rooted upon this Divine achievement, the believer awaits whatever comes. His Master has conquered death and sin. He sees Him as His disciple saw Him,[1] clothed in the garments of a glorified High Priest ; He has the snow-white hair of eternity ; and the flaming eyes of omniscience, from which no secret can be hid ; His feet of burnished brass affirm the immovableness of His authority, and the voice as the sound of many waters His right to command ; He holds in His hand the seven stars, for He is the sustainer of the universe and the constellations move at His bidding ; the tongue-like sword proceeds from His mouth, for every word He speaks is judgment ; His countenance as the sun shining in His strength proclaims the Majesty of Him who dwells in the light that no man may approach unto. He is the Lord of Life and Death ; He is Guide of all human history ; and nothing can be done but under His supremacy.

[1] Rev. i.

# CHAPTER XXIV

## THE CHURCH AND CHRISTENDOM

"The office of the Nation is by stern and righteous punishment to restrain men's self-will when it breaks out into acts; the office of the Church is, by gracious and loving methods, to bring out the true free will of which it is the base counterfeit."—F. D. MAURICE.

AFTER the Ascension of Christ there was left in the world a small group of people banded together by their discipleship to Him. There were especially eleven men, who proceeded at once to make up their number to the original twelve, who had been chosen out from among the disciples in a special sense and appointed as His ambassadors. They were the representatives of the King of the Divine Kingdom. Upon them as they were gathered together in prayer there came a new power which the Lord had taught them to expect, and in that power they became the founders of the Christian Church. For three centuries the Christian Church was a body separate from the rest of the world, consisting of men and women who were to some extent drawn out of the world as they became members of it. They were not therein made morally perfect; but they realised that in the fellowship of the Church there was at work a life and a power which were of God. This life and power were not really other than the energy which created and sustained the national States; for these latter, in our modern jargon, are the operation of God immanent in history, while the life of the Church is the energy of God transcendent. This Divine life within the Church, nourished perpetually by the reception of the human life of Christ, His Body and Blood, might be obscured and hampered by the presence in the same individuals of much that belonged to the world and even to what was definitely bad in the world. But it was not these lower qualities in them which made them a Church ; the whole essence of the Church was its supernatural and divine life. It was this alone which maintained its separate existence and gave it its essential characteristics. For the maintenance of these, and that too especially in connexion with the means of their nourishment, there grew up an order of the Church symbolising the unity of its life in all times and places, and the fact that this life is not something which men have generated out of themselves in their strivings after righteousness, but is the gift of God.

Yet this period of the Church's history is always looking forward to something more. The prayer, which the Lord had taught, contained the petition that God's Kingdom might come and His will be done in earth as it is in heaven. It could not be sufficient that groups of people in different parts of the world should be drawn out from the life of the world to become recipients of the life Divine. This would cut apart the new Covenant from the old altogether ; it would suggest what the heretic Marcion definitely taught, that the God of the New Testament is different from the God of the Old. It would suggest, what the Manichean heresy taught, that this world of matter is not God's world at all. The world itself must be won for Christ.

Gradually the leaven worked. At last the Emperor himself professed conversion. We do not know for certain what his motives may have been ; there was great political convenience in the adoption of Christianity ; but whether he was personally sincere or not, the conversion of Constantine and the Edict of Milan represent one of the great stages in the coming of the

Son of Man. It was a submission to Christ as Lord of mankind on the part of the great political power of the world. From that moment a new epoch begins, and side by side with the Church we have Christendom. From the time of the Reformation onwards, with the growing insistence on nationalism both in politics and religion, the idea of Christendom has been sinking into the background. It may be hoped that the great catastrophe which has now overtaken the world may turn men back to believe again in Christendom.

In the first three centuries of the Church's life we had the Church on one side confronting a world often hostile and always alien. Christendom is precisely the world as no longer alien, but as seeking to conduct its secular affairs in the power of that life of which the Church is the channel and trustee. In this approximation of the world to the Church there was implicit a great danger, the danger of a reciprocal approximation of the Church to the world. To a deplorable degree those who were primarily responsible for the witness to the Church's Divine life yielded before this temptation, the Church becoming, at least in outward appearance, an earthly kingdom. And yet the Divine life was always there, and in the times of deepest corruption could still express itself in the lives of individual saints and their immediate followers. It was only when the Church ceased to trust to its own distinctive life and behaved like any ordinary State, that the world itself could become relatively indifferent to the application of the Divine life to its own daily affairs. This is now again being altered. In England we had Lord Melbourne, Queen Victoria's first Prime Minister, who remarked as he left a church where he had heard an evangelical preacher, "Upon my soul, if religion is going to interfere with the affairs of private life things are come to a pretty pass." And there are many in recent years who have said the same thing concerning the interference of religion with our public life. Yet the pressure continues, and as the spiritual life of the Church is deepened, the nations whose citizens are very largely members of the Christian Church inevitably come under the influence of that spirit, and public life is changed. Christendom should be a real conscious unity grounded upon the unity of that fellowship of the Holy Spirit which in its deepest essence the Church must always be, even though there has hardly been an age when the pettiness of men has not obscured that unity with disputes and controversies. The nations of Christendom must learn to feel themselves united to one another in their common dependence upon the life which the Church preserves and through which they become different from the surrounding nations. Europe in its political sense, as the assembly of nations that have tried to make politics an expression of the moral nature of man, is the heir of ancient Greece ; the Church is the heir of ancient Palestine. The idea of Christendom is the fusion of these two ; it is only through the realisation of the idea of Christendom that the Kingdom of God can become a complete reality, and the Lordship of Christ over all the affairs of man become an actual fact in the world.

Much of the history of Christendom hitherto has consisted in the reciprocal influence of its two constituent factors, the universal Church and the National State. In the greatest age of medieval Europe the Church endeavoured to be a sort of spiritual successor of the old Roman Empire, and to exert direct authority of a political kind by means of its spiritual censures over the national governments. Like so much else about the Middle Ages, this attempt is characterised by a kind of reckless idealism. Men realised that if the Church is at all what it claims to be, it ought to control the secular life of men. An effort was therefore made to give it direct authority over this life. But while the goal was noble, the method was essentially false. The result of this attempt was to secularise the Church and to leave the Nation without any consciousness of divine sanction or mission. In exercising the authority which it attempted, the Church inevitably fell back upon the use of those instruments which are only appropriate in the hands of the secular government. It made itself incapable of providing on any universal scale that appeal to the spiritual nature of men which it is its peculiar prerogative to make. The proceedings of the Inquisition are only the logical working out of the whole scheme, and they show how false in principle the whole scheme was. Meanwhile, inasmuch as the Church was claiming to direct everything about human life that had any spiritual significance, the State became inevitably a mere machine for administration ; and this theory of the State is still upheld by certain ultramontane theologians.

The Reformation is in part at least the rebellion of the national State against the universal political authority of the Church. So far as it is such, it frequently appears to be a mere claim for independence on the part of the State, and this claim has often been advanced by men who cared only for the independence itself and not for the spiritual values whose realisation it made possible. None the less it was a true instinct that led men to demand for the national State freedom from the political authority of Rome, and the State was gradually appreciated as a truly moral and spiritual force. The reaction, however, as is customary with reactions, went too far, and as the Church had attempted to subordinate the State to itself, so now the State attempted to subordinate the Church. Such a position for the Church was inevitably felt by earnest Christians to be intolerable. A society which claims a divine origin and a world-wide membership cannot consent to be a department of any national State ; hence there arose the conception of the free Church within a free State. Each was to perform its own functions without interference from the other, though, of course, there would be mutual influence. But this view of the matter still fails to do justice to the Church's universal claim. It inevitably renders very weak the sense of full fellowship existing between Churchmen who are subjects of different States, and it would never enable the Church to perform one of its highest functions, the binding of the nations together in one fellowship of the Holy Spirit. We need to press forwards to the idea of the free State within the free Church. The State must be free ; that is, the Church must not try to exercise any political domination over it. The Church must be free ; that is, the State must not attempt to determine in any way its faith, its modes of worship, or its ideals. But the States which constitute the world must come to recognise themselves as provinces in the spiritual Kingdom of Christ and as therefore deriving their own welfare from the welfare of the whole Kingdom. The Church itself must become wholly free from worldliness in order that it may be fit to inspire the nations so to serve the Kingdom which it represents and on behalf of that Kingdom to receive their homage.

When in the Middle Ages the Church definitely claimed the homage of the nations, it did not at all adequately realise the meaning of that claim. Rome has been throughout in the last resort absolutely individualist ; it appears to sacrifice the individual to the ecclesiastical machine, but that is only because by means of this sacrifice the individual is fitted for eternal salvation. In the end of the day this and this alone was the concern of the medieval Church, and as far as I can judge is still the sole concern of the Church of Rome. It is presumably with reference to this tendency in Rome that there is a proverbial paradox in the Orthodox Church, that Rome is the only real Protestant. I would suggest that in this particular Rome has followed the weakest point in the Platonic philosophy. I have pointed out elsewhere[1] that while for Aristotle the State

---

[1] In *Plato and Christianity*.

and its constitution are ends in themselves so that the test of a good constitution is stability and durability, for Plato politics is always absolutely subordinated to ethics. His one real concern is the eternal salvation of the soul. The true philosopher in this miserable life will cower behind a wall as out of a storm of sleet and rain, happy if he can escape unspotted to the other world. The political constitution is to be estimated by the moral condition in the souls of the citizens from which it springs, and which in the next generation it reproduces. In all of this Plato is vastly superior to Aristotle and yet fails to do justice to all sides of human nature. He is often credited with sacrificing the individual to the State because he seems to take away liberty and most possibilities of pleasure in his ideal Republic, but this after all is simply for the sake of the individual soul in its eternal destiny. Justice in the State is for him a mere image of justice in the individual soul. He is right here in the main and only fails so far as justice falls short of love. How far it is true that this doctrine, as mediated through St. Augustine's *De Civitate Dei*, actually moulded the outlook of the Roman Church, I have not the necessary knowledge to determine ; but there can be no doubt that the outlook is the same. One deplorable result of this has been that religion in the West has tended to become individualist almost in the degree in which it is spiritual. Before there can be again such a thing as Christendom existing in the world as a living fact, we must recover, or possibly learn from the Eastern Church, the idea of a moral and spiritual corporate life which, if not the whole of the end of man is none the less part of his end, and therefore to be regarded in proper proportion as a true end in itself. For this purpose we must first of all realise the spiritual character of the State even in its most material functions.

As far as it is possible to forecast, there will always be need for State and Church, for the Law and the

Gospel. Even Christ's most exalted precepts are given not as setting aside the old law but as completing it. His Sermon on the Mount gives the legislation by which men are to live in the realised fellowship, but His teaching perpetually recognises the possibility that the fellowship itself may be broken so that men may be externally members of it, but yet not filled with its spirit; and in such a case the process of the Law becomes requisite.

All men as a matter of fact are in private life quite familiar with the two levels upon which we all live. There is the legal relationship in which we are bound to stand as regards people whom we do not know and between whom and ourselves there is no bond of fellowship at all; and there is the relation of friendship in which competing claims no longer exist. We know that in ourselves we are perpetually upheld in our purpose of living in a manner that befits loyal citizens by the penal sanctions of the law. He would be a rash man who would dare to say that he would certainly remain free from all tendency to overreach his neighbour or to indulge in various evil courses if there were nothing at all except his love of God and man to keep him straight. The ape and tiger die hard; and, as Bishop Creighton remarked, even when they are dead there is still the donkey, who is hardest of all to kill. We are in fact definitely assisted towards the freedom of the spiritual life by the enforcement of minimum standards. God alone knows how great a part is played by the different motives which determine our conduct; but there are those of us who know quite well that for us certain wrong actions are ruled out because of their legal or social consequences. The spiritual capacities of our nature have thus a freedom for development which would otherwise not be given to them. This foundation supplied by law is necessary for the superstructure which love would build. The primary requisite of any one who would live by love is simply that he should observe the law. It has lately been pointed out that the driver of a motor-car best shows his love for other motorists upon the road by keeping to the left. If he allows deep yearnings to divert his attention he is likely to cause a collision which will be as disastrous to them as to him. Keeping the law is not the whole of love, but it is in almost all cases the beginning of it.

The State and the Church are the channels through which these two forms of the one spiritual influence play upon men. The State gives men security against certain evils in themselves or in other men, so that they may be set free for the higher life of the spirit. The Church exists precisely to elicit that higher life of the spirit. If either Church or State tries to perform the function of the other, disaster must ensue. In the Heavenly Jerusalem, as there is no temple set apart for worship, so there is presumably no State enforcing the law with penalties. But we are not yet living in the New Jerusalem, and we need both State and Church for the building of our spiritual life so long as we are ourselves partly animal, or have tendencies needing to be checked ; and we are also under the necessity of perpetually renewing our spiritual life in worship if it is not altogether to decay. We may expect then that the course of history will continue in the future, as in the past, to consist in the conversion of nations, the building of the Christian State, and the incorporation of the Christian States within the fellowship of the Church, until at last Christendom and Humanity are interchangeable terms. Then, as the Divine Life of which the Church is the channel leavens all things, the Holy City will be realised, descending from God, the New Jerusalem which is the moral and social life of mankind made perfect in the love of God.

All considerations however combine to show that this result can never be attained, at least in anything approaching perfection, by any one part of humanity in isolation from the rest.  The Body of Christ has many members and the functions of all the separate members must be exercised if the Body is to display the fulness of its power.  At present many races with their peculiar gifts are outside the Church of Christ ; the body therefore remains incomplete ; it is something, which in St. Paul's phrase, we are to be "building up" ; and the life in those parts of the body which are already something like fully grown is none the less defective because the whole organism lacks the services of those members which are at present wanting.  The merely European Church can never do even for Europe what the universal Church must do for the nations of the world, and the Church will only have full power even in those regions where it is completely established when it is also established in all other parts of the earth as well.  Only then will the royalty of Christ be complete in fact as it is eternally complete in right and title. It is thus that the Church is not only His Body or the instrument of His will, but is also the "completeness of Him who all in all is being completed."[1]  We are to look forward to a time when all men of all nations will be linked together in the pursuit of a common purpose, and that the purpose of Christ, so completely that all mankind will be a single moral personality, "one perfect man."  That will be "the measure of the stature of the completeness of the Christ."[2]  Meanwhile what members there are must hold fast by the head, submitting themselves to its directions both in their influence exerted upon the civilisation which has already accepted Christ in name and in the work of extending His Kingdom and building up His Body.  "From Him all the body fitly framed and knit together through that which every joint supplieth, according to the working in due measure of each several part, maketh the increase of the body unto the building up of itself in love."[3]

---

[1] Ephesians i. 23 ; cf. Armitage Robinson, *ad loc.*
[2] Ephesians iv. 13.    [3] Ephesians iv. 16.

The Church will only manifest the whole power of Christ when it embraces all mankind ; here and now it fully manifests His Spirit only in the degree in which it is missionary. Christendom will only be complete when it is all the world, and now is only truly Christian so far as it is concerned for the bringing of the world into the Kingdom of God, of which it is at once the earnest and the servant.

# CHAPTER XXV

## THE KINGDOM OF GOD AND THE HOLY SPIRIT

"Jesus came into Galilee, proclaiming the good news of God and saying, The time is fulfilled and the Kingdom of God is come near ; change your hearts and trust in the good news."—St. Mark.

"They came together, then, and asked him, saying, Lord, dost thou at this time restore the Kingdom to Israel? And he said to them, It is not your business to know times and seasons which the Father has put under his own authority. But you shall receive power, the Holy Spirit coming upon you."—Acts of the Apostles.

The account of our Lord's teaching which is given in the Synoptic Gospels represents Him as fastening attention upon the coming Kingdom of God. One long discourse, the subject of a whole critical controversy by itself, declares the Kingdom to be imminent even as He speaks, and other sayings express the same conviction. In the Fourth Gospel the whole emphasis is laid upon the gift of the Spirit, and the place, which in the other three is occupied by the discourse just mentioned, is here given to another discourse in which the gift of the Spirit is the central theme.

It has often seemed that these two pictures are portraits of different originals. If the doctrine of Christ is that recorded in the synoptists, then it is not also that recorded in St. John, and *vice versa*. "It is only by considering the Fourth Gospel as a highly idealised work that we can claim for the Jesus of the Synoptic Gospels any historical reality whatever." [1]

We shall see, however, when we look more closely,

[1] Percy Gardner, *Exploratio Evangelica*, p. 167.

that this is an entirely false view of the matter, for the Kingdom of God is the sphere of the Spirit's operation, and the effect of the Spirit's operation is the building of the Kingdom of God. We have already seen that our Lord at the outset of His ministry repudiated all the ways in which it is possible to control men's conduct without first winning the allegiance of their hearts and wills. He used as the best available expression of His meaning the symbolism of the apocalyptic writings, and particularly that of the Similitudes of Enoch. He spoke of Himself as the Son of Man, and many of the contexts suggest that it is the conception of the Son of Man as set forth in that book which is chiefly in His mind ; but it is quite equally clear that He is correcting the conception even while He makes use of it. It was altogether contrary to His whole method of teaching that He should say in so many words, This prophecy or that was true in one respect, but inadequate in another ; or, to be more precise, that He should say quite plainly that His Kingdom was to rest solely upon the power of love. To say such things in the form of direct instructions would frustrate the very object in view ; it would set up a theory of the Kingdom before the Kingdom itself was there. But He would live among men and die before men, manifesting Himself after His Resurrection, so that those who had been witnesses of these things would be banded together in an actual Kingdom long before they had any theory about the nature of that Kingdom or its basis. In this way their whole natures, their aims and purposes no less than their intellectual ideas, would be won for His service, and this could be accomplished in no other way.

Even to the disciples He makes no claim of Messiahship until at Cæsarea Philippi St. Peter, in answer to His question, hails Him as Messiah. Immediately He declares that the Son of Man, the Messiah in His glory, must suffer, and immediately He starts for Jerusalem upon the journey that ends in the

Passion.    On that journey little children come to Him as they had done before ; and the disciples, supposing that He would be occupied with greater and more engrossing concerns, tried to drive them away ; but He says, " Let the little children come ; do not forbid them ; they are the kind of people that my Kingdom is made of."    He deliberately and specifically contrasts His Kingdom with other kingdoms.    In all others the great ones exercised authority.    It is not to be so here ; here the greatest is to be servant, even as the Son of Man—again the title of the Messiah in glory—came not to be served but to serve.    In other words, authority is to be exercised, not against hostile and recalcitrant wills, but only through winning a free allegiance.    He declares that the power of the Kingdom is now about to be manifested ; as He speaks it is at hand ; and before the High Priest He claims that in that moment its power begins.    For its power is the power of love to call forth answering love.    This it does by its own one method of sacrifice, so that when the sacrifice is completed the power of love, which is the authority of God, reaches its completion also.[1]

Probably the accomplishment by this power of the end which is set before it, will take long centuries. There are many sayings of the Lord to show that He did not expect the accomplishment of God's purpose in the world to be reached in its fulness immediately. What was to appear immediately was the power sufficient for that accomplishment, so that from thenceforward the victory in principle was already won.    In the long process there would be both gradual development and great catastrophes.    Upon these latter in particular He fastens, and among them chiefly upon the fall of Jerusalem.    That would be the next great cataclysm in the spiritual history which begins with the call of Abraham, and continues through the whole divine guidance of Israel, down to the birth of the Christian Church,

[1] See *Church and Nation*, I.

Z

and beyond that to the perfect realisation of God's rule. The fall of Jerusalem was the sweeping away of the last stronghold of the nationalist religion of Israel, and so was in a peculiar degree a coming of the Son of Man in His Kingdom. The collapse of a civilisation which is failing to live according to the Spirit of Christ is such a coming of the Son of Man ; for it is the manifestation of the inherent futility of every order that is not His. Whenever He comes it must be in judgment, though this is not the purpose of His coming ; His purpose is always to establish the Kingdom of God and to draw men into it ; but as they refuse or reject His invitation and His claim they condemn themselves. The Gospel of St. John has been described as the Gospel of the Judgment, and so indeed it is. From one point of view it seems to be full of self-contradictions. The Lord is represented as saying, "For neither doth the Father judge any man, but he hath given all judgment unto the Son" (v. 22). "For judgment came I into this world" (ix. 39). But on the other hand He is also reported as saying, "I judge no man" (viii. 15). Perhaps the solution is supplied by the fullest of the statements on the subject : "For God so loved the world, that he gave his only begotten Son, that whosoever believeth on him should not perish, but have eternal life. For God sent not his Son into the world to judge the world ; but that the world should be saved through him. He that believeth on him is not judged: he that believeth not hath been judged already, because he hath not believed on the name of the only begotten Son of God. And this is the judgment, that the light is come into the world, and men loved the darkness rather than the light ; for their works were evil" (iii. 16-19).

Here it is made clear that the purpose of God is salvation, and that not so much from the consequences of sin as from the sin itself, and thereby incidentally, no doubt, from its consequences also. To reject this salvation is to accept condemnation, or indeed to choose it, so that he that believeth not is condemned already, or rather, therein.   There can be no condemnation beyond this ; life has been offered and refused, and this is the judgment.

This doctrine is part of the whole reversal of man's ordinary beliefs about religion, which is involved in the Christian revelation.   The work of the Spirit will be to prove men wrong in their ordinary notions about these things. ;  " When he is come he will convict the world in respect of sin and of righteousness and of judgment " (xvi. 8).    Men think of sin as consisting in wrong acts and are liable to suppose that if they have avoided wrong acts they are virtuous ; but sin is the self-centred will, the will that cannot put its trust in Christ, the Incarnation of the Divine love, or perceive that because He is perfect Love He is one with the Father.   And similarly men think that judgment is the infliction of a specific penalty in punishment for wrong acts ; but it is rather the evil state inseparable from the self-centred will.   " This is the judgment that men loved darkness." And so the evidence of what sin is, is that the world does not believe in Christ.   The evidence of what righteousness is, is to be found in the fact that Christ goes to the Father.   The evidence of judgment is found in the fact that when the world supposed itself to be condemning Christ it was in fact falling under His condemnation.   " He shall prove the world wrong in respect of judgment, because the prince of this world hath been judged."   Men thought that the prince of this world was pronouncing judgment upon the Lord ; but it was not so ; it is Caiaphas and Pilate, not Christ, who lie under the condemnation.

But further, this rejection of Christ by the world, which is the condemnation of the world, is also the means by which the world is rescued.   " Now is the judgment of this world : now shall the prince of this world be cast out.   And I, if I be lifted up from the earth, will draw all men unto me " (xii. 32). The very act in which the world, and the evil that is in it, puts forth its utmost effort against the manifestation of love, is the means by which love completes that manifestation and thereby puts forth its full power. This is the supreme act in the foundation of the Divine Kingdom.

From the moment that the manifestation of the Divine love was perfected in the completion of the sacrifice, the power of the Kingdom in its fulness was at work in the world. His coming from then onwards is a present fact, though its universal realisation lies still in the future, and there is much in slow development and in violent catastrophe that must take place before that final achievement. " Behold he cometh with the clouds " ; the tense is present : " And every eye shall see him " ; that is future. The great appeal of " Come," with which the Bible closes, is answered by the words, " Surely I am coming fast."

That great book with which the Bible closes sets before us the whole course of human history as a struggle between two forces, the one represented by the Lamb that had been slain and by the Holy City, New Jerusalem ; the other represented by the Great Beast and Babylon the Great. It is Love with its instrument of sacrifice upon the one side, and Pride with its instrument of force upon the other. Our actual society rests upon both. So far as it is symbolised by the police force and the law courts it rests upon the necessity for restricting men's selfish desires, even in order that they may attain their selfish ambitions. If all men were selfish, society would arise ; otherwise we should have the state of nature in which, as Hobbes describes it, the life of man is " solitary, poor, nasty, brutish, and short." So soon as any man obtains what he desires, he finds that the hands of all are against him ; and as this is true of each in turn, all will combine together in an agreement neither to commit nor suffer injustice. That is the basis of Babylon the Great.

But society would also arise if men were entirely unselfish ; for men have different gifts and each needs the services of all.   And so the very fact of our mutual dependence upon, and fellow-membership with, one another, will lead to an ordered society for the widest possible sharing of the produce of our varying gifts. As has been said, society as we know it, and as it appears in any stage of human history, rests upon both of these at once.   Political progress is the growing predominance of fellowship over antagonism, and therefore also of love over pride.   It is the perpetual triumph of the sacrificed Lamb over the Great Beast, the perpetual fall of Babylon, the perpetual descent of the Holy City, the New Jerusalem coming down out of Heaven from God.   This is the inner meaning of the whole drama of history.   But the Holy City descends from God ; for love is the very nature of God, and men possess it only so far as it is given them from Him.   " We love, because he first loved us."   The power of love has indeed been in the world from the beginning, for the world was made by the God of love in order that He might have children on whom to lavish His love, and from whom He could win answering love.   But this power of God could only reach its own plenitude by manifesting itself in a form that men could understand.   God was guiding human history before the Incarnation ; the Holy Spirit " spake through the prophets."   But the power of God over men's hearts and wills could not in the nature of the case be complete until it had revealed itself intelligibly.   For God had made men so that their full response could only be given to what they understood.

Before the Incarnation they were, as always, like clay in the hands of the potter.   He guided their destiny then as now ; then as now He gave His commands, and disobedience to those commands involved destruction.   But to be guided thus, or to be commanded thus, was to be in the position of a puppet or at best a slave. The aspiration of the divinely guided human spirit reached out towards a faith in a real sonship but could not make sure of its goal. The Incarnation changed all this. " I have not called you servants," the Lord says, " but I have called you friends. For the servant knoweth not what his Lord doeth." So St. Paul tells his converts that " we have not received the spirit of slavery again so that we should fear, but we have received the spirit of adoption whereby we cry Abba, Father." Only through the historic Incarnation can the spiritual power reach its own fulness, and in order that this Spirit might be in its fulness operative in the world, Christ came, and died, and rose again. St. John would seem to confine the name of the Spirit to this power in its plenitude, so that before the Passion, Resurrection, and Ascension it could be said that He was not in the world. " There was not yet Spirit, because Jesus was not yet glorified " (vii. 39). It was only by His appearance in the flesh that the Spirit could come, so that he is anti-Christ who denies that Jesus Christ is come in the flesh. Yet it was positively desirable that this presence should be withdrawn in order that the power of the Spirit might come. " It is expedient for you that I go away : for if I go not away, the Comforter will not come unto you ; but if I depart, I will send him unto you " (xvi. 7). And, indeed, the little band of disciples who had been so slow to understand the Lord when He was among them, and whose faith and loyalty were shattered by His arrest, became through the gift of that Comforter the nucleus of the Church militant and triumphant.

The sphere of the action of one spirit upon another is chiefly that region of the sub-conscious where most of our thinking takes place. That is why the influence is so seldom recognised. Whether we are most sensitive to good or evil suggestion depends on our whole moral character, and this again depends mainly on the

moral standards of our civilisation.[1]   In the old world
God's Spirit found here and there a man who could
receive Divine truth which was as yet out of reach for
most men ; they became prophets.   But when once the
full revelation of God's love had been given, there was a
Body of believers, the Church, which by its knowledge
of the Divine love was made permanently receptive of
the Spirit's influence.   The main function of the
Church is religious education, that is to say the building up of thought and character, conscious and subconscious, in the knowledge of the Love of God, so
that the soul is always open to the operation of the
Holy Spirit.

The Kingdom shares with the King the dual aspect of
" immanence " and "transcendence," as the phraseology
of recent discussions has expressed it.[2]   As the Divine
Word was always in the world and yet was only fully
manifested when it became incarnate in the person of
Jesus Christ, so the Divine sovereignty or the reign of
God has always been the ultimate truth about the
universe and about human life.   His Law has always
been supreme, so that whoever offended against it
perished, just as the Law of Gravitation operates
whether it is known or not.   Men found the Law by
sinning against it, and this was so ordained because
experience is better than instruction for teaching moral
truth.   But because the spiritual power of God over the
spirits of men could only be completed when its nature
was revealed in an intelligible form so that men should
render it a free response, so the Kingdom comes with
power only through that revelation.   All history has been

---

[1] Hence the greater evidence for the existence of devils in heathen as compared
with Christian countries.

[2] From this follows the variety of ways, all quite correct, in which the expression
can be used : (a) all progress is a sign of the presence of the Kingdom ; (b)
catastrophes in which evils are destroyed are Comings of the Kingdom ; (c) the
final consummation is, par excellence, the Kingdom.   Aristotle says that a
" process " may be described as "complete " either with regard to the whole time
which it takes, or with regard to the moment in which its result is reached.   So it
is with the Kingdom, except that here we must remember that the very value of
the result is given to it partly by the process leading up to it.

guided by the Divine providence ; the growth of nations
and the institutions of social life and all that went to
build up fellowship among men, not only in Israel but
in every nation under Heaven, was the working of the
Divine Spirit immanent in the processes of human
nature. But the truth of the processes was not known
until the supreme revelation was given ; consequently
from that moment the process itself is altered in those
who have received this knowledge. For it now becomes not a mere unconscious movement in obedience
to a divinely implanted instinct, nor a straining aspiration after an ideal not yet in any sense realised, but the
response to a love made known and the fulfilment of a
duty which arises from the act of that love. Consequently there is a difference, impossible to exaggerate
in its importance, between those whose aspiration after
holiness or fellowship is something undertaken on what
must seem to them their own initiative, and those in
whom it is something called out from them by the
knowledge which has been given them of the love of
God. In one sense, therefore, the Kingdom of God
which Christ proclaimed is His eternal sovereignty,
which never could become more real than from the
beginning to end of history it was and is. In another
sense that Kingdom is only realised in those who,
knowing God's love, respond with answering love ;
love which, because God Himself is Love, goes out
to all men as to God Himself ; for He loves all men,
and our love for Him will lead us to love for His
sake all whom He loves. Again, the Kingdom is in
one sense the permanent leaven in human life, alike
in Christian and heathen countries ; yet in its fulness it
is only seen where men know God and live by that
knowledge. Thus it is said of the Holy Spirit that
He is the sanctifier of the elect, that is of those to
whom through no merit of their own has come the
knowledge of the Gospel, because only in their lives is
it possible that the Spirit of God could have that

fulness of power which is derived through the revelation of God given in His Son. Thus the Holy Spirit proceeds not only from the Father but also from or through the Son.

We have seen already that the Church, as a Divine organism distinct from the rest of the world, exists to be the vehicle and channel of the Divine life given by God to men rather than sought and found by men. If the nation and all that is good in its life is the working of God immanent in history, the Church is the medium of God transcendent, breaking in upon history. Its whole order and organisation is devised to fit it for this function. This is the meaning of its hierarchy and sacraments ; the life that constitutes the Church, so far as it is something distinct from the world, is that life of God transcendent which in the Incarnation was offered to men. But there are not two Gods, one immanent and one transcendent ; and therefore there is no cleavage between the spiritual movements in what we ordinarily call secular life and those within the Church ; all is the work of one God, one Holy Spirit. It is perfectly possible, as indeed it frequently happens, that, in this respect or that, the operation of the Holy Spirit is more potent among those who are not members of the Church than among those who are, for while the life of the Church is itself the very life and power of the Kingdom of God, that Kingdom is something wider than the Church and greater. But the Church remains the normal channel for the influence of the Spirit. The operation of the power of the Spirit in those who stand apart from the outward fellowship of the Church could not be so great as it is, if there were not in the world the organism which was created and adapted to be the organ of that Spirit.

Consequently, until the final consummation when every eye shall see the Christ as in very truth the Lord of life and death, it is impossible to say of the Kingdom, Lo here, or, lo there ! It is all about us and at work everywhere ; we are its citizens by right of our sonship to God, alike in nature and by our adoption in Christ. It has no outline, nor can it be contained in anything narrower than humanity itself. But within humanity there is planted the organism of the Church to be the channel and vehicle of the life of the Kingdom, until at last the Church includes mankind, and all nations, coming into the Church, make Christendom co-extensive with the world, when at last the Kingdom of God will be come.

In one sense this will be the sum and climax of all history and the fulfilment of its goal, and so far the presentation of the matter by the " liberal " theologians of the nineteenth century is justified. But in another sense it is the new creation of God through the transcendent life and power which broke in upon the world in Christ, and which is perpetually available for bringing about cataclysms and catastrophes which sweep away all that in Church, or nation, or civilisation as a whole, may be hostile to His cause and impeding its advance.

Meanwhile, however, the point of practical importance is this, that while the Spirit of God is in all the world and no man is ever for a moment without His guidance, yet that guidance is especially given to those whose hearts are attuned to Christ. That this should be so is natural enough ; it is fundamental to the Christian conception of prayer that while God always gives us what is good for us, what at any time is really good depends upon our own condition and relation to Him. Food which is wholesome to a healthy man may be poison to a man suffering from disease. The deepest of all diseases in the soul is forgetfulness of God and a belief that man can live independently of Him ; consequently, to men suffering from this spiritual sickness, gifts, which would be blessings to those in spiritual health, may be turned into occasions of stumbling. In particular, they might heighten the disease itself by leading the man to suppose more than ever that without any thought of God he none the less obtained all that he needed. The supremest of all blessings is reserved for those who know the source from which the blessing comes ; and even for them the direct guidance of the Spirit comes most definitely in those times when their spiritual relationship to God is strongest. Experience establishes beyond the possibility of question that the deepening of the spiritual life is the surest way of winning clear guidance from God with regard to practical duties. The man who, knowing God as the God of love, is keeping his soul perpetually strengthened by communion with God, finds himself used, often in ways which he only afterwards understands, for the loving purposes of God.

But this again leads to the very practical belief that the matter of most vital import for the life of the individual or for the advance of the Kingdom is that the growing character should breathe an atmosphere that is truly Christian in faith and hope and love, so that it will become attuned to Christ and thus fitted to be the channel of the Spirit. Here is the supreme function of the Church—to be the home in which the children of God grow towards perfection from infancy to old age, breathing in His spirit, so that in all their activities they are under His guidance. If this is what is meant by religious education, then religious education is more important than any other one thing in the whole world. But it must not consist of mere instruction (though instruction is indispensable), nor must it be supposed that it ceases with childhood or at any other time. It begins with earliest infancy and, going on to extremest old age, is the perpetual nurturing of God's children so that they may be worthy to live in His home.

We have thus the following factors playing their part. First, there is the secular organisation of society in tribe, and nation, and state, representing attempts made under the guidance of God towards that fellowship which is the life of love. Then there is the Church, which consists of the same persons as make up the world, and may, therefore, through their infidelity have its own life obscured and merged in the life of the world, but which, so far as it is anything at all distinct from the world, is the society of those who share in the life of perfect love, not as something that man in his search has found, but as something that God in His mercy has given. Beyond this there is Christendom, which is the secular life leavened and moulded by the life that comes through the Church from God. At last, in one sense including all of these, and in another sense lying beyond all of these, there is the Kingdom of God, which is seen first in the whole process towards the life of love embracing all humanity, and then in the realised achievement, when all humanity is united by the grace of our Lord and the love of God in the fellowship of the Holy Spirit.

Whether or not this ideal is capable of realisation upon this planet is a question of comparatively small interest. Much of the language of the New Testament, and emphatically one phrase in the Lord's Prayer, encourages a hope of the coming of the Kingdom upon earth. But there are other sayings which suggest that the perfected Kingdom either finds its place elsewhere or, if upon earth, only after a " renovation " of both heaven and earth, whatever may be implied in this. But there is one sense at least in which, so far as we can now tell, that consummation is unattainable under the conditions of terrestrial life. If we suppose that some generation of mankind, either next year or in the year $x^{(x-1)}$, should arrive at a quite perfected form of life, still that would not for us, who have lived in the process of attainment, bring complete satisfaction of the soul, and even for those who lived in the perfected world there would be a lack if they were cut off from fellowship with those by whose struggles and labours their own happiness had in part been won. It was such

a thought as this that led to one of the earliest of Jewish
expressions of the hope of immortality.   The redeemed
Israel would itself be imperfect if the patriarchs and
heroes of old could have no part in it, and this leads the
seer to exclaim : " Thy dead shall live ; my dead bodies
shall arise.   Awake and sing, ye that dwell in the dust :
for thy dew is as the dew of herbs, and the earth shall
cast forth the dead." [1]   The fellowship which Christ
founded upon the rock of such faith as that which St.
Peter showed when he confessed our Lord as Messiah,
was said to be immune from the separation caused by
death.   "On this Rock will I build my Church ; and
the gates of the grave shall not prevail against it."
That death is not the end of the individual life is
guaranteed by the Christian revelation of the love
of God.   Love is always of individuals, and God who
made men for Himself will not let them merely pass out
of existence through a failure of their physical strength.
And there is already a real Communion of Saints, a
fellowship of the living and the departed, so that as we
lift up our hearts to the Lord in the service of the
Holy Communion or Communion of Saints, it is " with
Angels and Archangels, and with all the company of
heaven that we laud and magnify His glorious Name."
Yet this fellowship at present is incomplete.   There is
not now that interpenetration of personality between
those on earth and those who have died which we do
to some extent experience in our relations with those
whom we love most on earth.   It can only be when
freed from the limitations of our earthly existence that
we enter into the very fulness of the joy of the Lord,
which is the joy of perfected love.   That this earth can
become, and shall become, something worthy to be called
God's Kingdom we may believe and affirm.   But the
final satisfaction of the soul which can only be reached
when, filled by God, it finds its own fulfilment in living
for and in others, and all others, cannot be expected

[1] Isaiah xxvi. 19.

under the conditions of this life. It was by Death and Resurrection that Christ Himself became, as it were, universally available, so that His sphere of work was no longer limited to that part of the earth in which His physical presence was ; it must be so too with those whom He has redeemed. " We have not here an abiding city, but we seek after the city which is to come."

Suppose for a moment that all human beings felt permanently and universally to each other as they now do occasionally to those whom they love best. It would follow that all the pain in the world would be swallowed up in the joy of doing good. Then go further, and suppose every particle of energy in the world animated by the equivalent spirit to "love" in the particular form of energy which we call human consciousness.

So far as we can conceive such a state, it would be one in which there would be no "individuals" at all, in the sense in which "individuality" means mutual exclusion : there would be a universal being in and for another : where being took the form of "consciousness," it would be the consciousness of "another" which was also "oneself"—a common consciousness. Such would be the "atonement" of the world.[1]

When that is reached we shall know in its fulness that fellowship of the Holy Spirit which is the realised Kingdom of God.

[1] R. L. Nettleship, *Philosophical Remains*, p. 42.

# CHAPTER XXVI

## CHRISTUS CONSUMMATOR

Ἐν αὐτῷ εὐδόκησε πᾶν τὸ πλήρωμα κατοικῆσαι.—St. Paul.

In our consideration of human religion we found that
the aspiration which is its root could only find its goal,
and therefore the human soul only find its rest, in a
God who should be the union of absolute power and
absolute love. It appeared, moreover, that the hypothesis of such a Being's existence was alone adequate
to explain the existence of the world. No principle
known to human experience could offer such an
explanation except that of an all-ruling will. And
such a will would seem to be self-contradictory if it is
not perfectly good, for it would be a will which, having
perfect freedom of choice, none the less chose the
smaller rather than the greater satisfaction. Either,
then, there is a God of Love, or else the universe is in
the last resort inexplicable. But the fact of the world's
evil seemed fatal to this hypothesis ; or, at any rate, it
seemed that the hypothesis could only be maintained if
it could first be shown that evil overcome of good con-
tributes to a greater good than was otherwise attainable,
and further, that the evil of the world is, in fact,
overcome by the goodness of God, who through His
love took upon Himself its burden. At making this
further step reason hesitates until it finds some actual
fact of history which seems to require just that step as
its only possible explanation. The fact of the Life and

351

Death and Resurrection of Christ is just such a fact as is required. The dogma of the Incarnation, which is that fact interpreted in the light of its consequences, gives to the aspiration of all human religion just the resting-place it seeks.   •

At an earlier stage of the enquiry we had found that the moral good for man consisted in the life of love and the fellowship of which that love is the binding power. After such a fellowship all civilisation is striving ; all legislation has this as its ultimate goal. But the very methods upon which secular civilisation relies are proof that this attempt can never by itself be successful ; for the obstacle to fellowship is self-will, and self-will cannot be ejected merely by the restraint which law can exercise. There is needed some power, akin to the spirit which moves and guides secular progress, which shall break in alike upon the individual and upon society from without, capable of effecting not only change but renovation. There is only one power known to men which is capable of producing such results ; it is the power of an entirely self-forgetful love expressing itself, as love always expresses itself, in sacrifice, that is to say, in the doing or suffering of what apart from the love would not be done or suffered. The hope of progress seemed to lie in a society whose atmosphere should be permeated by this influence. The fact of the Life and Death and Resurrection of Christ again supplies exactly what is needed. The dogma of the Incarnation, which is that fact interpreted in the light of its consequences, gives to man's moral effort alike the impetus and the goal which it requires.

A still earlier stage of the enquiry had shown us that that effort of Mind to apprehend the world, which goes under the name of Art, points forward to an ideal experience in which there should be offered to the con- templating soul some image truly adequate as an expression of the whole world's ruling principle, in gazing upon which the soul would be rapt in that meditation which is already worship. But we also found that unless the full depths of tragedy were sounded this impulse of the human will would remain still unsatisfied. Once more the fact of Christ's Life and Death and Resurrection supplies our need. In the clash between the claims of the old dispensation divinely instituted, and the new revelation divinely given, there is seen tragedy at its very highest. If the story had ended with the Cross we should have said that Christ had fallen a victim to His own sublime idealism, and that His cause had suffered because just at that moment the very quality of His virtue was disastrous. We should revere Him as earth's noblest hero ; but there would have been no Church to carry on His work. His cause would have perished with Him in the Death which He voluntarily suffered. The whole depth of tragedy is plumbed ; and out of it the light of the Resurrection breaks. Once more the dogma of the Incarnation gives man the fulfilment of his hope, for the figure of Christ is the express image of the Eternal God.

Going back to the earliest stage of our enquiry, we remember how the intellect in its purely scientific procedure led us to the belief that the world is perfectly coherent and forms a single system, but could not find what is the actual principle of unity that holds that system together. And yet we found also that intellect would welcome as the crown of its own edifice the revelation or discovery of that principle which the rest of our enquiry declared must take the form of a loving will. And though from the point of view of human science the dogma of the Incarnation is mere hypothesis, yet it is an hypothesis which explains all the facts, and there is no other such forthcoming. Reason cannot prove it ; we live by faith and not by demonstrative knowledge ; but Reason welcomes it as the needed completion of its own work.

When we see how Science and Art and Ethics and

the Philosophy of Religion present converging lines which though converging can never by the human mind be carried far enough to reach their meeting-point, but that that meeting-point is offered in the fact of Christ as Christians have understood it, we have no longer any reason to hesitate in proclaiming that here is the pivot of all true human thought ; here is the belief that can give unity to all the work of mind. The creative mind in man never attains its goal until the creative mind of God, in whose image it was made, reveals its own nature, and completes man's work. Man's search was divinely guided all the time, but its completion is only reached by the act of God Himself, meeting and crowning the effort which He has inspired.

# EPILOGUE

## CHAPTER XXVII

### ALPHA AND OMEGA

" I am the Alpha and the Omega : saith the Lord God, which is, and which was and which is to come, the Almighty."—THE APOCALYPSE.

WE have completed our survey, and the argument of the book might be left to stand upon such merits as it may have. But certain questions emerge from the survey itself, of which it is as well to say something further. Throughout our argument we have been trying amongst other things to ascertain in what sense the world is many and in what sense it is one. We have tried to reach unity also with regard to the process of Time, for that which more than everything else seems to condemn both thought and action to futility is just the transitoriness of things.

We found that Science reached unity over against multiplicity by discovering principles which, unchanged themselves, hold good of many different facts, and that in regard to Time the principles, which Science seeks and, so far as it is successful, finds, are the unchanging principles which govern the processes of change. But the unity here was felt to be too abstract for a perfect satisfaction. The mind by its own scientific method rather grasped that the world is one, then apprehended it in its unity. This further step was taken by Art ; here the mind seemed not only to

355

be emancipated from Time, but to have achieved a mastery over it and over all other forms of multiplicity. The object of æsthetic contemplation is grasped as a perfect unity, and the experience seemed to become more and more itself as the object of contemplation became more and more adequate as a symbol of life. In contemplation the mind is not only freed from Time, but is superior to it ; for it can grasp a whole process in a single apprehension whose value is determined by the course of the process. This we found to be part of the meaning of both music and drama. And yet still the achievement was not finally satisfactory, for the contemplating mind was left outside the object of contemplation. The artistic experience occurs in the course of a life which passes from stage to stage. It does indeed seem to show the possibility in principle that the Eternal can be adequately symbolised in a limited period of time, but in itself the artistic experience is simply an episode. The conquest of Time and the satisfaction in perfect orderliness is a passing event in a life that is transitory and in an experience that is full of chaos. It is necessary, if satisfaction is to be reached, that the contemplating mind shall realise itself as a work of art, which itself forms an element in the great artistic whole.

The lives of the greatest men, while not reaching a perfect achievement in the period of earthly life, yet point unquestionably to the realisation of just this ideal. There is about them a relative completeness ; the whole life in all its changing stages is a single whole which through its devotion to service fits in with the process of the world around it. Yet just the greatest and best men are most conscious that the ideal remains unrealised, that they have in themselves no power to achieve it, and that if such efforts as theirs are all that is available for the purpose, there is little hope that either in the individual or in society will the perfect harmony be reached.

So Morality points forward to Religion, the supreme activity of finite Creative Mind.   Here we find Morality combined with Science and with Art ;  man postulates an absolute perfection which he can worship.   But to this the evil in the world presents an obstacle which would appear insuperable, unless there is some evidence, other than mere human longing, that the infinite perfection is indeed a reality, and not only so but the dominating and governing reality of the universe.

The possibility that this should be so is shown by the recollection that the value of the past is alterable. This is proved by every drama that was ever written. I venture to give once more the illustration of this. The real value and meaning of the first act of a play is not known until the play is ended.   The cheerful opening of a tragedy may merely heighten the gloom of a total effect, or the gloom in which some tale of triumph opens may heighten the exhilaration that the story as a whole affords.   So it may be with the evil in the world.   Nothing can make it other than evil, but there may be a stage which we can reach in which we shall look back upon it and feel that while it was evil and in itself remains evil, yet it is now good that there should then have been something evil.   Let us take the extreme instance at once.   It is conceivable that Judas Iscariot should become so wholly delivered from all self-concern that he may pass through the shame of his treachery and be able in perfect self-abnegation to rejoice that he was allowed to play a part, although a shameful part, in completing the manifestation of his Lord's glory.

The whole course of our argument points to the suggestion of an experience that should include in a single apprehension the whole course of Time, even though that course be endless in both directions, in the same way in which the mind of a spectator at a play grasps in a single apprehension the whole course of the play.   This would be Eternity.   To this, as far as we

can tell, the finite mind can never rise ; but we achieve
it to some extent with regard to the history of the past,
and we achieve it with regard to selected passages,
whether of history or of fiction, which the dramatist or
the novelist may set before us.　Yet to the end and for
ever, man's trust in such an absolute apprehension must
be a belief in a Mind other than his own of which his
own is a finite counterpart.　If then he finds upon the
very plane of history, and occurring in the process of
Time itself, an event which seems to him capable of
being regarded as a revelation, though at a moment of
Time, of the eternal principle of things, which is now
conceived as an eternal all-embracing Mind, he will
welcome it as giving him just what his own finite
mind most needs—the link between itself and the
infinite Mind.　Here is Eternity offered in the midst of
Time in the way that the experience of Art leads us to
believe is possible.　But here too is Eternity revealed in
course of Time to the finite mind in a form which the
finite mind itself can fully grasp.　The revelation,
moreover, contains just that one essential requirement
which man's mind in Religion, which is its highest flight,
desiderated.　For here is shown the evil of the world
not only made an opportunity for greater good, but
becoming the very material out of which the greater
good is furnished.

We are here on the borders of the old problem
about free-will and omnipotence.　It would be absurd
to introduce anything that professed to be a serious
discussion of that great problem in the last chapter of
a book, but it may be well to indicate the treatment of
it which would appear to follow from the position to
which we have been led.　Man's moral experience we
found to affirm freedom in the sense of real responsibility.　A man is in some degree the origin of his own
actions and author of their consequences.　We also
found that this responsibility is social quite as much as
individual, inasmuch as the human environment of a

character, and also its material environment, which is largely the result of human action, play a great part in determining its development for good or for evil. But this freedom did not mean an absolute indeterminism. When a life is looked at from the end to which it led, it is seen to have run a real course, and not to have moved by a series of disconnected jerks. Moreover, in just those men who most of all seem to possess moral freedom and strength of will, the unity of life is greatest. This is all in harmony with the picture of freedom given us by Shakespeare in his profoundest artistic intuitions. Part of the gloom of his tragedies arises from the fact that while the characters are free, inasmuch as the origin of their actions is themselves, they are yet bound hand and foot inasmuch as from themselves there is no escape. It is not indeterminism, but self-determinism which seems to be supported by the evidence of the moral consciousness, and that a self-determinism of real growth and not a mere determination by the past.

The artistic consciousness, with which we found the moral consciousness to be so fully in accord in principle, gives us illustrations within an extremely limited sphere of what we can conceive to be the eternal experience of God. When we hear a piece of music which we know, or watch a play whose plot is familiar to us, we do indeed perceive a real growth from stage to stage and watch real choices being made by the composer or by the characters of the play. The theme need not have been developed in just that manner at that point ; the hero or the villain need not have made precisely the decision which he did. By the end of symphony or play a perfect unity is achieved for the constitution of which every element is necessary in its place ; but it is only in the whole that the ground of this necessity is shown, and therefore at any given moment during the course of the play there is as yet no necessity. It would appear that this analogy has some real value for our understanding of the Divine in its relation to the world, if we remember one great difference, namely, that the Divine Author is, so to speak, writing the play while it is being acted, and therefore we cannot throw back, or at least have no grounds for throwing back, the course of history into a previous determination in the Author's mind.[1] Hamlet on the stage has to do what he does in the printed book, for Shakespeare wrote it so long ago ; it is rather the experience, as it grew in Shakespeare's own mind in the process of writing, which supplies the real analogy. But even this is incomplete and to it must be added the analogy of a father training his children. He may be the perfect artist leading them step by step to a perfection of life, but his material is the living will and he has perpetually to adjust his action to the action of this living will. His influence may be so great that he can be perfectly sure of ultimately producing the result that he wants, and yet it may be that his will is perpetually thwarted and can only reach its end as the mistakes of the child work themselves out in their destructive consequences, and as he takes upon his own heart both the evil which is represented by those mistakes and the whole suffering which results from them.

We are now perhaps ready for a statement in set terms of the relation to the Divine to history. We are ourselves set in the mid process of Time ; we are actors in the middle of a drama whose goal we ourselves only dimly perceive or do not perceive at all. The Author of the play, who is also the Father of us His children, is watching at every turn, always countering our mistakes, and even as each arises making of it the material through which He more abundantly shows His love,

[1] This point is vital. When the human mind tries to conceive the Eternal and Omniscient God, it always pictures Him as knowing all Time *at a moment of Time*,—as, for example, knowing *now* all the past and future. But the whole point of the argument is that while all Time is the object of the Eternal comprehension, the comprehending Mind is extra-temporal and therefore does not grasp it now or at any other Time, but precisely Eternally. Thus we turn the flank of Bergson's argument that Finalism is "only inverted mechanism" (*Creative Evolution*, p. 41), and that by means of a treatment of Time which is based on his own.

and therefore calls out from us a better response. Sin itself is made to turn to blessing ; and yet it remains sin, purely and utterly evil—not to be attributed to the Divine choice, but to human error and self-will, or perhaps beyond that to diabolic suggestion. Because a universe bound together by mutual love is the goal, therefore all forces which are alien to love are by Divine law self-destructive. He who hates will call forth hate, until in the resulting conflict men learn that hate is the enemy of their own souls. This result may be called the Divine judgment, for it is the dispensation of the Divine mercy by which man is enabled to learn out of his own experience, and therefore to appreciate more fully than otherwise he could, how evil a thing is hatred, and how excellent a thing is love.[1] Both sin and the pain it brings are part of the process by which finite man learns that only in union with the infinite, and in the fellowship with all else that is finite resulting from that union, can anything that is good be reached. And the process exists because love that has won against hatred has in it for evermore a nobility which positively consists in that conquest of hatred, and which is therefore otherwise not obtained. The evil remains evil, but there is promise of a time when it will be good that the evil should have been ; and Eternally it is good that there should be evil in the course of Time.

Man is always wanting to imagine for himself a God who shall exactly suit his need. Some think that they have found this in an attenuated Christianity. They are liable to argue that Christianity suits them, but that perhaps it may not suit Indians or Arabians ; it is not clear, they say, that Foreign Missions have good results, and it is better (as it is certainly cheaper) to leave the unconverted nations alone. But Christianity is not a

---

[1] So the Great War came as God's judgment. And He let it come. Why was the Emperor of Germany a William II. and not a Frederick I.? God who inspires the heart could have stopped the war. But it may have been more merciful to let Europe learn even thus the true nature of its life of materialism, ambition, and self-indulgence if it would learn in no other way.

drug which suits some complaints and not others. It is either sheer illusion or else it is the Truth. But if it is the Truth, if the Universe happens to be constituted in this way, the question is not whether the God of Christianity suits us, but whether we suit Him. A sane man does not say, " The Law of Gravitation does not suit me, so I can ignore it and walk over the edge of this cliff in security " ; nor will a sane man say, " A God who requires me to love my very tiresome neighbour and even my most wicked enemy does not suit me, so I will pursue my selfish interests in security." If God is love, selfishness is enmity against omnipotence —a foolish enmity. We may reject Him if we like, but it makes no difference to His achievement of His purpose. " The stone which the builders rejected, the same was made the head of the corner. . . . He that falleth on this stone shall be broken to pieces, but on whomsoever it shall fall, it will scatter him as dust."

But the Power is also Love. To all that is selfish the Love of God is infinitely terrible ; to realise that Love is the law of the Universe, and that, whether we will or not, we are being used and used up for the good of the whole society of spirits, must be to the selfish soul an agony of torture. Pride is offended to utter misery at the thought of our impotence to change the issue ; even our utmost assault on the Divine Love merely enables it to manifest itself more fully.[1] But Love rejoices in the union with all things living wherein it finds itself. The realisation of this same truth about God is Heaven or is Hell according as Love or Pride is uppermost in the heart.

But the Divine Love cannot be content with using as puppets of its purpose the souls whom it created to be worthy of itself. The kind of power that God exerted in the world before the birth of Christ was not enough. Not only events, but hearts and wills must

---

[1] Imagine the rage of Caiaphas when he first realised that he had been used to further the cause of Christ and to heighten His glory.

be ruled. So the Love was made known in an intelligible form through Life and Death, so that omnipotence should be complete, and, by the responding love called forth, the free allegiance of hearts and wills be won. By Power and by Love God would deliver us from Pride, which is the one poison of the soul, and bring us into union with Himself.

This union, however, means something more than the Divine control of our conscious wills and affections. In such union the whole nature becomes receptive, and deep in the subconscious nature divinely given thoughts are planted, even as in the same depths of the selfish nature other evil spirits, human or diabolic, plant the thoughts of which it is receptive. We saw at the outset of our enquiry that all living thought, or almost all, is subconscious. We hardly ever know the origin of those thoughts which we call our own, as distinct from those which other men have given to us by speech or writing. Probably it is by suggesting thoughts to the subconscious minds of His servants that God most normally directs the course of History, even as by similar suggestion the evil powers try to thwart His purpose. Probably the good seed and the bad are sown by the Sowers in all hearts ; but only those grow to conscious thoughts or plans of action which have found congenial soil. But the evil device, as we have seen, always leads to its own defeat and the greater exaltation of good, while the good will possesses the one supreme and lasting joy of union with the eternal God.

At every moment God is controlling the results of human choice and turning them to the fulfilment of His own purpose ; but the choice is human and the wrong choice is an evil thing. But if the whole of history is indeed an ordered system such as the intellect demands for the satisfaction of its ideal of coherence, we are led of necessity to believe in an Eternal Knowledge to which the whole process, endless though it may possibly be, is present in a single apprehension.

For the Omniscient Mind every episode is grasped as an element in that glorious whole of which it is a constituent part. "Everlastingly in the life of God death is swallowed up in victory."[1] It is in the absolute perfection of that eternal experience, in which the whole process of Time is grasped in a single apprehension, that the ultimate ground of all that happens in history is to be found. To those who have seen in the Life and Death and Resurrection of Christ the manifestation of the eternal omnipotence, this experience can already be in a small measure shared through faith. "The Eternal God is thy refuge, and underneath are the everlasting arms."

> It fortifies my soul to know
> That though I perish, Truth is so ;
> That howsoe'er I stray or range,
> Whate'er I do Thou dost not change ;
> I steadier step when I recall
> That if I slip, Thou dost not fall.

It is clear that this conception of God requires for its statement the Doctrine of the Trinity ; indeed, without that Doctrine the universe is completely unintelligible. Many have regarded this Doctrine as an unfathomable mystery, a sort of revealed enigma ; and this has led others to regard it as mere word-jugglery. The unfathomable mystery is the Nature of God ; this doctrine is merely the furthest that man has gone in the rational apprehension of that mystery. We have found ourselves compelled to affirm concerning God propositions which could not all be true of a single personality such as ours. He is the Eternal and Omniscient, to whom all History in its infinite range is present in a single apprehension—the Father of an Infinite Majesty ; He is that Father self-revealed in the processes of Nature and of human effort, and above all in Jesus Christ who is the express image of His Person ; He is that Father winning the love of His children by the

[1] Canon Streeter in *Concerning Prayer*, p. 39.

guidance of their inmost thoughts, and pre-eminently the thoughts of those whose hearts have been won to free allegiance by the knowledge of the revelation which is in Jesus Christ.  But while in all of these activities there is one God, there must in each be seen a distinct Person—to use the word which, though misleading,[1] is the best that human language affords.  In One Person we see the Eternal Knowledge of the world wherein Love conquers Pride ; in Another we see the Infinite cost at which the Victory is won ; in Another the age-long struggle in which the fruits of the Victory are secured.  These could not be combined in a single experience such as our experience is.  God in Eternity and God in Time—one God ; but not one Person. For God in Eternity all is perfect in the triumphant harmony of the whole ; but for the very perfection of that triumph God in Time must suffer real disappoint-ment and defeat in order that defeat itself may be defeated and captivity led captive.  God, the Father, of an Infinite Majesty ; God staggering beneath a load too great for Him on the way from Jerusalem to Calvary ; God struggling with many a disappointment and defeat against the brutality of Nature and the selfishness of Man : these are the Three Persons of the One Godhead.

Of necessity the distinction between God in Eternity and God in Time is clearer than that between the Son and the Spirit who are both active in Time.[2]  Indeed, the early Church often drew no distinction here at all.  And St. Thomas himself declares that the Spirit is only distinguishable from the Son because of His pro-ceeding from Him : *Si Spiritus Sanctus non esset a Filio, nullo modo posset ab eo personaliter distingui.*" [3]  Apart from the Incarnation the distinction could not be

---

[1] Because Person generally connotes Individual, a thought which is here irrelevant and whose introduction is heretical because nonsensical.

[2] On the whole Doctrine see my lectures on *The Nature of Personality*, viii.

[3] *Summa*, Pt. I. xxxvi. 2.  Clearly the Eastern formula " through the Son " means just the same as the Western " from the Son," while more adequately safeguarding the primacy of the Father.

drawn.  To say that the Holy Spirit "spake through the prophets" and to say that "the Word of the Lord" came to them is to say the same thing.  But by His self-revelation in the Son God makes our hearts receptive of His Spirit, who is known to be other than the Son, while yet one with Him, because being within us He inspires us with devotion to Christ as One also without us and above us.

This is not to make the doctrine of the Trinity merely "economic."  Unless we regard the Incarnation as an accident so far as the Being of God is concerned, the Revelation in the Son, and the consequent activity of the Spirit uniting the world with God, are the very means by which God Himself guides to its goal that process of History which in its entirety is the object of His Eternal Love, the occasion of His Eternal Joy, the ground of His Eternal Peace.

But while belief in the Eternal so conceived is the one thing that can at last give peace beyond all understanding to the mind which truly enters into the miseries of this tormented world, it would seem to be an untenable faith except for those who have found in the Cross and Resurrection of the Word Incarnate the pivot of their thought.[1]  We are always trying to reach the Eternal and Almighty by a leap, and then to make use of Him for our temporal and finite purposes.  But if we are to enter into the life of God we must eat the flesh and drink the blood of the Son of Man, making His human life our own.  God in His eternal omnipotence is only to be found by union with God in the sacrifice of Gethsemane and Calvary. We pray, like the sons of Zebedee, " We would that thou shouldest do for us whatsoever we shall ask of thee " ; and to that there is only one answer : " Can you share my adventure and my sacrifice ? "  The cry of Moses is the cry of all mankind—" I BESEECH THEE, SHOW ME THY GLORY."  The answer to it is not

---

[1] See pp. 291, 292.

that which he himself or any other of mankind would expect ; but it is the only answer which for a moment meets the human need or vindicates the omnipotence of love. "THEY CRUCIFIED HIM, AND THE MALE-FACTORS, ONE ON THE RIGHT HAND AND THE OTHER ON THE LEFT."

HAVING, THEREFORE, BRETHREN, BOLDNESS
> *For it is a venture, not a certainty, to which we are called ;*

TO ENTER INTO THE HOLY PLACE
> *The Presence of God, which is Love ;*

BY THE BLOOD OF JESUS
> *In the inspiration of His sacrifice ;*

BY THE WAY WHICH HE DEDICATED FOR US
> *He has trodden the path Himself ;*

A NEW AND LIVING WAY
> *None could travel it before He came ; and it is found by life, not by thought alone ;*

THROUGH THE VEIL, THAT IS TO SAY, HIS FLESH
> *His Human Nature conceals His Divinity, until we share it by living in His strength His sacrificial life ;*

AND HAVING A GREAT PRIEST OVER THE HOUSE OF GOD
> *In the innermost Presence of Love there is One to represent us when we stay away, to welcome us when we come ;*

LET US DRAW NEAR WITH A TRUE HEART IN FULNESS OF FAITH
> *Though it is a venture, and faith is not demonstrative knowledge, we can live by this faith in unalloyed confidence.*

## "*MY LORD AND MY GOD.*"

*Printed by* Lowe & Brydone (Printers) Ltd., *London, N.W. 1.*